HALLOWED

in

TRUTH

and

LOVE

Spirituality in the Johannine Literature

DOROTHY A. LEE

WIPF & STOCK · Eugene, Oregon

HALLOWED IN TRUTH AND LOVE
Spirituality in the Johannine Literature

Published by permission of Mosaic Press, 508 High Street, Preston Vic. 3072, Australia.

Wipf & Stock
An imprint of Wipf and Stock Publishers
199 W. 8th Avenue, Suite 3
Eugene OR, 97401
www.wipfandstock.com

ISBN 13: 978-1-62032-275-8

Manufactured in the U.S.A.

for Eric Francis Osborn
(1922 - 2007)
inspiring scholar, mentor, friend
and
for Barbara Sinclair Lee
(1919 - 2010)

much loved mother

Table of Contents

List of Illustrations

Preface

There are a number of people and institutions without whose support I could not have written this book. Most obviously, I thank Trinity College, for its welcome of me some four years ago, and its encouragement of my research and writing. I thank especially the Warden, Andrew McGowan, and my colleagues within the Theological School. I am also grateful to colleagues within the Melbourne College of Divinity, and in particular to Christiaan Mostert, who listened patiently to my changing plans and offered advice. I am conscious I owe much to my New Testament confreres in Melbourne, especially Brendan Byrne SJ, Frank Moloney SDB, and Mary Coloe PBVM.

The staff of the Dalton McCaughey Library have been indefatigable in their help and encouragement, especially in sourcing inaccessible books and articles.

I am grateful to my students within the United Faculty of Theology and at Trinity College who constantly stimulate me, and help me to see the Fourth Gospel from ever-new angles. They keep my interest alive, and their questions compel me to take seriously other points of view that are not necessarily my own.

I owe much to my publisher, Hugh McGinlay, for his fine editorial touches, his theological astuteness, and his gracious support of my work.

I am grateful most of all for the gift of a loving family, especially Edwin, Ruth, Emma, Miriam, Philip, Irene, and Jemima Joan. Their acceptance and care goes beyond all that I could want.

Last of all, I dedicate this book to two people, recently deceased, who have had, in entirely different ways, a profound affect on my life: one my colleague and mentor, Eric Osborn, and the other my mother, Barbara Lee.

Dorothy A. Lee
Feast of St Aidan
August 2011

Trinity College
MCD University of Divinity
Australia

Introduction

In the confusion of meaning over the term 'spirituality', it may seem futile to write a book concerned with New Testament spirituality. In the popular view, in secular circles where 'spirituality' is part of a common vocabulary, there is no necessary connection to any identifiable religious life, Christian or otherwise. Its scope hardly seems to go beyond the notion of interior, individualistic well-being. Ideas of tradition or discipline are generally absent, as is involvement in religious ritual. Above all, such spirituality is disconnected from theology and religious text. As a consequence, some may conclude that to speak of spirituality at all is so broad a concept as to be meaningless; the word is corrupted by over-use and muddied by a loose and disconnected assortment of ideas.

In the world of Scripture study, spirituality is often dismissed as subjective and pietistic, outside the realm of critical enquiry. In this view, spirituality is not interested in the objectivity of the biblical text, but rather the reader's individual response to the text, which is beyond the purview of scholarly study. Spirituality is seen as personal, private and external to critical analysis. It is relegated to the prayer desk rather than the library—an empathetic response to the text that can stand in the way of objective analysis. In such biblical scholarship, the study of Scripture is confined to textual analysis, social-scientific understandings of the world behind the text, historical settings, and the ideologies which emerge from the text. Perhaps the difficulty of defining the word 'spirituality' explains in part its dismissal from many theoretical studies of the Bible.

In more recent years, spirituality has asserted its own status within the world of scholarly study as a distinct discipline. Sandra Schneiders, herself a New Testament (Johannine) scholar, has had a significant role in this development, seeing spirituality as a field within its own right: the study of human spiritual experience across a wide range of religious traditions.[1] As a discipline, spirituality endeavours to unite the objective and the subjective. Other writers who support this view emphasise the interdisciplinary nature of spirituality, its engagement with other branches of theological study, such as Scripture studies, history, theology, liturgy, and ethics.[2] Spirituality has its own identity in the study of theology, in this view, its own place within the field of academic study and research. While it may cross disciplines, it possesses its own, distinctive identity. If this is the case, and spirituality is more than just subjective experience, then the spiritualities of the Bible are also worthy of study and analysis.

It is possible, therefore, to identify several dimensions of spirituality. In the first place, and most importantly for this book, spirituality may be studied in the writings of Scripture, where it is seen as part of the content of the biblical text.[3] In this case, there is no single, monolithic biblical spirituality but a number of different spiritualities in the variety of biblical writings—sometimes complementing, sometimes overlapping, sometimes in tension with one another. There is a certain objectivity to this definition, authenticating the need for critical study of spiritual themes in the Bible, regardless of the researcher's personal views. Secondly, spirituality describes a personal and transformative connection with the biblical text, for individuals and communities. This latter definition, in particular, articulates the subjective aspects of spirituality where it is concerned with the interpretation and application of the text. Thirdly, spirituality may be defined as a way of living informed by the Bible, where the Bible is interpreted as a profoundly spiritual text that offers a basis for living. This view deals with the content of biblical spirituality but seeks to understand it within a broader framework.

To speak of spirituality in this last sense means engaging, not only with Scripture, but also with systematic theology in general. Samuel M. Powell argues that several aspects of theology lie at the basis of authentic spirituality, aspects that can be drawn from the biblical writings: the incarnation, with its implications for understanding God, revelation and the human person (including cross and resurrection); human existence and its significance, lived in the context of community; the incoming reign of God, already realised in Christ; and participation in the triune life of God.[4] These points reveal the interconnection between the two disciplines, theology and spirituality. John R. Tyson offers a similar perspective in his anthology of ecumenical Christian spiritual writings from the early church to the present. He identifies nine theological themes that, in his view, undergird spirituality across the Christian tradition: creation and redemption, sin, justification, the presence of God, the saving work of Christ, the Spirit, the Trinity, the communion of saints, and the final kingdom of God.[5] These central theological affirmations emerge from the tradition and from Christian spiritual reflection on the Bible over centuries. In some Christian traditions, markedly that of the Eastern Orthodox church, there is no sharp line between theology and mysticism, experience and doctrine: each is concerned to articulate divine mystery.[6] In Christian understanding, therefore, theology and spirituality ideally belong together: 'A theology that is alive is always grounded in spiritual experience. If it is to be complete, theology needs to be *lived* just as much as it needs to be studied and explained.'[7] Equally, spirituality needs theology to give it shape and form, like the banks of a river directing its flow; it requires the biblical witness, in all its diversity, to elucidate its own foundations. To avoid unhelpful bifurcations, each stands in need of the other.

In the Pauline writings, from which the term is derived, spirituality is invariably connected to the divine Spirit. The adjective *pneumatikos*, from the noun *pneuma* ('spirit'), usually signifies something given by the Spirit (e.g. Rom 1:11; 15:17; 1 Cor 1:7; 2:13; 12:1), though it can also refer to the human spirit (e.g. Rom 2:29; 7:14; 1 Cor 3:1). This is a good basis for a biblical definition of spirituality, which is concerned fundamentally with the role of the Spirit in engagement with the human spirit.[8] Such a definition makes it clear that we are dealing with theology and with texts in their objectivity, as well as with faith. Spirituality, in this sense, is part of the substance of Scripture and not simply a matter of its application. With this understanding, spirituality becomes an important aspect of New Testament theology,[9] as well as possessing implications for transformative living. Stephen Barton has argued, in general terms, that Christian spirituality 'is about the sense of the presence of God and living in the light of that presence.'[10] Studying New Testament spirituality means examining how different texts conceive of that divine sense and presence; how they present the Spirit in engagement with the human spirit; how they imagine transformation. As a consequence, it is not only gainful but necessary to comprehend the spirituality which is present in biblical texts. This is as authentic a form of study as examining other aspects of the Bible's structure, history, and theology.[11]

In this study, we are concerned to outline the spirituality which emerges from the Johannine writings—the Gospel of John, the Johannine epistles, and the Book of Revelation—in a way that opens the text to further explorations within the mind and heart of the reader. We examine the spirituality of the Johannine writings from the vantage-point, not only of their theology but also their symbolism, assuming that symbol lies at the heart of theology—unfolded through narrative and discourse, dialogue and misunderstanding, letter and vision. As Alfred Plummer said of the Fourth Gospel over a hundred years ago, an assertion that can be extended to the epistles and Revelation: 'the whole Gospel from end to end is penetrated with the spirit of symbolical representation'.[12] These symbols are not decorative elements to adorn the text but part of its core substance, with cognitive meaning as well as theological and religious content. Spirituality, in these texts, is thus quintessentially symbolic, based on the presumption that symbols, in their dramatic projection and engagement with the reader, form the backbone of the text, the heart of its meaning and message.

The Gospel of John

In the third century the Gospel of John was famously termed by Clement of Alexandria as the 'spiritual Gospel' (150—215 AD).[13] The Synoptic Gospels too have their wealth of spiritual meaning, yet the Fourth Gospel's rich tapestry, teeming with symbol and metaphor, with characterisation and personal encounter, with long, meditative discourse and lengthy narrative, seems to lend itself to the description. This is a profoundly spiritual Gospel, arising from John's unique theological insights, his plentiful symbolism and his unique focus on the Spirit. There is a mysticism to this text, an awareness of the divine,[14] that has the capacity to 'reverberate into the present of any reader.'[15]

However, to imply that the Synoptic Gospels—Matthew, Mark and Luke—are closer to history while John is more other-worldly is a dangerous and inaccurate division.[16] Not only have the Synoptics their own understanding of spirituality, but the Gospel of John also lays claim to an equally strong and complex connection to history. As D. Moody Smith points out, the Fourth Gospel 'presents an unusual weaving together of historical data and theological interests.'[17] Johannine spirituality is rooted in the events of history, in the life and death of Jesus of Nazareth and in the ongoing religious life of the community. Spirituality in its Johannine sense, therefore, is neither ethereal nor insubstantial, but earthly and earthy: grounded in the stuff of human history. If the description of John as the 'spiritual Gospel' carries with it a sense of historical location and grounding, then it is still apt.[18] Apart from anything else, it points to the distinctive role of the Spirit.[19]

This study of the spirituality of the Fourth Gospel takes for granted a number of assumptions that are part of its rootedness in history. It assumes, for example, that John's Gospel was written later than the Synoptic Gospels and most likely in the last decade of the first century. The authorship and provenance are not indicated directly in the text, but there is a long and venerable tradition of Ephesus as the place of writing. Given that Ephesus was a Roman-Hellenistic city with most likely a Jewish community, this tradition is probably correct (cf. Acts 18:18-19:40).[20] While John is writing from a community with specific issues and needs, it would seem that he writes with an awareness of the wider Church—as is the case for the other Gospels, which are local without being parochial, local yet possessing universal appeal.[21]

As for the author, the 'beloved disciple' who appears in the Gospel and claims authorship is never named in the text (Jn 13:23-25; 19:26-27; 20:3-10; 21:7, 20-23).[22] The superscription to the Gospel, 'according to John', has been traditionally associated with John the apostle, the son of Zebedee; Irenaeus (c.130-c.200 AD) takes this view, tracing his information back to Polycarp (c.65-c.155) who personally knew the apostles.[23] On the other hand, the early church seems to know of another John, a Christian teacher and leader ministering in Ephesus, and it is possible that Irenaeus has confused the two. Papias, the bishop of Hierapolis in Asia Minor in the second century (c. 60-135), speaks of this figure as someone outside the Twelve but a follower of Jesus during his life-time. Whether John the Ephesian elder or John the apostle—or whether the two are one—the author seems to be identified with the mysterious beloved disciple who is responsible for the Gospel, and who claims eyewitness testimony.[24] If that is the case, the author must have written as an old man but knew Jesus as a young man, and was associated with Judaea and Jerusalem rather than Galilee.[25]

John's Gospel, as with the Synoptic Gospels, is not biographical in the modern, chronological sense. However, in the terms of the ancient world it seems to qualify as a 'life' (*bios, vita*) and thus a biography,[26] though not one necessarily concerned with literal chronology and depiction. This type of biography is explicitly interpretative, its role not simply to inform but more significantly to transform. Yet this classification does not deny the differences between the Gospels, particularly on points of detail. For example, did Jesus call the first disciples as fishermen (Synoptics) or did they come to him as disciples of John the Baptist (John)? Did Jesus cleanse the temple at the beginning of his ministry (John) or at the end (Synoptics)? Did Jesus go to Jerusalem three times throughout his ministry (John) or was there only one significant journey (Mark)? Was the Last Supper a Passover meal (Synoptics) or a special fellowship meal on the night before Passover (John)? Did Jesus wash the feet of the disciples on this occasion (John) or institute the eucharist (Synoptics)? We could go on.

The point is that these tensions, wherever or not we can resolve them, highlight the interpretative nature and stance of each Gospel. While the Johannine tradition seems to reach back to its own witness of the ministry of Jesus, there are signs of a vibrant connection to Synoptic traditions. For all the differences between John and the Synoptic Gospels, there are significant points of correspondence and overlap: in specific stories, such as the miraculous feeding with the boat journey immediately following (John 6:1-21; Mark 6:3-52, 8:1-21); and in the overall shape of Jesus' ministry, beginning with John the Baptist and concluding with the Passion, death and resurrection stories. The Fourth Gospel has a level of independence from the Synoptic Gospels but there are signs of influence and cross-fertilisation, at the very least—if not direct knowledge.

It is not impossible that the fourth evangelist was acquainted with one or other of the Synoptic Gospels. Arguments for this view, or its opposite, have tended to go back and forth in critical circles, and it is difficult to mount an unassailable case either way.[27] But the fourth evangelist does make certain assumptions in his Gospel that imply a store of prior knowledge on the part of the implied reader. Whether that pre-knowledge is based on text or tradition is hard to know, even where the oral has precedence over the literary. However, the evidence for the former is strong. Early Christian leaders, as we know from Acts and the Pauline epistles, were remarkably mobile, and communication between one community and another was not infrequent. The oral medium of missionaries and preachers became more and more dependent on written text—Gospel and epistle—which was 'published' in oral form, via memory and recitation. It is hard to imagine a community where so foundational a document as the Gospel of Mark—widespread enough to become a major influence on the writing of two further Gospels— was unknown.[28] These points have greater weight if the geographical origin of the Fourth Gospel is a major centre such as Ephesus.

One of the issues critical scholarship has also discussed is the question of whether only one edition of the Gospel was produced, or whether there were two or more editions, thereby accounting for some of the irregularities in narration.[29] This remains a distinct possibility. This remains a distinct possibility. The unevenness at several points suggests, either a clumsy synthesis of several traditions, which hardly fits with other evidence that points to careful and sensitive narration, or a text in more than one edition, produced over a fairly short period of time. Most problematical here is the place of John 21 in the overall schema of the Gospel, which to many scholars still seems to be a later, uneasy addition to the resurrection stories—although this assumption can be insensitive to important literary connections.[30]

A further issue is the shape of the early Christian community within its own cultural and religious setting, involving awareness of the world to which the Fourth Gospel belongs. As F.J. Moloney has pointed out, 'The Fourth Gospel … is a difficult text, and a great deal of this difficulty comes from its strangeness when read in our present cultural context.'[31] This perspective raises questions of cultural values that are very different from our own, highlighting the danger of uncritically turning the ancient worldview into a reflection of our own. Different models of kinship, honour, patronage, and individual identity need to be taken seriously in reading an ancient text, which suffers sometimes from a sense of superficial familiarity.[32] This point is as true for the Jewish background of the Gospel as for the Hellenistic—though, in John's context, the two worlds overlap.

For some time, scholarly approaches to the text have focused on the Jewish background and setting of the Gospel: the relationship to the Old Testament world, as well as the contemporary Jewish environment, and rabbinic methods of exegesis and biblical interpretation. More recently, the focus has shifted to include the Graeco-Roman environment in which the Johannine community—like much of the early Christian community in general—had its place, especially in the political situation of the imperial cult and the uneasy relationship between Christians, on the one hand, and Roman imperialism and state religion, on the other.

Readers of the Fourth Gospel have shown interest in the historical circumstances within the Johannine community that might have given rise to the composition of the Gospel.[33] There have also been challenges to the notion that we can discern the shape of a community lying behind the Gospel.[34] It is certainly difficult to sketch a profile of a community—its structures, membership, worship life, and so on—where the text provides so little evidence, and studies have tended to be highly speculative, if not actually tenuous.[35] A further challenge is to the assumption that the Gospels were written for their own geographical community only, rather than a wider audience.[36]

One thing is certain: it is necessary to read John's Gospel within its own literary and theological framework. Sometimes readers do not trouble to make this kind of distinction but read without awareness of the differences among the Gospels—without reference to the distinctive flavour of each. As a consequence, in the popular mind one Gospel

Illustration 1. St John the Evangelist. Lindisfarne Gospels, eighth century AD
The British Library, Cotton MS Nero D.iv. f. 209v

In the image of the Lindisfarne Gospels above, the fourth evangelist is seated on the left-hand page, opposite the text which is the Latin Vulgate, though a later scribe has thoughtfully provided a translation in Anglo-Saxon between the lines. The eagle is perched just above the evangelist's head—emerging almost from his brain—and about to take off in flight, a book clutched in its claws. The halo that surrounds the evangelist's head is repeated for the eagle. Pertinent biblical imagery associated with eagles include the maternal eagle hovering over its nest and carrying its chicks to safety, its great strength, power, mystery and beauty, its capacity to mount high in the sky and swoop down upon the earth, and its metaphorical relationship to worship and the saving presence of God (Deut 32:11; Prov 30:18-19; Jer 48:40; Ezek 17:3-7; 2 Esdr. 11:5; Rev 12:14). It is these aspects—particularly the ability to sweep effortlessly between heaven and earth—that led the early Church to identify the flying eagle with John the evangelist.

converges on another, all four mixed together in a hotch-potch of indistinction. John is a skilful story-teller and theologian—as can also be said of the Synoptic evangelists—and needs to be heard and read in his own right. His spirituality is not identical to the other Gospels; indeed within the biblical canon it is unique. It is John's distinctive perspective that this book seeks to explore, while recognising at the same time that there are other overlapping New Testament spiritualities equally deserving of attention. We address here the unique shape of Johannine spirituality through the study of the narration and symbolism of the text, asking what its spirituality might have to offer the lives of readers who profess the same faith.

The traditional symbol for John's Gospel, among the other Gospels, is the eagle. The four symbols—the lion, the man, the bull and the lion—derive originally from Ezekiel and the Book of Daniel. In Ezekiel the four living creatures with the jewelled wheel are a symbol of the presence of God, whereas in Daniel they are associated with four kings and kingdoms (Ezek 1:4-28; 10:14; Dan 7:2-8). The imagery of Ezekiel is picked up in the Book of Revelation where the four beings reside in the celestial court: 'the first living creature like a lion, the second living creature like an ox, the third living creature with a face like a human face, and the fourth living creature like a flying eagle' (Rev 4:7).[37] Along with the twenty-four elders, they worship God and the Lamb in the heavenly sanctuary (Rev 4:6b-11, 5:6-14; 7:11-12; 19:4).

Johannine Epistles

It may seem a simple matter to group together the Gospel and epistles of John, but their precise inter-relationship is not easy to determine. There are certainly close similarities in language and metaphor, suggesting at least a common community behind them, if not the same author: incarnation, love, abiding, light and darkness, truth, believing, birth from God, water and blood, knowing God, eternal life.[38] Yet there are also a number of differences—a greater emphasis, for example, on sin and forgiveness, a concern with 'antichrist', an emphasis that is somewhat more future-oriented than the Gospel, the absence of reference to Jesus as the Word, polemic that is aimed at those who have left the community rather than the Jewish authorities, the theme of the discernment of spirits, and a less explicit concern with theology and more pragmatic direction for the life of the believing community.

The Johannine epistles are puzzling for a number of reasons, including the issue of composition. 1 John, for example, completely lacks the usual introduction and conclusion to a letter (unlike 2 and 3 John), making it seem more like a tract than an epistle, except for the explicit and frequent references to writing elsewhere in the text. Although there has been much debate on the context and setting of 1 John, there are not many explicit markers in the text itself.[39] 2 John is addressed to 'the elect lady', concluding with greetings from her 'elect sister' and it is unclear whether this refers to an actual woman, the head perhaps of a house-church, or is metaphorical for the Christian community. The third is addressed to 'Gaius', an otherwise unknown Christian, presumably a leader in the community; two other members are mentioned by name, Diotrephes critically, as failing to acknowledge the writer's authority, and Demetrius favourably, as one who holds fast to the truth. Yet neither epistle gives the identity of the writer, using the first person ('whom I love in the truth') without qualification, as if he is well-known and needs no further identification. That too is an unusual feature of epistles and particularly of those within the New Testament. On this basis, a number of scholars have argued for a 'Johannine school', a tradition going back to the beloved disciple and carried forward by his disciples.[40]

Whether the Johannine epistles were written before or after the Gospel is likewise difficult to determine: a case can be made either way. The signs of schism in the community suggest to some a later context than the Gospel, where the community seems unified.[41] Admittedly, the Gospel, with its broader appeal and its focus on the narrative of Jesus, may have moved on from earlier divisions; its emphasis on unity may have arisen from bitter experience.[42] In any case, we need not assume the three letters were all written at the same time; they may have been composed at different times, and in relation to an earlier edition of the Gospel. Either way, there is a close connection between the perspectives of Gospel and epistles, regardless of the order in which they were composed.[43]

More pertinent and problematical is the question of authorship and whether the same hand is responsible for both Gospel and epistles. If it is the one author, then the reference to the death of the beloved disciple at the end of the Gospel—with its reference to his death (21:22-23)—might suggest that the epistles were earlier, unless we assume either that John 21 is a later, if sympathetic, addition or that the evangelist is not dead by the end of the Gospel.[44] Alternatively, the author of the epistles may have been a close companion of the one whom the Gospel describes simply as 'the beloved disciple'. The sense of both presupposed knowledge of that identity and anonymity certainly coheres between Gospel and epistles; indeed, the reticence suggests the same personality dominating both.[45] The thematic differences may be explained by a later different context and focus.

At the same time, we should not ignore the effect of difference in genre. This, after all, is the only example in the New Testament of a Gospel and epistles bearing the same name, and we need to make due allowance for the considerable difference between the narrative form of a Gospel, with a wider audience in mind, and a letter addressed to a small group of people or an individual in very specific circumstances (as is the case particularly with 2 John and 3 John). No-one would claim that the epistles reach the heights of the Gospel. Their genre dictates a more practical and even pragmatic focus, explicitly pastoral rather than strictly theological, showing a concern for the living out of the gospel in the immediacy of believers' lives.

Revelation

If it is not easy to group together the Fourth Gospel and the Johannine epistles, it is more difficult with the Book of Revelation. Technically, it perhaps should not be included under the rubric 'Johannine', because, in the judgement of most, the authorship of the Book of Revelation cannot be confused with that of the Gospel and/or epistles.[46] Nonetheless there are sufficient similarities, not to mention geographical and socio-cultural affinities, to link the three texts, despite their obvious differences.[47] The writer of Revelation is most likely an unknown visionary and leader of the church in the Roman province of Asia Minor. Although traditionally associated with John the apostle, even in the ancient world there was not complete unanimity on this point (linked to controversy over its place in the canon).[48] Modern commentators generally view the author 'John' as distinct from either the apostle or the elder—an unknown Christian prophet associated with the churches in Asia Minor.[49] The consensus is based on differences of language and theology. The Greek of Revelation has a wider vocabulary but lacks the simple dignity of either the Gospel or the epistles; it is rougher and less sophisticated in grammar and syntax. Moreover, the theological standpoint is apocalyptic in Revelation, a perspective rather different from the more fully anticipated perspective of the Fourth Gospel and epistles. This book therefore makes the assumption that the authorship of Revelation is distinct.

For all that, there are distinct points of overlap: a partial commonality of symbolism and theology. Both the Gospel and Revelation are connected with an author named 'John'—the Gospel in its superscription and Revelation within the text itself (Rev 1:1, 4, 9; 22:8). In the tradition, the two were traditionally considered to be authored by John the apostle, and even those who continue to argue for the apostolic authorship of the Gospel and epistles do not these days necessarily extend the argument to include Revelation. Furthermore, both texts are connected, in some way, with the city of Ephesus and the Roman province of Asia Minor—either by tradition (as in the case of the Gospel) or within the text itself (Rev 1:11; 2:1-7). The overlap in symbol and theology is apparent in motifs such as the title of 'Lamb' used of Jesus, or the reference to God's dwelling among mortals (Jn 1:14; Rev 21:3). There would thus seem to be religious and geopolitical links between these texts, even if this is confined to their inhabiting the same geographical environment —although that in itself makes them subject to mutual influence. Between them there are mysterious links yet also significant differences.

Just as difficult to determine is the dating of Revelation. Opinions of the date of composition vary, the most popular being some time in the

90's, while Domitian was the Roman Emperor (81-96 AD), an opinion that goes back to Irenaeus.[50] A minority have argued for an earlier dating, associating Revelation with the period during or immediately after the reign of the Emperor Nero (54-68 AD) who was the first to persecute the Christians in Rome, a persecution in which the apostles Peter and Paul perished.[51] One possibility within this earlier dating is the year 69 AD, the 'year of the four emperors' (Galba, Otho, Vitellius and Vespasian), during a brief period of civil war in Rome.[52] Either way, Revelation seems to have arisen out of a turbulent period within the Roman empire, with either the threat or the reality of persecution for the Christians in the seven churches.

Whatever we conclude about the date of Revelation, the context of the communities of the seven churches are set within the political and economic environment of the Roman Empire. Rather than being a simple blue-print of the future and the end of time, Revelation is perceived more and more as 'an indictment of empire'.[53] Whatever it may say about past and future, the Book of Revelation is set firmly against the Roman Empire and all that it stands for. This opposition has political and religious, economic and spiritual implications; indeed, it defines the spirituality of the letters and visions. Rome and its imperial prowess, its divinisation of empire and emperor, its wealth and trade, and its oppression of those outside its embrace, form the context of Revelation. Here we confront the theological, spiritual and ethical dilemma of Christians struggling to live out their faith in what John the Seer sees as the idolatrous and oppressive environment of the Roman province of Asia Minor.

Shape of this Book

There is more than one perspective from which to view the spirituality of these writings, and no single perspective can claim to be comprehensive. The Gospel of John, for example, is often described as a pool in which an infant can paddle and an elephant can swim.[54] This is one way of saying that the Gospel has a mysterious quality to it: easily graspable, in one sense, but profoundly elusive in another. This book offers several approaches to Johannine spirituality, with some overlap between them: the same material, but seen by tracing different themes and symbols through the Gospel, epistles and Revelation. It is like a series of photographs of a building or a mountain or a tree, taken from different angles and set alongside each other. Despite the differences, each should be identifiable as one and the same object of view.

We begin with the motif of the 'Word' in the Fourth Gospel, a major title for Jesus in the Prologue but implicit also in the rest of the Gospel (chapter 1). The title implies a spirituality that arises from God's self-communication with the world in creation and redemption, which is apparent particularly in the way John uses 'word' and 'words' throughout the Gospel. But study of the Johannine Word (and the words) leads to a fundamentally symbolic reading of the Gospel narrative. This reading begins with the incarnation as the fundamental symbol of the Fourth Gospel and embraces the main symbols of the narrative which are closely tied to the incarnational motif. There is a kind of 'sacramentality' to the Gospel—broader than actual sacraments—in its apprehension that revelation is always in some sense mediated and material.

From there we move to a consideration of worship and the role of the Johannine Jesus within the worship of God (chapter 2). Since the goal of Christian theology and spirituality in the New Testament is doxology, it seemed vital to devote space to the significance of worship within the Fourth Gospel. Here we see that, for John, Jesus as Word and Son plays a pivotal though complex role in the authentic worship of the Father. In many ways, this role defines the mission of the Johannine Jesus. Through explicit terminology for worship, and through parallel Johannine imagery of 'glorification' and 'honour', John sets worship as the purpose and end result of the Gospel narrative.

It is a natural step to move from there to the theme of the Spirit in John's Gospel, since the Spirit by definition lies at the heart of New Testament spirituality (chapter 3). John has a unique theology of the Holy Spirit who appears throughout the Gospel, from the ministry of John the Baptist to the gathered disciples on Easter Sunday behind locked doors. In particular, John's unique perspective on the Spirit is characterised by the term 'Paraclete', a title used exclusively in the

Farewell Discourse and invariably obscured in English translation. To recognise the significance of the Paraclete as integral to John's presentation of the Spirit is essential for grasping John's spirituality.

The discussion on the Spirit-Paraclete leads, somewhat indirectly at first, to a consideration of the theme of absence, a theme not generally considered part of John's spirituality (chapter 4). Yet it is present in the Fourth Gospel, above all in the theme of Jesus' departure which takes up so much of the second half of the Gospel. Indeed, the theme of Jesus' absence—and therefore divine absence—may be a major factor in John's motivation for committing the Gospel to writing. John recognises the pain and loss of this absence but also offers consolation and hope for the community, both in the present and the future. This hope is tied inextricably to the role of the Spirit, and has significant implications for the continuing life of the believing community. From there we look at discipleship in John's Gospel, evidenced in themes of believing, following, gazing, abiding, loving, and obeying (chapter 5). The last chapter of Part I examines more embodied aspects of the Gospel's spirituality, particularly in relation to the senses: seeing, hearing, touching, tasting and smelling (chapter 6). These enlarge John's understanding of spirituality in bodily ways, requiring the use of image and imagination.

Part II begins with an outline of the main themes and images of the Johannine epistles, and relevance of such imagery for understanding their spirituality, as connected to, and distinct from, the perspective of the Fourth Gospel (chapter 7). Life, light, love, abiding, forgiveness, and the discernment of spirits are key concepts, threading their way through the letters. The spirituality is focussed particularly on the life of the community of faith, those who have retained their commitment to what the author sees as true faith, as against the apostates. Finally, we examine briefly the Book of Revelation in its dynamic symbolism and imagery, as these relate to understanding the complex and rich theology of John the Seer (chapter 8). Grasping the code of its somewhat bizarre language enables us to enter its spiritual and liturgical domain, encountering a spirituality that has remarkable political and economic implications. The last chapter attempts to draw all these threads together into a final statement that sets out the meaning and significance of the spirituality of these Johannine texts.

End Notes

[1.] See Bruce H. Lescher & Elizabeth Liebert (eds.) 'Introduction', in *Exploring Christian Spirituality. Essays in Honor of Sandra M. Schneiders* (New York: Paulist, 2006), 1-7.

[2.] Judith A. Berling, 'Christian Spirituality: Intrinsically Interdisciplinary' in Lescher & Liebert (eds.), *Exploring Christian Spirituality*, 35-52.

[3.] See John R. Donahue, 'The Quest for Biblical Spirituality' in Lescher & Liebert (eds.), *Exploring Christian Spirituality*,73-97.

[4.] Samuel M. Powell, *A Theology of Christian Spirituality* (Nashville: Abingdon, 2005), 26-48.

[5.] John R. Tyson, *Invitation to Christian Spirituality. An Ecumenical Anthology* (New York/Oxford: Oxford University Press, 1999), 4-45.

[6.] Vladimir Lossky, *The Mystical Theology of the Eastern Church* (ET: Crestwood, New York: St Vladimir's Seminary Press, 1998), 7-14.

[7.] Philip Sheldrake, *Spiritiuality and Theology. Christian Living and the Doctrine of* God (London: Darton, Longman, & Todd, 1998), 3 (3-32)

[8.] For a contemporary understanding of 'spirituality' within the context of Christian theology, see especially Philip F. Sheldrake, *Explorations in Spirituality: History, Theology, and Social Practice* (New York: Paulist, 2010), 1-14. For an outline of various definitions, see Lawrence S. Cunningham & Keith J. Egan, *Christian Spirituality. Themes from the Tradition* (New York: Paulist, 1996), 5-28.

[9.] See Powell, *Christian Spirituality* 2, who argues that theology 'deals with the essential and normative features of spirituality'.

[10.] Stephen C. Barton, *The Spirituality of the Gospels* (London: SPCK, 1992), 113. Barton (114-133) goes on to describe the Fourth Gospel's spirituality as personal, corporate, christocentric, bound up with history and its interpretation, 'a gospel for tough times' (123), and charismatic (in the true sense of association with the Spirit).

[11.] See especially the opening comments by Peter Adam, *Hearing God's Words. Exploring Biblical Spirituality* (Downers Grove: InterVarsity Press, 2004), 15-46, who bemoans the neglect of the Bible in Christian understandings of spirituality.

[12.] A. Plummer, *The Gospel According to St John* (Cambridge: Cambridge University Press, 1905), xliii. In this respect, Plummer considers the evangelist a greater genius than Shakespeare.

13. Quoted by Eusebius in *HE* 6, 14, 7. On Clement's use of the Johannine writings, see Charles E. Hill, *The Johannnine Corpus in the Early Church* (Oxford: Oxford University Press, 2004), 121-8.

14. So L. William Countryman, *The Mystical Way in the Fourth Gospel. Crossing Over Into God* (Valley Forge PA: Trinity Press International, 1994), 1-8.

15. Barton, *Spirituality*, 114.

16. The use of author's names in this study — 'John', 'the elder', 'John the Seer' — is a matter of stylistic variation, and does not denotes the flesh-and-blood author, to whom we have no access, but rather the text itself.

17. D. Moody Smith, 'John: Historian or Theologian?' *BR* 20 (2004), 31.

18. See the summary essay by Paul N. Anderson, 'Aspects of History in the Fourth Gospel: Consensus and Convergences' in P.N. Anderson, F. Just, & T. Thatcher (eds.), *John, Jesus, and History, Volume 2: Aspects of Historicity in the Fourth Gospel* (Atlanta: SBL, 2009), 379-386.

19. Craig R. Koester, *The Word of Life. A Theology of John's Gospel* (Grand Rapids: Eerdmans, 2008), 133.

20. There is, as yet, no archaeological evidence of an actual synagogue building, but that does not negate the presence of a Jewish, synagogual community in the city, nor of an actual building.

21. See Richard Bauckham, 'For Whom Were the Gospels Written?' in Richard Bauckham (ed.), *The Gospels for All Christians: Re-thinking the Gospel Audiences* (Grand Rapids: Eerdmans, 1998), 9-48.

22. Some have argued that the notion of 'author' does not necessarily imply the writer of the Gospel, but can mean the creative mind behind the tradition. Certainly, we know that it is unlikely that John physically wrote the Gospel, since scribes were usually employed for the task (cf Rom 16:22; Gal 6:11). On the role of a secretary or *amanuensis*, see, e.g. Ian J. Elmer, 'I, Tertius: Secretary or Co-author of Romans' *AusBR* 56 (2008), 45-60.

23. For a brief survey of Patristic arguments on authorship, see Maurice F. Wiles, *The Spiritual Gospel. The Interpretation of the Fourth Gospel in the Early Church* (Cambridge: Cambridge University Press, 1960), 7-12. Hill argues that the attribution of the Gospel to the Apostle John goes back to Papias in the early part of the second century (*Johannine Corpus*, 385-96).

24. Richard Bauckham, *Jesus and the Eyewitnesses. The Gospels as Eyewitness Testimony* (Grand Rapids, Michigan/Cambridge, UK: Eerdmans, 2006) 358-411. Some argue that the eyewitness language is metaphorical rather than literal: that the beloved disciple attests to the truth of the events he describes rather than their strict historicity. See, e.g., Andrew T. Lincoln,

'The Beloved Disciple as Eyewitness and the Fourth Gospel as Witness' *JSNT* 85 (2002), 2-36, who argues that the language of eyewitness is a literary device.

25. Martin Hengel, *The Johannine Question* (ET London: SCM, 1989), 24-108, argues that the author of the Gospel and epistles is John the elder. For the view that John the apostle is still the most likely candidate for authorship, see Andreas J. Köstenberger, *John* (Baker Academic, 2004), 6-8. For the view that the Fourth Gospel is anonymous, see, e.g., Lincoln, *Saint John*, 17-26. On the beloved disciple, see James H. Charlesworth, *The Beloved Disciple: Who Witness Validates the Gospel of John?* (Valley Forge: Trinity Press International, 1995) esp. 225-287, who sets out the variety of theories on his identity, concluding that the beloved disciple is Thomas.

26. Richard Bauckham argues that the Fourth Gospel has more in common with ancient historiography than the Synoptic Gospels ('Historiographical Characteristics of the Gospel of John' *NTS* 53 [2007], 17-36).

27. Further on the relationship between John and the Synoptics, see D. Moody Smith, *John among the Gospels* (2nd ed.; Columbia: University of South Carolina Press, 2001), Paul N. Anderson, 'John and Mark—the Bi-Optic Gospels' in Robert Fortna & Tom Thatcher (eds.), *Jesus in Johannine Tradition* (Philadelphia: Westminster, 2001) 175-88, and *The Fourth Gospel and the Quest for Jesus: Modern Foundations Reconsidered* (Edinburgh: T & T Clark, 2007).

28. For a summary of the historical issues in John's Gospel, see D. Moody Smith, 'The Problem of History in John', and the response by Craig S. Keener, 'Genre, Sources and History' in T. Thatcher (ed.), *What we Have Heard from the Beginning. The Past, Present, and Future of Johannine Studies* (Waco, Texas: Baylor University Press, 2007), 311-320, 321-323.

29. See Raymond E. Brown, *The Gospel According to John* (AB29; 2 vols.; New York: Doubleday, 1966), 1.xxxii-xxxix; Barnabas Lindars, *The Gospel of John* (London: Oliphants, 1972), 46-54; John Ashton, *Understanding the Fourth Gospel* (2nd ed.; Oxford: Oxford University Press, 2007), 82-86, 199-204.

30. See Majella Franzmann & M. Klinger, 'The Call Stories of John 1 and John 21' *St Vladimir's Theological Quarterly* 36 (1992), 7-15, and Peter F. Ellis, 'The Authenticity of John 21' *St Vladimir's Theological Quarterly* 36 (1992), 17-25.

31. F.J. Moloney, *The Gospel of John* (SP 4; Collegeville: Liturgical Press, 1998), 18.

32. For a brief summary of these values, see especially Jerome H. Neyrey, *The Gospel of John* (NCBC; Cambridge: Cambridge University Press, 2007), 15-27.

[33.] See, e.g. Ben Witherington, *John's Wisdom. A Commentary on the Fourth Gospel* (Cambridge: Lutterworth, 1995), 37-41, D. Moody Smith, *John* (ANTC; Nashville: Abingdon, 1999), 33-9, and Andrew Lincoln, *The Gospel According to Saint John* (BNTC; London: Continuum, 2005), 82-9.

[34.] See Edward W. Klink, *The Sheep of the Fold. The Audience and Origin of the Gospel of John* (SNTSMS 141; Cambridge: Cambridge University Press, 2007), 42-106.

[35.] See Craig S. Keener's careful study of what he entitles the 'social contexts' of the Fourth Gospel, which begins by acknowledging the 'tenuousness of past historical reconstructions', but nonetheless demonstrates something of the general social and religious milieu behind the Gospel (*The Gospel of John. A Commentary* [Peabody: Hendrickson], 2003), 1.140 (140-232).

[36.] J. Louis Martyn argues that the Fourth Gospel is a two-level drama which reflects as much, if not more, of the life of the ongoing community that produced it, than of Jesus' own ministry (*History and Theology in the Gospel of John* [2nd ed.; Nashville: Abingdon, 1979). Against this, see, e.g., Klink, *Sheep of the Fold*, 185-246.

[37.] Translation of biblical texts, unless otherwise indicated, are my own.

[38.] For a helpful outline of the similarities between the Gospel and 1 John, see John Painter, *1, 2, and 3 John* (SP18; Collegeville: Liturgical Press, 2002), 64-73. Painter himself argues that 1 John was written after the Gospel by a different, though dependent, hand.

[39.] See the note of warning in Judith Lieu, 'Us or You? Persuasion and Identity in 1 John' *JBL* 127 (2008), 805-7.

[40.] See, e.g. R. Alan Culpepper, *The Gospel and Letters of John* (Nashville: Abingdon, 1998), 42-61.

[41.] As argued, for example, by Raymond E. Brown, *The Community of the Beloved Disciple. The Life, Loves, and Hates of an Individual Church in New Testament Times* (New York: Paulist, 1979), 103-144. Most scholars take this view of the writing of the Johannine epistles.

[42.] A minority argue that the Johannine epistles were written prior to the Gospel, either in whole or part. See, e.g., Kenneth Grayston (*The Johannine Epistles* [Grand Rapids: Eerdmans, 1984], especially 7-14); also Judith Lieu, *The Second and Third Epistles of John* (Edinburgh: T & T Clark, 1986), 166-216, who argues for the relative independence of the several Johannine writings. C.H. Talbert sees the epistles as earlier than or possibly contemporaneous with the writing of the Gospel (*Reading John. A Literary and Theological Commentary on the Fourth Gospel and the Johannine Epistles* [London: SPCK, 1992], 3-17).

43. For those who support a significant level of dependence by 1 John on the Gospel, see, e.g., I. Howard Marshall, *The Epistles of John* (Grand Rapids: Michigan, 1978), 31-42, Raymond E. Brown, *The Epistles of John. A New Translation with Introduction and Commentary* (New York: Doubleday, 1982), 30-35, 69-115, S.S. Smalley, *1, 2, 3 John* (Waco, Texas: Word Books, 1984), xxii-xxxii, David Rensberger, *The Epistles of John* (Louisville: John Knox, 2001), 1-7, and Painter, *1, 2 and 3 John*, 58-74.

44. It is possible that the evangelist is clearing up a misapprehension that he is immortal and not subject to death, especially if he is rapidly aging. See Keener, *Gospel of John*, 2.1240-6. Nevertheless, the first person narration of 21:24 implies the hand of another, confirming the testimony of the beloved disciple.

45. For a succinct argument in favour of a single authorship for both, see Robert W. Yarbrough, *1-3 John* (Baker Exegetical Commentary on the NT; Grand Rapids: Baker Academic, 2008), 5-15; Yarbrough argues in favour of John the apostle, son Zebedee, as the author.

46. The conclusions of David E. Aune are representative (*Revelation* [3 vols; WBC52; Dallas: Word Books, 1997], 2.lvi): 'it is not possible to identify [the author of Revelation] with any other early Christian figures of the same name, including John the son of Zebedee or the shadowy figure of John the Elder.'

47. On the theological similarities between the Fourth Gospel and Revelation, see Stephen S. Smalley, 'John's Revelation and John's Community' *Bulletin of the John Rylands University Library of Manchester* 69 (1987), 549-71.

48. This was, however, a majority view. See Joel C. Elowsky (ed.), *John 1-10* (ACCS NT IVa; Downers Grove, IL: InterVarsity Press, 2006), xxiv-xxvii, who argues for John the son of Zebedee as the author of Revelation.

49. For a good summary of the issues surrounding authorship, see Aune, *Revelation*, 1.xlvii-lvi.

50. See especially the summary in G.K. Beale, *The Book of Revelation. A Commentary on the Greek Text* (NIGTC; Grand Rapids: Eerdmans, 1999), 4-27.

51. E.g. Arthur A. Bell, 'The Date of John's Apocalypse: The Evidence of Some Roman Historians Reconsidered' *NTS* 25 (1978), 93-102.

52. For arguments supporting this dating, see, e.g., George H. Van Kooten, 'The Year of the Four Emperors and the Revelation of John: The 'pro-Neronian' Emperors Otho and Vitellius, and the Images and Colossus of Nero in Rome' *JSNT* 30 (2007), 205-48.

53. David R. Barr, 'John's Ironic Empire' *Int 63* (2009), 20.

54. The quotation seems to originate in Gregory the Great's *Moralia in*

Iob, Bk 1.4, where it refers to the Bible in general; the image is that of a lamb rather than an infant. http://www9.georgetown.edu/faculty/jod/texts/ moralia1.html.

Part I: The Gospel of John

Chapter 1
Spirituality and the Word

To understand the symbols of John's[1] spirituality requires laying bare the foundations of the writer's theological vision. To do so is to grasp not just the language John uses but also his understanding of how that language operates. John's Gospel, on the one hand, is essentially symbolic, revealing itself in Johannine 'sign', image, and metaphor. These elements form the basis for what we may call the 'sacramentality' of the Gospel: its communication of the invisible through the visible, spirit through matter, glory through flesh. Yet the Fourth Gospel is a theology of *word*, in content as well as formal expression. To some, that may seem to take us out of the realms of spirituality altogether, and towards reason and cognition. But 'word' in this Gospel is closely allied to symbol, so that the two can only be understood in relation to each other.

Word and Words

Since 'the Word' is where John's Gospel commences, so also should we: the word that comes from God and the Word that is God. To make such a beginning is noto say something about both theology and spirituality. The theological centre of the Fourth Gospel is also its spiritual heart. Jesus is explicitly named as the Word (*Logos*) only in the Prologue, although the opening verses of the Gospel provide the theological underpinnings for the whole Gospel (1:1-2).[2] Whenever we encounter the Johannine Jesus in this Gospel, we are aware that we are in the presence of the Word, the one who shares the nature of God and has entered the reality of the world. 'Word' is about communication, and that is precisely the Fourth Gospel's concern: God's communication with, and revelation to, creation.[3] As it transpires, this communication is self-communication: a revelation that draws the world into the intimacy of relationship. The Prologue is, in the words of Udo Schnelle, 'the history of God's care for the world'.[4]

There is more than one way to structure the Prologue and a number of suggestions have been proposed, some of them quite complex.[5] Perhaps the simplest is in three movements, with a chiastic pattern, the first and third paralleling each other. Parts A and A[1] describe the Word who is associated with light and the source of all life, whose glory radiates the humanity he has taken as his own. The one who will later claim of himself that he is 'the Light of the world' (8:12) is the one who brings life and light to creation, a light that no darkness then or in the future can quench: 'in him was life, and the life was the light of all people' (1:4). Just as in Genesis, light is the first created substance (before the sun and moon), being manifest through God's dynamic speech—'God said, Let there be light; and there was light' (Gen 1:3)—so in John light is the first manifestation of the world's re-creation through the divine Word, and a core symbol of the Fourth Gospel. Part B deals with the response of human beings to the revelation of the Word and Light, beginning with the witness of John the Baptist and concluding with those who accept the light and are born of God (1:5-13). This represents an inclusio, with the rejection of 'his own' in the middle (1:10-11), emphasising that, for John, tragedy has neither the first nor the last word but is enclosed by those who recognise the light and turn gladly towards it. Here again the light 'shines in the darkness but the darkness has not overcome it' (1:5):[6]

> Jn 1:1-5 The Word in the beginning   *A*
> • with & as God
> • as Creator
> • as life and light
>
> Jn 1:6-13 Response to the Word   *B*
> • testimony of John the Baptist
> • rejection by 'his own'
> • acceptance by children of God
>
> Jn 1:14-18 The Word in time   *A[1]*
> • glory dwelling in flesh
> • testimony of JBap
> • Moses and Jesus
> • Son as narrator of Father

Within this structure, the Prologue has several things to say about the Word, which the reader is to bear in mind throughout the subsequent Gospel narrative.[7] First of all, the Word exists in intricate relationship with God, a relationship that is later captured in the imagery of Father-Son: 'In the beginning was the Word, and the Word was with God, and the Word was God. He was in the beginning with God' (1:1-2). In this way, John depicts the paradoxical unity, separateness and intimacy lying between the 'word' (*logos*) and 'God' (*theos*). In the distinction between heaven and earth, between 'above' and 'below', the Word belongs in the former, existing in intimacy with God in the celestial realm. The preposition 'with' (a somewhat unusual choice) suggests that the Word is face-to-face, 'turned towards' or beside, God in love and union.[8] So the opening verses make clear that the Word and God are both one and the same ('the Word was God'), and also distinct and in relationship to one another ('the Word was with God'). This complex association, which is not yet clear to the reader, pre-exists creation; 'in the beginning' (*en archê(i)*, the first words of the Greek Old Testament, LXX Gen 1:1) refers to the eternity before time began.

Secondly, the Word relates to creation and not just to God. God's self-communication manifests itself in the making of the world through the agency of the Word: 'All things came into being through him [the Word], and without him not one thing came into being' (Jn 1:3). Note the emphasis of the text: nothing of substance in the world is outside the Word's creative, embracing power.[9] The source of the world's life, physical and spiritual, is the divine Word, the one who exists from all eternity face-to-face with God. Thus the Word interacts with God and the world, dwelling in relationship with God and bringing the world into being. As in the first creation account where God speaks and each intricate part of creation springs to life ('God said', Gen 1:3-31), so John reveals that the Word, closely affiliated to God, is no less than the divine utterance through which the world exists. Creation and redemption are inextricably linked: the one God, the one Word, the one domain.

So far, John has made no explicit reference to Jesus: he will not name him until later in the Prologue (1:17). For the Hellenistic Jewish reader, well-versed in the Old Testament, John in the opening verses could well be speaking of certain Old Testament motifs. In some Jewish circles, the Law (Torah) was thought to exist before creation,[10] and the giving of the Law on Mt Sinai the most significant expression of the divine word outside creation (Exod 23, 34). God's word on the mountain is a manifestation of the covenant, a gracious, life-giving gift to Israel, in which God offers the choice between life and death (Deut 30:11-20), blessing and curse, the former sealed with the promise of the land. This dynamic, life-giving word is also a major theme in the prophetic literature, where 'the word of the Lord' comes to the prophets, a word of salvation and judgement, speaking out against idolatry and injustice, calling the people of Israel back to the covenant as set out in the Torah.

The manifestation of the divine word that bestows life on God's people in the Prologue is thus not alien to the Jewish reader or the Gentile reader well-versed in the Old Testament. The word of God is a major symbol in Old Testament theology, a word that not only creates the world but recalls God's people to their true identity and heritage again and again, saving and rescuing them in exodus and exile, in disobedience and failure. Unlike human words which fall empty to the ground, the word of God in Israel is fecund and productive, whether in Genesis, Isaiah or the Gospel of John, whether with a small 'w' or a capital:

> For as the rain and the snow come down from heaven, and do not return there until they have watered the earth, making it bring forth and sprout, giving seed to the sower and bread to the eater, so shall my word be that goes out from my mouth; it shall not return to me empty, but it shall accomplish that which I purpose, and succeed in the thing for which I sent it (Isa 55:10-11 RSV).

In this sense, God's word is one and the same, undivided: the same speaking, the same desire for communication, the same creative zest and determination, the same unity of speech and act.

It is significant that, when Jesus is named later in the Prologue, it matches John's first reference to Moses: 'The law indeed was given through Moses; grace and truth came through Jesus Christ' (1:17). There is no discrepancy between Jesus and Moses here, between law and grace; Moses is a positive figure in the Fourth Gospel. Although the giving of the Law is not God's last or ultimate gift, it has great import for John. In the Johannine understanding, the old points to the new, while the new is rooted and grounded in the old. Later in the Gospel, Moses will turn out to be on Jesus' side (5:45-47) and, even in his sabbath healing—an apparent breach of the Torah—the Johannine Jesus does not contravene the Mosaic Law. Indeed the figures of both Moses and Jesus are indispensable in the revelation of God's creative and redemptive word, according to John—though Jesus is the greater figure for, whereas Moses gives God's first word to Israel, Jesus *is* God's last Word for the world, the fulfilment of Torah and the reality to which it symbolically points.

But there is a further aspect of the Old Testament that is vital to John's picture of the Word of God in the Prologue. John's presentation of the Word existing with God before creation and acting as the source of life for creation suggests, not only Torah, but also the figure of Holy Wisdom (Sophia). Wisdom exists with God before creation (Prov 8:22-26; Sir 24:9; Wisd 6:22), is the agent of creation (Prov 8:27-30a; Wisd 9:1-2), faces both God and the world simultaneously, delights in each (Prov 8:30b-31), radiates divine glory (Wisd 7:25-26), and nourishes the hungry with true food, being both the giver and the gift (Prov 9:1-6; Sir 24:19-21). Wisdom acts as a bridge, in other words, between the heavenly and earthly realms (Wisd 7:27).[11] These same qualities can also be said of Word and Torah in the Old Testament, since wisdom is linked inextricably to the Law as the manifestation of God's communication with, and guidance of, Israel in the covenant. Indeed, many of the qualities ascribed to Wisdom, especially in the later traditions, are divine qualities.[12] Wisdom thus expresses God's immanence to creation, and it is this rich tradition upon which John draws for his portrait of the Word in the Prologue, a portrait that underlies the rest of the Fourth Gospel.

It may seem strange, therefore, that after the Prologue Jesus is not once named as the Word in the rest of the Gospel. Other titles Jesus has in abundance, but this one is curiously lacking.[13] Many scholars explain this by arguing that the Prologue in its original form was a separate hymn, probably of the Johannine community, which John adapted for his own use.[14] Even if this were the case, there would be more to be said. As the key to the Fourth Gospel—in its present form— the Prologue sets the mood and tone for the Gospel.[15] All through the narrative, John presupposes that the reader knows that this person who speaks and acts, who lives and dies, who passes through the darkness of death into the light of light, is the divine Logos, the Word of God before time began. This is particularly apparent in the prayer of John 17, where the stance of the Johannine Jesus is that of the Word 'turned towards God', the one who was in the beginning, whose origins and destiny are 'from God', who is sent by God, and whose destiny is to return to God.

But there is another reason that 'Word' is absent from the main narrative of the Gospel: it is superseded by the title of 'Son'. That superseding takes place within the Prologue itself, where the somewhat abstract language of 'God' and 'Word' (1:1-2) is transformed into the more colourful, concrete and intimate language of Father and Son (1:14, 18).[16] For John, 'Son' is the preferred title for Jesus, becoming a core symbol in the Fourth Gospel. The title contains a wealth of spiritual meaning not apparent in other terminology, including that of 'Word'. In the Johannine worldview, believers become sons and daughters, children of God, through the filiation of Jesus, drawn into his relationship with the Father, as the risen Jesus indicates to Mary Magdalene in his careful use of the possessive adjective: '*my* Father and *your* Father, *my* God and *your* God' (20:17). That means that, wherever we encounter 'Son' in the rest of the Gospel—and the title occurs frequently, either as Son, Son of God or Son of Man, which though not precisely identical are closely linked[17]—we assume we are dealing with the 'Word', the latter taken up into the former and transformed. For this reason, it is not strictly accurate to describe the 'Word' as absent from the rest of the Gospel. When the Prologue is read aright, the appellation endures in the 'Son' title which encloses it. Nevertheless, the notion of the 'word' in a more general sense is far from absent from the rest of the Gospel. The Johannine Jesus not only *is* the Word but also *speaks* the word, a word that summons people to

Illustration 2: Romanian glass icon of Christ the Word[18]

In the Romanian icon above, the pomegranates in the background emphasise the role of the Word in creation, the source of all life. Holding the Word in his left hand, he is the Word, the divine Logos from all eternity. His palpability in flesh is implicit in the very form of the icon itself: as in the incarnation, matter once again symbolises spirit; flesh commemorates glory.[19] The form of this particular example is Byzantine but the execution is the work of eighteenth century peasant art, painted on glass: a combination of classical iconic form and popular interpretation.[20]

faith. Authentic spirituality is demonstrated in those Johannine characters in the Gospel who show belief in the efficacy of Jesus' word. Most notably, in the first 'Cana to Cana' sequence (2:1-4:52), the mother of Jesus and the royal official evince exemplary faith in the word of Jesus: the one instructs the servants to 'do whatever he tells you' (2:5) while the other immediately accepts Jesus' assurance of his son's health (4:50). Even under apparent rebuke, their faith persists and, in the case of the wedding story, nurtures the faith of the newly-formed band of disciples in pointing to the power of Jesus' word, as the mother of Jesus instructs the servants. Indeed, the glory of Jesus is manifest precisely through such faith in the creative, healing utterance of Jesus—in whom speech and deed are one, as with the God of creation and exodus.

This faith in the word of the Word-Son is intrinsic to Johannine spirituality. Indeed, it is the first and necessary step on the spiritual path, according to John. For the reader, it means believing all that the Johannine Jesus says of himself as the giver of living water, the bread of life, the light of the world, the Good Shepherd, the resurrection and the life, the way to the Father, and so on. Equally it means accepting, not only the revelation of Jesus' own complex identity, but also human identity in general, since Jesus represents a universal humanity. Thus he reveals the hunger and thirst for life, the yearning for truth, goodness and beauty, exposing the tragedy of enslavement to sin and death, the anguish of languishing in self-enclosing darkness. The Johannine Jesus articulates the truth of what it means to be human as well as what it means to be divine. And faith, in the first place, is the trust that that dual self-revealing utterance of Jesus is true—true enough to build one's life upon: 'Very truly, I tell you, anyone who hears my word and believes him who sent me has eternal life, and does not come under judgement, but has passed from death to life' (5:24); 'the words that I have spoken are spirit and life' (6:63).

John has different ways of expressing the notion of faith in relation to the word, or words, of Jesus. For example, Jesus speaks of abiding in his word(s) (8:31, 15:7)—or his word abiding in disciples (15:7)—of hearing it (8:27, 43, 14:24), keeping it (8:51-52, 14:23-24,

15:20, 17:6), remembering it (15:20), and even being cleansed by it (15:3). All these verbs describe something more than intellectual assent or notional agreement; they express a fundamental orientation of life, a rock on which to stand, a foundation on which to build. We will see later how central the notion of 'abiding' is for John's understanding of discipleship and spirituality, with its focus on resting in Jesus and being at home in him. For the time being we note the import of other verbs. To hear, for the fourth evangelist, is not just a literal hearing but a listening of the heart, an apprehension that goes deep within, that allows the self to open itself more and more, little by little, to the divine, healing voice. The connotations in the imagery of *keeping* Jesus' word suggest guarding and treasuring that which is of incalculable value: like cradling a precious jewel in one's hands or standing guard over an ancient treasure. Likewise the idea of *remembering* is not something superficial, not just a feat of memory, a clever ability for verbal recall, but rather (like hearing) a profound bringing to conscious mind of the liberating word of Jesus. Less comprehensible perhaps is the notion of being *cleansed* by the word or words of Jesus. Yet John indicates the sheer power of language to transform and hallow, to purify the intentions, to centre on what really matters, to forgive imperfection and failure. There is something very receptive about 'being cleansed': like a small child washed clean of dirt and grime.

All these verbs, abiding, hearing, keeping and remembering, suggest that to sit in silence before the word of the Johannine Jesus, letting everything else go—to sit before the *word* of the *Word*—is simultaneously to be refreshed, nurtured, cleansed, and renewed. For this evangelist, it means coming face-to-face with the source of life and drawing nurture from it, a life that ultimately overcomes death. No great effort required, this seemingly passive holding of the word, day after day, and allowing it to reach down into the depths, yet perhaps the hardest to achieve. The call is not so much, or at least not primarily, to heroic deeds and strenuous effort. Rather it is a matter of living in the word which enfolds, consoles and renews, especially where human effort falters. By this word believers in the Johannine worldview are fed and renovated, recognising in it the voice of God making its home within. Although not named in the Fourth Gospel, silence has by implication a place in Johannine spirituality: the silence of listening, of waiting upon God.

In John's Gospel, of course, hearing is not the only response to the Word and words. Disciples are also called to speech: to bear witness, to speak on behalf of Jesus as John the Baptist does, and the Samaritan woman (4:39), and above all the beloved disciple in the composition of the Gospel (21:24). There is also a speaking addressed to God, the intimacy of conversation in which disciples share the Son's freedom of speech before the Father. But the priority lies in listening, in opening the ears (inner and outer) to allow the Word to penetrate the deepest places.

There is another implication, to which we have already in part alluded. This deceptively small act of holding and guarding the word of Jesus is what it means, for John, to be a restored child of God. As the Johannine Jesus, the Son, holds the word of the Father (8:55), so too do those who have been re-made as children of God: they too hold the word of Jesus and are sustained by it. *They* are sons and daughters because *he* is the Son. They share in his filiation, his status, and so enter the Father's love: they dwell in the household of faith as free children, not slaves (8:34-36). To keep the words of the Word is one definition of what it means to be a child of God in this Gospel, to be part of the community of God's children who enter confidently and freely into the Son's communion with the Father. In this sense, we can speak of prayer in John's Gospel as entry into the status of God's children—through meditation on the word—knowing that the Word himself purifies and renews, especially where the words and deeds of disciples fail. For John, this movement requires a miracle of re-birth (1:13; 3:1-9), to be confirmed again and again.

The notion of the Word who is Jesus, and the life-giving words which come from Jesus, however, can be taken a step further. The words spoken by Jesus in this Gospel are seen to occupy the same position as the words of Scripture. In the Cleansing of the Temple, for example, the narrator tells us that the disciples 'believed the Scripture and the word which Jesus had spoken' (2:22), implying an equivalence to both. Elsewhere in the Gospel, Jesus fulfils the words of the Old Testament, both in his ministry and above all in the glorification of his death. The words of Scripture find fulfilment in the rejection that Jesus experiences (12:38), in the betrayal of Judas (13:18; 17:12), in the abiding unity of the disciples even in a context of disarray and disunity (18:9), in the form that Jesus' death will take (18:32), and in the events of the Passion: the casting of lots, Jesus' thirst, and the wholeness of his bones (19:24, 28, 36). Thus both the words of Jesus himself and, by implication, the words of the Gospel as a whole share parity of status with the typological words of the Old Testament. The beloved disciple sees himself as authoring Scripture in his witness to the Word. The words of testimony attempt to make the Gospel of John, in effect, Scripture.[21]

Symbol and Incarnation

So far we have discussed the spirituality of the Word/word without explicit reference to the incarnation. Yet it is impossible to bypass this, the central motif and climax of the Prologue:[22] that the Word is revealed in and through material flesh.[23] The term 'flesh' here refers not just to the body but to the humanity of Jesus, body and soul. It is a form of synecdoche in which the part stands for the whole. As the centre of the Fourth Gospel's understanding of salvation, the flesh of the incarnate Word expresses the Johannine conviction that God has become human in Jesus Christ.[24] The divine word in the Old Testament—the word of creation, the prophetic word, the word of wisdom and Torah—is enfleshed, crossing the impassable gulf between Creation and creation. God has definitively entered the material world in a way unprecedented, yet nonetheless prepared for, in the Old Testament. Divine glory now shines through the Johannine Jesus, in flesh and blood, as the locus of the divine self-communication, emerging as new while cocooned in Israel's past.

Thus not only is the Word articulated in the Son, but the Word is also incarnate, enfleshed. The divine glory, once shining from within the heart of Israel, now expresses itself in the humanity of Jesus—a widening and narrowing of God's self-revelation at the same time: not narrowly in Israel but now in universal human flesh; not broadly in Torah, prophet and Wisdom, but now more narrowly in the one Child of Israel. The flesh of Jesus, in this Gospel, is precisely how the divide between divine and human is traversed. That such a divide exists is implied in the Prologue, as well as throughout the Gospel. But there are two very different dimensions to that divine-human gulf. On the one hand, the separation is inevitable: 'no-one has ever seen God' (1:18). By definition God is beyond created reality—its source and sustainer, but also outside its bounds, utterly other in character and being. This distinction involves all created reality, physical or spiritual. By implication it is as pertinent for the soul: all belong on our side of the divide, with God uniquely on the other. John expresses this distinction in the Prologue by the use of the verb 'to be' for the divine side and the verb 'to become' for all aspects of created reality.[25] God simply *is* but the world is in a perpetual state of *becoming*.

There is a further division between God and the world, one created by the intrusion of sin and death, which John depicts symbolically as 'darkness'. No explanation is given for this disjunction, but it adds an irresolvable complication to the abyss that separates the Creator from the created. As a consequence we discover in the Prologue two parallel realities: first, that, as a consequence of the division, creation has tragically and inexplicably failed to recognise, if not outright rejected, its Creator; and secondly that, again in consequence of this painful disjunction, human beings have lost their created status as children of God and must regain it, a status that can only be restored by God.

In this context John makes dual use of the important term 'flesh'. Within the Prologue there is a careful distinction between the *flesh* that is ineffective—though never intrinsically evil in this Gospel—and the *flesh* that is redemptive, that heals the breach and mends creation. The first reference to flesh refers to that which cannot effect the requisite new birth: 'who were born, not of blood or of the will of the flesh or of the will of man, but of God' (1:13). The second reference, coming significantly straight after,[26] is to the incarnation: what mortal flesh cannot of itself achieve, the creative power of the enfleshed Word can. A similar contrast is drawn, this time between 'flesh' and 'spirit' (*pneuma*), in Jesus' dialogue with Nicodemus: 'What is born of the flesh is flesh, and what is born of the Spirit is Spirit' (3:6). There is nothing innately pejorative about flesh in either of these references. Rather, John at one level is making a simple statement of fact, that there are two realms, the heavenly and the earthly. To this he adds a theological point, that no force of earth can mend the rupture in the fabric of the world. In the same way, in the bread of life discourse, Jesus draws a contrast between the two different kinds of flesh, this time in reverse order. Jesus' flesh and blood are necessary for life: 'unless you eat the flesh of the Son of Man and drink his blood, you have no life in you' (6:53). But, at the same time, flesh is ineffective, of no avail compared to the Spirit: 'It is the Spirit that gives life; the flesh is useless' (6:63). Of itself, then, as the symbol for created existence in its intrinsic materiality, flesh cannot cross the abyss or re-forge the broken links that bind Creator to creation. Only a divine miracle can re-create what is lost.

The early church speaks of this kind of theology as the divine image lost in the fall. The language is consonant with the Gospel of John. Just as children can be said to be the 'image' of their parents, so human beings were created in the 'image' of God, an image lost but renewed by the grace of the one creating and re-creating God. Yet both creation and re-creation take place through the agency of the Word-Son, at the instigation of the Father. Just as the Word represents the hand of God reaching out into the chaos and primordial darkness to give form and life to creation, so the Word represents the speech of God resonating in the darkness of the world, entrapped in sin and death, calling it to new life and re-creation. This latter is effected, not simply by divine fiat, but more radically (and completely) through incarnation. This time the Word does not merely reach out to touch creation but enters into it, becomes intrinsic to it, joins himself to it as in a marriage. Creator becomes creation. That which is utterly other, unlike and spirit, now becomes alike and matter. Like the symbol of the snake in the wilderness, which heals the deadly bite of the snake with a bronze snake lifted up on a pole (3:14-15), so in order to heal flesh the Word himself becomes flesh. The Father crosses the gulf, making of the flesh of the Son the bridge between heaven and earth. Flesh is healed by flesh. In this Johannine worldview, the flesh which is ineffective and mortal, unable to mend creation, becomes the flesh disclosing divine glory, in sight of which the viewer is restored once more to the status of child of God—like the Word, and through the Word, now able to reflect the same glory. That glory is manifest throughout the Gospel.[27]

In the post-Easter period, John speaks of the Spirit emerging both from Jesus' death and his resurrection (19:30, 20:19-23). As we will see in more detail later, that same Spirit, abiding on Jesus from the beginning and manifest throughout his ministry, is now bestowed on the disciples to comfort, defend and guide them in the absence of Jesus. More than that, the Paraclete, as we will see in chapter three, will actualise the presence of Jesus for the community after the resurrection. How then does such a promise ensure the pertinence of the incarnation? Does so tangible a theology, grounded in the confirmation of materiality and uniting so completely the heavenly and the earthly, become in the post-Easter context a merely spiritual faith, cut off from its material roots by the ascension of the body/flesh of Jesus? If the stories of Mary Magdalene and Thomas (20:1-18; 24-29) join hands across the central narrative of Jesus' gift of the Spirit (20:19-23),[28] so that the desire of each disciple to hold and see—to behold—is not rejected but rather redefined, then no such conclusion is possible. Christian faith, according to John, always remains palpable, fleshly, incarnate. This palpability is extended, for John, to the ongoing life of the church.[29]

All of this is linked in the tightest way to John's symbolic theology. Symbols in this Gospel are neither decorative nor arbitrary but substantial, part of the coherence of the good news. In general terms, symbolism can manifest itself in different forms—in metaphor, art, music, dreams—but at the same time symbols, and especially religious symbols, do not simply point to another reality separate from themselves. Rather, in pointing to that otherness, they are also the means of access to it; not just a sign-post beside the road pointing elsewhere, but the form of transport that takes us to a destination otherwise inaccessible, ineffable, transcendent: 'no-one has ever seen God'. As the linguistic form of symbol, the metaphors of the Gospel create new meaning, bringing together in extraordinary ways elements that, at face value, have no correspondence.[30] They need, therefore, to be carefully interpreted. To make the Johannine statement that Jesus is the Way (14:6) brings together two unlike elements: a human being and a pathway. Yet we cannot interpret the metaphor literally—Jesus is not literally to be identified with a road—and must therefore attempt to find the metaphorical and symbolic meaning. We might then say that the Johannine Jesus is the means by which we reach God, that he reveals who God is, that he gives direction, that he enables us to move into life, that he makes possible our journey 'towards God'.[31] But it is nowhere as concise or as vivid as the metaphor itself. Nothing can really substitute for it. In this sense, within the Johannine worldview, symbolic reality in its Christian understanding *is* truth.

In the Fourth Gospel, there are certain symbols in particular that have core value within the narrative.[32] They are generally not confined to the one story, but recur throughout the Gospel, sometimes with new dimensions and shifting meanings. In this sense, not all symbols are equal. Light, water, lamb, Father-Son, are examples that belong to the heart of the Gospel; to dispense with such symbols as these, as if peeling a piece of fruit and discarding the peel, is impossible without losing the core. Form and content belong intimately together. This does not mean that the Johannine core symbols cannot be articulated in other language—paraphrased, explained, explored—but it does mean that such explication is never a substitute for the symbol itself. When we are dealing with symbolism in this Gospel we are dealing, for John, with truth.

The palpable nature of John's understanding of salvation— intimately tied to creation as its background, pattern and scope— is apparent in the narrative of the Gospel through its multifarious symbolism. It is evidenced, for example, in the metaphorical 'I am' sayings which represent the fusion of divine and human, heaven and earth, beginning and ending in the incarnation: they represent 'the presentation of christological affirmations in pictorial form'.[33] The divine 'I am' associated with God's unique being—the glory which pre-exists creation and is the source of life, love, truth and goodness— is married to the ordinary realities of material life, producing an extraordinary clash, yet union of opposites, a union that only God could ever hold together. Jesus, who can say of himself uniquely, 'I am', is thus the bread of life (6:34), the gate of the sheepfold (10:7, 9), the shepherd of the sheep (10:11, 14), the light of the world (8:12; 9:5; 12:46), the pathway to God (14:6). In an extension of that association with the divine source of life, he is also the giver of living water. His body and blood are the source of nourishment for believers who feed on him to have life. Out of that same body, though dead on the cross, life-giving blood and water flow (19:34). Thomas beholds the glory in the flesh—flesh, that though risen to new life and triumphant over death and darkness, nonetheless retains the marks of crucifixion, the wounded side unhealed because these very wounds are the source of the community's faith and life (20:27).

This means that, in the light of the incarnation, the flesh of the Johannine Jesus is the ultimate, core symbol of the Gospel. Just as a religious symbol points to divine reality and also takes us to it—just as it partakes in the reality of that which it indicates—so the flesh of Jesus points to, and communicates, divine glory. Jesus is the definitive Symbol of God in this Gospel, the visible manifestation of the invisible God, the bearer of divine glory, a glory that discloses itself in human form. Elsewhere the New Testament speaks of Jesus as the Image of God (2 Cor 4:4, Col 1:15), which is more or less the same thing. According to John, the only way we can see the unseeable God is in the face of Jesus, the only way we can touch the unattainable God is in the tangibility of Jesus' flesh and blood, the only way we can hear the reverberations of God's voice is in the one who is himself God's speech to us, God's Word.

John's understanding of incarnation itself ensures this. Just as the divine glory is actualised for believers through the flesh of Jesus, so the meaning of the Gospel is actualised through the symbols of the Johannine narrative. In this sense, form and meaning are inextricable, mirroring one another as reflection and reality, each necessary to the other's existence.[34] The symbols of the Fourth Gospel represent the theological foundations of the text, the shape and form of its expression. They give voice to the Johannine apprehension that, in becoming human, God has spoken through the medium of creation itself. Matter thus redeemed has a new capacity to verbalise the reality of God, just as human beings now possess the 'authority' to 'become God's children', born of God and of God alone (1:12-13), and to speak on God's behalf (15:26-27; 20:17-18; 21:24).

Symbol and Sacrament

In this sense we can speak of a kind of symbolic spirituality in the Fourth Gospel. Indeed, we may go further and perceive the incarnation as the nub of John's sacramental spirituality. If a sacrament, at least in later tradition, is said to consist of the visible presentation of an invisible grace, the exterior manifestation of divine life, then the ultimate sacrament in this Gospel is the Johannine Jesus, the Word made flesh. The word must always be enfleshed in human experience; that is intrinsic to John's spiritual theology. This issue concerns more than actual sacraments. The more fundamental issue is the sacramental nature of John's theological understanding, arising from his incarnational theology.[35] This may involve sacraments but it is a broader category, a horizon of meaning that pervades the Fourth Gospel and its spiritual vision from beginning to end.[36]

To take one example: through the experience of the children of Israel in the wilderness and the gift of the manna, the image of bread serves to symbolise for John the nourishment that the flesh of Christ, as Holy Wisdom, both is and gives.[37] In this sense bread finds its truest and highest expression in the eucharist. There, as a mother nourishes her children with the milk of her body, Jesus the Lamb of God feeds his disciples with the food and drink—the bread and wine—of his own flesh and blood. When John becomes explicit about the eucharistic meaning of the Feeding, he speaks of it as sustaining an intimate relationship between Jesus and believers. It is the source of life, both in the present and for the age to come (6:53-54), because it connects the believer to the one who is the source of life: within the community, through Jesus, to the Father (6:57). This sacramental connection is intimate and relational—the resting of the believer in Christ—which is at the same time the mutual abiding of the one in the other (6:56).

The evangelist's understanding of water also partakes of the same 'sacramentality'. The early chapters of the Fourth Gospel establish the link between baptism and the Spirit: the baptizing of John the Baptist which is continued by Jesus' disciples (1:25-28, 3:23, 4:1-2; also 10:40), the imagery of birth that is 'of water and the spirit' to enable entry into eternal life (3:5), the gift of living water offered to the Samaritan woman (4:7-15), and the association of water with the Spirit in the context of the call to discipleship at the feast of Tabernacles (7:37-39). In its development, the symbol of water takes a new turn in the footwashing where, while retaining its sacramental overtones,[38] it is linked now to cleansing rather than drinking.[39] The placing of the Footwashing narrative where the institution of the eucharist occurs in the Synoptic Gospels is significant in this respect. Within its literary context, John interprets the washing of the feet as first and foremost about cleansing as a ritual preparation for, and participation in, the saving death of Jesus: 'unless I wash you, you have no share with me' (13:8). Only in a secondary and consequent sense is it about service to others in the community (13:12-15). The Farewell Discourse which follows makes it clear that this participation is loving and intimate: God at home in the life and heart of the believer, and the believer finding a true home in God.

Forgiveness and reconciliation are likewise vital aspects of the relationship between the Johannine Jesus and believers. It is the gift the risen Jesus gives the gathered disciples on the evening of Easter Day. The disciples receive the gift of peace and the gift of the Spirit which enable them to take reconciliation with them on their mission: the releasing and retaining of sins (20:19-23). Although forgiveness does not appear as a major theme in this Gospel—at least in explicit language—it is implicit in the references to cleansing. There is mention of sin, though generally it refers to the one fundamental sin of rejecting life and turning instead to darkness. Reconciliation, peace and forgiveness represent tangible ways in which 'life in abundance' hallows the community of faith in truth and love. Thus water moves from that which is drunk in order to quench thirst—metaphorically speaking, the thirst for life—to that which cleanses the body— metaphorically, purifies the soul. Note that, in both senses, John is using fundamental human needs to underscore his conviction of the spiritual needs and longings which he sees as equally fundamental to human life. Thirst needs to be quenched and bodies need to be washed. These basic human needs become metaphors for the thirst-quenching and cleansing gift of water which Jesus bestows in the Spirit. The sacramental theology of the Fourth Gospel means that divine truth and grace are always mediated and always christological: always the flesh redeemed and renewed by flesh, apprehended through the core symbols of the Johannine narrative.

Spirituality, Word and Symbol

Perhaps the best visual image that depicts the holding together of word and symbol, as presented in the Gospel of John, is found in the Orthodox icon of Christ the Word, often called 'Pantocrator' (all-ruling or all-holding one). In this iconic tradition Jesus gazes directly at the viewer, face-to-face, holding in his left arm the book of the Gospels, while raising his right hand in blessing, his fingers poised to represent both the trinity and his own dual nature. The words, 'The One who is', adorn the halo around his head. Icons are not essentially works of art but rather 'windows on the eternal',[40] means by which the viewer is taken—via the 'flesh' of colour, pigment and form—from the earthly to the heavenly. The viewer participates in that to which the icon symbolically points, effecting transformation. This spirituality is close to John's theology, especially in his understanding of the Word that is Jesus, the words that come from Jesus, and the written words of the Gospel. The icon depicts what lies at the core of John's symbolic theology. Jesus in this iconic depiction is the divine Word, the authentic Image or Symbol of God, the agent of creation and source of life, the giver of plenitude and blessing, as revealed in the pages of the Fourth Gospel. John's spiritual theology begins in the one who is Word, Symbol and Son, before whom the reader stands, transfixed by his gaze and his sublime identity. The spirituality of this kind of viewing brings transfiguration and life, since 'from his fullness we have all received, grace upon grace' (1:16).

'Lord, to whom can we go? You have the words of eternal life' (6:68), says Simon Peter to Jesus after many in the crowd have left Jesus, alienated by his self-revelation as the Bread of heaven. These words, centred around Johannine images—bread, water, wine— appeal directly to human needs: for food and drink, for nourishment, protection and shelter, and lead step-by-step to an apprehension of deeper spiritual needs. To allow the Johannine symbols to address the heart is, in Johannine terms, to find life within them. Words, after all, are not just expressive; they also create meaning. The Johannine words and symbols are intended to beat a pathway between God and the reader, a bridge between heaven and earth, a structure to create union not only with heaven, but also with others. The words do so because—and only because—the incarnate Word, in John's vision, inhabits human language as he indwells humanity, bearing divine glory so that the human mind can reverberate with the wondrous speech of God, heart-to-heart, face-to-face. God's light leads out of darkness and God's voice summons creatures into being. The 'Word' expresses a fundamental dependence on God for all that humanity is and can be. As Rowan Williams puts it, discussing the need of God yet God's freedom from us:

> Before we are looked at, spoken to, acted on, we are, because of the look, the word, the act of God. God alone (as supremely free of the world) can bring a hearer into being by speaking, by uttering (making external "outering") what the life of God is, in a creative summons ... We are here ... because of God's "word": our reality is not and cannot be either earned by us or eroded by others.[41]

At the end of his retelling of the Greek myth of Psyche and Eros, C.S. Lewis has his chief character, Queen Orual, addressing Eros just before her death at the end of her story:

> I ended by first book with the words No answer.
> I know now, Lord, why you utter no answer.
> You are yourself the answer. Before your face
> questions die away. What other answer would
> suffice? Only words, words; to be led out to
> battle against other words.[42]

This dynamic, life-forming divine word which speaks all things into being competes against the wordiness of human speech, the re-tracing of old words that burden the spirit. The distinction is between meaningless words and the Word, between the empty words that go on and on, incommunicative, like dead leaves caught on autumn winds, and the vibrant words—simple and few—that conjure life as if from nowhere, filling the spirit with hope and life. In this sense, the Johannine 'answer' to the futility of word-making is the incarnate Word. This Johannine understanding of 'word' does not stand over against silence, any more than it is opposed to symbol. On the contrary, just as in music the pauses are as significant as the notes, so too this living speech implies, by definition, the silence as part of the hearing.

In his poem 'Ash Wednesday', T.S. Eliot speaks of the distinction between the needless words and the one word needful, between the jangled sounds that stifle and the true living voice. For him, the word must be heard but cannot, without silence: 'Where shall the word be found, where will the word / Resound?', he asks. The answer is, only where there is 'enough silence', where people no longer prefer noise and cease denying 'the voice'.[43]

In this theology, so consonant with the Gospel of John, spirituality involves the cultivation of silence, not as an end in itself, but in order to hear the voice, to trace the true form of the animating words, to meet the Johannine Word. He is linked to his words, which alone bear the imprint of his divine humanity in this Gospel, shaped in his likeness, descending like rain from heaven yet rising up also from the earth: the spirited words that share flesh and blood yet speak a celestial word—the one word needful. In this theology, silence is part of communication, not something beyond it. Reflecting on Derrida's understanding of language and silence as both forms of rhetoric, Graham Ward makes this point well:

> Silence becomes analogous to the blank margins of a page, the space beneath the vaulting of a Cathedral, or a musical interval. The margin frames and focuses the text. The empty spaces here establish a certain tension between the arrangement of the letters, the words and the syntax into a communication and the empty margins which a space for the cessation of intellection. It is a space for/of breathing. The margins, therefore, articulate ... a certain rest, a certain Sabbath, a space for the activities of prayer and meditation. In silence a rest is written into the fabric of creation.[44]

Silence, in this sense, is integral to language, the rest that makes possible the utterance, the openness of heart that enables the hearing of the Word even in the most luminous moment of self-manifestation.[45] The bond between word and symbol is likewise of primary significance in Johannine spirituality. It would, of course, be absurd to depict words as the expression only of reason: words can be as intuitive as art or music. John's understanding of the Word, in its Old Testament associations, has to do as much with action and intuition, with imagination and sanctification as it has with reason. As the iconic presence of God, the Johannine Jesus—incarnate, crucified and risen—is intimately linked to the symbols of the Fourth Gospel; the whole Gospel is a 'symbolic narrative' appealing to the imagination and heart of the reader as much to the head, enticing him or her to new life, a new way of being, a re-birth. John's spirituality is sacramental, in the wider sense of that term, as we have seen, grounded in the communication of spirituality through matter.

This Johannine sacramentality has two implications. In the first place, it means that, according to John, theology is quintessentially symbolic, straining inadequately always to that which is beyond, mysterious, indescribable. The God of revelation in creation, Law and incarnation is no less enigmatic; indeed, in one sense the more God is revealed the more inscrutable God seems. The incarnation is not a riddle to be solved but a mystery to be entered. Rational ideas and language have their place, a vitally important place, but not to replace the power of theological symbol which has precedence over all efforts at paraphrase. We need such paraphrase because the symbols require explication and evaluation, but what we offer in interpretation can never take the place of the original, any more than commentary on a piece of music, or even the score, can substitute for the performance. The Johannine God remains unfathomable.

Secondly, by implication, John's symbolic vision takes sacraments seriously. We have to proceed carefully here, especially historically. The place of later church sacraments in the Johannine community is a disputed matter, and not easily resolved. It has seemed possible to some to discern any number of sacraments, or only two, or more if the footwashing is included. But that is not our concern here. We read John looking back over centuries of debate and disagreement, where the number and meanings of sacraments has been spelled out on either side of ecclesiastical divides. The Fourth Gospel precedes this process of definition and debate, although it also arguably stands at its head. John's symbolic worldview lends itself to an appreciation of sacraments as fundamentally connected to incarnation, where the divine glory is perceptible in flesh. Theologically, in a Johannine understanding, the meaning of sacraments is the conveying of divine presence in materiality, the transfiguration of matter into a vehicle for the divine glory.

This theology resounds particularly with the eucharist, as the evangelist explicates it in John 6, in a narrative that explores sapiential and sacramental motifs around the theme of faith. In revealing Jesus as the Bread of life, whose flesh and blood effect eternal life in union with him, John conveys a sense of the symbol and its import. Bread already has a religious tradition for the people of Israel, a tradition that John exploits, picking up the Passover and exodus connotations in the feeding itself and throughout the ensuing dialogue. The manna in the wilderness is miraculous, given by God, but is mortal, material, unable to protect against death. Its true role, according to John, is to point symbolically to Jesus, the Manna from heaven whose flesh given for the world on the cross nourishes believers, body and soul, so that death—though painfully real—may never overcome them.

In the Greek myth of Demeter and Persephone, the young girl while picking flowers is taken by force from her mother, the corn goddess, by the god Hades, Lord of the Underworld. There she is compelled to reside, till the inconsolable Demeter, wandering the earth in search of her beloved daughter, demands her return by refusing to give growth to the crops. Unfortunately, Persephone has already tasted the fruit of death by eating pomegranate seeds in the Underworld, and she can never permanently abandon the realm of the Dead. As a compromise, Zeus ordains it that she spend half the year with Demeter (hence spring and summer) and half with Hades in the Underworld (autumn and winter), when her mother once again mourns her loss. Persephone, in a sense, stands for the human condition unable to escape death; her ruptured relationship with her mother, painfully partial, signifies the alienation in our relationships.

In John's spirituality of the word, there is no need for such compromise. What the Johannine Jesus promises is an eternal summer, a release from the dread grip of Hades, offering believers the seeds not of death but of life, a life won by his own descent to the Underworld. These 'seeds' are the words of everlasting life. They thrive in the core symbols and narrative of the Gospel which are conveyed to the Johannine believer through the senses—through sight, hearing, taste, touch and smell[46]— bestowing fecundity and life. The vital presence of life, joy and freedom indicates that, for John, believers no longer live in the grip and fear of death. The words of the Word who is 'the resurrection and the life' germinate and grow within them.

The symbolic and sacramental life which the Johannine Jesus communicates through faith—where he is host at the banquet, the giver of the food of eternal life and the food itself—cannot be overcome by death; it contains the seeds of life that will never wither but, like a well of water, 'spring up to eternal life' (4:12). But the imagery also connects the implied reader with his or her own hunger. The sapiential revelation communicates not only the reality of God but also the truth of the human spirit. At the banquet in Proverbs 9, Lady Wisdom (Sophia) the gracious hostess who invites all to taste her munificent food and to drink her well-aged wine contrasts with Dame Folly who has her own unappealing 'banquet' of stale bread and water, with ghosts as fellow-guests. The imagery of hunger and thirst discloses the truth of what human beings devour to fill the aching void, so often the food of folly rather than wisdom. The physical craving points symbolically, in a Johannine sense, to a spiritual hunger and thirst, enabling perception of the deepest desires of the heart, the hunger for God and for the nourishment which only God can satiate. Augustine's famous words at the beginning of *The Confessions* are apposite here: 'you have created us for yourself, and our heart cannot be quieted till it find repose in you.'[47] In John's spirituality the incarnation becomes most palpable in the self-gift of the one who is son of Joseph and Son of God, true bread and true flesh, giver of living water, nurturing relationship and life in the believing heart, a life that death cannot overpower.

At the core of John's spirituality lies the notion of Jesus as the divinely human Word who speaks the words of the Father, words that give life and nourishment to those who hear them. The Word is the Symbol of God, the Icon of divine presence and indwelling, whose face turns towards the believer in grace and truth, drawing him or her into a godly circle of love. The palpability of word and sacrament, manifestations of the one reality, conveys the incarnation to the Johannine community, enfolding them in its embrace and sharing the divine life through the instruments of human life—through matter. To hear, to touch, to eat: these are themselves vibrant symbols of communion, where true identity is confirmed and believers are given a share in the life of the Johannine Jesus, his filiation, his glory. The Word speaks from God in ways that address and transform the imagination, using symbols that belong to human experience, and human needs and longings. The Jesus of John's Gospel both *is* and *speaks* the Word, just as he *is* and *gives* the true Bread. Word, symbol, sacrament, Scripture all unite in the Johannine gift of life, uttering the one word needful in the face of what John sees as death and darkness.

End Notes

[1] The Johannine 'signs' (*sêmeia*) are really symbols more than signs in that they do more than point in the direction of a divine reality: they convey and communicate it through the Gospel text.

[2] See Derek Tovey, 'Narrative Strategies in the Prologue and the Metaphor of *ho logos* in John's Gospel' *Pacifica* 15 (2002), 138-53, who argues that further instances of *logos* in John retain resonance with the christological title of the Prologue.

[3] John Calvin prefers the Latin *sermo* ('speech') for the Greek *logos*, in order to underline this point (*The Gospel According to St John, Part 1, 1-10* [Calvin's NT Commentaries; ET: Grand Rapids: Eerdmans, 1961), 7-9). Stephen W. Need argues that, to the first readers of the Gospel, *logos* would have meant 'the dynamic communicative speech of God on the one hand and the rational ordering of the universe on the other' ('Re-reading the Prologue: Incarnation and Creation in John 1.1-18' *Theology* 106 [2003], 402).

[4] Udo Schnelle, 'Johannine Theology: Introduction to the Christian Faith' in *Theology of the New Testament* (ET: Grand Rapids: Baker Academic, 2009), 671-4.

[5] See the helpful summary in John E. McHugh, *A Critical and Exegetical Commentary on John 1-4* (ICC; London/New York: T & T Clark, 2009), Excursus I, 78-90.

[6] Further on this structure, see Dorothy Lee, 'The Gospel of John: Symbol and Prologue', *Conversations* 2, no. 2 (2008), http://ctm.uca.edu.au/conversations, which includes an analysis of Josquin Deprez's, *In principio erat Verbum*. The motet employs the same structure ending with v. 14, as it does in Ben Witherington, *John's Wisdom. A Commentary on the Fourth Gospel* (Cambridge: Lutterworth Press, 1995), 47-59). A tripartite structure for 1:1-18 is also proposed by Francis J. Moloney, *The Gospel of John* (SP 4; Collegeville, MN: The Liturgical Press, 1998), 34, although he extends the second section to include v. 14. Eoin de Bhaldraithe sees a fourfold construction in the original poem, around the verb *egeneto* ('it/he became') which the evangelist has managed to preserve, despite his additions ('The Johannine Prologue Structure and Origins *AusBR* 58 (2010), 57-71.

[7] On the background to *Logos*, especially its Old Testament roots, see Craig A. Evans, *Word and Glory: On the Exegetical and Theological Background of John's Prologue* (Sheffield: JSOT Academic Press, 1993), 77-99, and McHugh, *John 1-4*, Excursus II, 91-96.

[8] This is how some have translated the somewhat unusual preposition 'with' in the phrase 'with God' in verses 1-2; *pros* literally means 'towards'. See Francis J. Moloney, 'In the Bosom of' or 'Turned towards' the Father?

AusBR 31 (1983), 63-71, and Ignace de la Potterie, 'L'emploie de *eis* dans Saint Jean et ses incidences théologiques' (*Biblica* 43 (1962), 366-387; see also Andrew T. Lincoln, *The Gospel According to Saint John*, BNTC (Peabody, MA: Hendrickson, 2005), 97.

9. Assuming, with Augustine, that evil is insubstantial and lacking in creative substance; *Confessions* (2 vols.; ET: W. Watts, LCL; Cambridge, MS: Harvard University Press, 1912), 1.VII.v.

10. So James D.G. Dunn, *Christology in the Making. A New Testament Inquiry into the Origins of the Doctrine of the Incarnation* (2nd ed.; London: SCM, 1989), 239-245.

11. There is a very close link between Wisdom, Word and Torah in this literature: they are virtually synonymous (e.g. Wisd 9:1-2; Sir 15:1; 19:20; 21:11); see esp. Craig S. Keener, *The Gospel of John: A Commentary* (2 vols.; Peabody, MS: Hendrickson, 2003), 1:347-363. A similar correlation is apparent in the writings of Philo, who shares the same religious environment as the fourth evangelist; see Evans, *Word and Glory*, 100-114.

12. On the influence of Wisdom/Sophia on John's Gospel, see, e.g. Evans, *Word and Glory*, 83-94; Witherington, *John's Wisdom*, 18-27; and Martin Scott, *Sophia and the Johannine Jesus* (Sheffield: Sheffield Academic Press, 1992).

13. The point should not be exaggerated, as Evans points out (*Word and Glory*, 185-186, n. 3).

14. For an outline of different views on the original form of the Prologue, see, e.g. Raymond E. Brown, *The Gospel of John* (2 vols.; AB; 29A & B; New York: Doubleday, 1966), 1.21-23; see also Matthew Gordley, 'The Johannine Prologue and Jewish Didactic Hymn Traditions: A New Case for Reading the Prologue as a Hymn' *JBL* 128 (2009), 781-802. Barrett disagrees and sees the Prologue as a Johannine creation from start to finish: *The Prologue of St John's Gospel* (London: Athlone Press, 1971).

15. The Prologue has also been aptly compared to a musical overture (Udo Schnelle, *Das Evangelium nach Johannes* [Leipzig: Evangelische Verlagsanstalt, 1998], 29. It is certainly integral to the Gospel; see P.M. Phillips, *The Prologue of the Fourth Gospel. A Sequential Reading*, (Library of NT Studies 294; London: T & T Clark, 2006), 5-6, who regards it as the beginning of the Johannine narrative rather than its preface.

16. See Dorothy Lee, 'John' in B.R. Gaventa & D. Petersen (eds.), *The New Interpreter's Bible: One Volume Commentary* (Nashville: Abingdon, 2010), 713.

17. See especially Andreas J. Köstenberger & Scott R. Swain, *Father, Son and Spirit. The Trinity and John's Gospel* (Downers Grove: InterVarsity

Press, 2008), 75-92.

18. http://www.tkinter.smig.net/PrincessIleana/JesusPrayer/images/
JesusTheTeacher.jpg

19. In the ninth century, St John of Damascus wrote a treatise defending
the use of icons, arguably against the iconoclasts (who asserted the
commandment against graven images, Exod 20:4; Lev 26:1; Deut 4:16, 23,
25; 5:8; 27:12; Isa 42:8), precisely on the basis of the incarnation. If the
Word radiates the divine presence in mortal flesh, then fleshly matter can
represent the divine, especially in the pictorial presentation of Jesus but also
for all the saints, especially the Theotokos (*On the Divine Images: Three
Apologies Against Those Who Attack the Divine Images* [ET D. Anderson,
Crestwood, NY: St Vladimir's Seminary Press, 1980]).

20. C. Irimie & M. Focsa, *Romanian Icons Painted on Glass* (London:
Thames & Hudson, 1970).

21. See especially F.J. Moloney, 'The Gospel of John as Scripture' *CBQ* 67
(2005), 454-468, and 'The Gospel of John: The "End" of Scripture' *Int* 63
(2009), 356-66.

22. On the centrality of the incarnation in the Prologue, see especially
Schnelle, 'Johannine Theology', 669-76.

23. Further on this, see Dorothy Lee, *Flesh and Glory: Symbolism, Gender
and Theology in the Gospel of John* (New York: Crossroad, 2002), 29-64.

24. Martin Hengel, 'The Prologue of the Gospel as the Key to Christological
Truth' in R. Bauckham & C. Mosser (eds.), *The Gospel of John and
Christian Theology* (Grand Rapids: Eerdmans, 2008), 268, describes 1:14 as
'the key to the twenty-one chapters that follow'.

25. Frank Kermode, 'John' in R. Alter & F. Kermode, *The Literary Guide to
the Bible* (London: Fontana, 1987), 443-8.

26. In the Greek, the word order is, 'who, not of blood … , but of God were
born', giving emphasis to the verb at the end.

27. For a study of glory within the concrete Johannine narrative, see e.g.
Jesper Tang Nielsen, 'The Narrative Structures of Glory and Glorification in
the Fourth Gospel' *NTS* 56 (2010), 343-66.

28. Dorothy Lee, 'Partnership in Easter Faith: The Role of Mary Magdalene
and Thomas in John 20' *JSNT* 58 (1995), 37-49.

29. See Mary Coloe, *Dwelling in the Household of God. Johannine
Ecclesiology and Spirituality* (Collegeville: Liturgical Press, 2007), 193-201.

30. For more details, see Lee, *Flesh and Glory*, 14-20.

31. See especially the book on spirituality by Michael Casey, its title
carefully chosen in light of John 1:1-2 (*Towards God. The Western Tradition*

of Contemplation [Melbourne: Dove, 1989, 1995], 1-9).

32. According to R. Alan Culpepper, *Anatomy of the Fourth Gospel. A Study in Literary Design* (Foundations & Facets; Philadelphia: Fortress, 1983), 190-197, the three 'core' impersonal symbols of the Gospel are light, water and bread. Craig S. Koester helpfully distinguishes between 'core' and 'supporting' symbols (*Symbolism in the Fourth Gospel: Meaning, Mystery, Community* [2nd ed.; Minneapolis: Fortress, 2003], 4-15, 257-64).

33. Schnelle, 'Johannine Theology', 687-8.

34. Dorothy Lee, *The Symbolic Narratives of the Fourth Gospel. The Interplay of Form and Meaning* (Sheffield: Sheffield Academic Press, 1994), 23-35.

35. The term 'incarnational theology' is sometimes used popularly (and inaccurately) to describe a theology that takes seriously the body and bodily existence. However, for John, the concept really concerns the bodily reality of *God*.

36. See Culpepper, *Anatomy*, 200-201.

37. Note the strong Wisdom overtones to this language: Sophia in Wisdom Literature both *is* and *gives* the gift (e.g. Prov 9:1-6; Sir 15:3).

38. Note the study by John Christopher Thomas, *Footwashing in John 13 and the Johannine Community* (Justus 61; Sheffield: JSOT Press, 1991), esp. 172-85.

39. On the symbolism of water in the Fourth Gospel, see Lee, *Flesh and Glory*, 65-87.

40. See Lee, *Flesh and Glory*, 20-22.

41. Rowan Williams, *On Christian Theology*, ed. G. Jones & L. Ayres (Challenges in Contemporary Theology; Oxford: Blackwell, 2000), 72.

42. C.S. Lewis, *Till We Have Faces. A myth Retold* (Glasgow: Collins, 1956) 319-320.

43. 'Ash-Wednesday' V, in T.S. Eliot, *The Complete Poems and Plays* (London: Faber & Faber, 1969), 96.

44. 'In the Daylight Forever? Language and Silence' in O. Davies & D. Turner (eds.), *Silence and the Word. Negative Theology and Incarnation* (Cambridge: Cambridge University Press, 2002), 179.

45. In icons of the transfiguration, the mandorla which surrounds the radiant figure of Christ, often with beams of light directed at each of the three apostles, is generally dark at its centre, signifying the ultimate unknowability of God. Further on biblical icons, see Solrunn Nes, *The Mystical Language of Icons* (2nd ed.; Grand Rapids: Eerdmans, 2005) and *The Uncreated Light: An Iconographical Study of the Transfiguration in the Eastern Church*

(Grand Rapids: Eerdmans, 2007).

[46.] So Dorothy Lee, 'The Gospel of John and the Five Senses' *JBL* 129 (2010), 115-127; see below, chapter 6.

[47.] Augustine, *Confessions*, I.I (LCL; 2 vols.; Williams Watts [transl], Cambridge, MS: Harvard University Press, 1912).

Chapter 2
Spirituality and Worship

At first glance, worship as a Johannine theme may seem to possess a marginal status within the Gospel. Explicit language is found in only one location, the story of the Samaritan woman's meeting with Jesus (4:16-31). On closer inspection, however, worship is so integral to John's spiritual theology that it merits consideration as a major theological theme of the Gospel.[1] While the majority of explicit references occur in the Samaritan conversation, the notion of worship is found in synonymous language and symbolism throughout the Gospel, particularly the vocabulary of glory. As the one sent into the world by the Father, the Johannine Jesus reveals the nature and significance of true worship, just as he reveals divine glory. His role in the Gospel is to point to the meaning of worship and to be himself its heart: the locus and object of worship.[2] John's spiritual theology is oriented towards worship, the praise of God as the heart of believing life. In this sense, worship is a central concern of John's spirituality. As Martin Hengel points out, to grasp appropriately the mystery at the centre of this Gospel—the mystery of Jesus—involves worship and liturgy.[3] The fundamental task of the Johannine community is the glorification of God, evident in the relationship of the Son to the Father, into which believers are drawn. Indeed, 'glory' is arguably the central theme of the Fourth Gospel, and it is closely allied to the notion of worship.

As with everything else, the Johannine theme of worship is clustered around a number of key symbols in the Gospel. Beneath these symbols stands the incarnation, the core Johannine symbol, in which the divine glory is apprehended through flesh—through the palpable, tangible materiality of the human person. Thus any discussion of worship must take seriously the symbols in which it is couched. In this sense, the symbols are the language of worship, its manner and method of articulation. As we shall see, the spirituality of John's notion of worship is fleshly, carnal—resisting the disembodiment of docetism and its discomfort with the humanity of Jesus. Worship may be 'in spirit and in truth' but, as we will see, a truly spiritual theology of worship begins in the incarnation and extends to the relevant symbols of the Fourth Gospel.

The Johannine Jesus as the Place of Worship

John's Gospel is essentially theo-centric:[4] that is to say, God stands at the centre of the narrative, so that everything said of Jesus is said always and only in relation to the God who is, above all else, 'the Father who sent me' (5:37; 6:44; 7:28; 8:16, 18, 26, 29; 12:49).[5] Indeed, the characterisation of Jesus and God are in one sense inseparable in John: neither makes sense without the other, as the Father-Son imagery makes plain.[6] There remains the closest possible relationship between them, an identity that is overlapping and interwoven. In this sense, John's *christ*-ology is a subset of his *theo*-logy. Although, ironically, the Father as a character in the narrative almost never appears and uses direct speech only once in the Gospel (12:29), all that happens revolves around the God who acts in and through the events of the narrative. As the divine Word, Jesus *is* the speech of God. In this sense, God does 'speak' throughout the Gospel: in an unending flow of 'sign', symbol, discourse, teaching, death, and resurrection. As the Symbol of God, the Johannine Jesus is the presence and utterance of God to the disciples, so that to know one is to know the other: 'The one who has seen me has seen the Father' (14:9). Worship of the Johannine Father involves at its core the presence and the work of the Johannine Son.

The role of Jesus in worship has three dimensions in the Fourth Gospel. In the first place, John presents Jesus as the *place of true worship*. In the Prologue, the evangelist uses temple language and imagery to describe the incarnation: 'the Word became flesh and lived among us and we have seen his glory' (1:14). The language of the Word 'dwelling' in the flesh (literally, 'pitched his tent') suggests the tabernacle in the Old Testament:[7] the root of the word contains 'tent' or 'tabernacle' (*skênoô, skênê*). This, in turn, suggests Old Testament Zion traditions, where the revelation of God's glory on earth, God's dwelling-place, is Mount Zion in the temple. For the Fourth Gospel, what we may call the 'sacred site' that radiates God's glorious, saving presence is the Word incarnate. The dwelling of the Word in flesh parallels the tabernacle as the temporal dwelling-place of God's glory. As one of the temple psalms expresses it: 'O Lord, I love the house in which you dwell, and the place where your glory abides' (Ps 26:8 NRSV). The theophanies of the Old Testament, especially those associated with the temple (e.g. Isa 6:1-4), are now manifest in the Johannine Jesus.[8]

But there are also overtones of Old Testament wisdom in the same language and symbolism. In the Jewish wisdom tradition, Lady Wisdom or Sophia, is pictured as 'a breath of the power of God, and a pure emanation of the glory of the Almighty' (Wisd 7:25 NRSV; cf. 9:8-11). Elsewhere Wisdom proclaims:

> my Creator chose the place for my *tent* (*skênê*).
> He said, Make your *dwelling* in Jacob,
> and in Israel receive your inheritance (Sir 24:8
> NRSV).

Here Wisdom is closely linked to the law, Torah, which in some Jewish traditions is thought to be pre-existent and eternal. As we saw in the previous chapter, the Word, Wisdom and Law of God in the Old Testament, which become so closely intertwined, for John all speak symbolically of Jesus. What 1:14 discloses is the movement of God's temple-glory, God's word and wisdom, from Mount Zion to the flesh of Jesus.[9] For John, the temple where God dwells is now found in Jesus, in whose flesh God's saving presence abides.

There is a similar theme in the Cleansing of the Temple, immediately after the gathering of the first disciples and changing of water into wine at Cana, at the beginning of Jesus' ministry (2:13-22). The Fourth Gospel interprets this episode so that its primary meaning is christological, reflecting the temple symbolism begun at 1:14. John sees the temple as an image pointing to Jesus' own body: 'he was speaking of the temple of his body' (2:21). The symbolic meaning of the temple emerges more fully here, establishing a connection with the verb 'dwell' used at 1:14. Here again, as with the Prologue, the flesh or body of Jesus reveals divine glory, just as the temple revealed the glory of God to Israel.[10] In this sense the Cleansing of the Temple (2:21) anticipates the Johannine Passion and resurrection narratives which bear witness to Jesus, the Lamb of God, and risen.[11]

There is some tension in the story, making it seem at first contradictory. At one level, Jesus cleanses the temple in order to purify what he calls, with characteristically Johannine authority, '*my* Father's house' (2:16). The emphatic 'my' shows also the uniqueness of Jesus' sonship (1:14, 18; cf. 20:17c). At the same time, at a deeper level, the real temple or sanctuary is Jesus himself: the resurrection signifies the metaphorical 'rebuilding' of this incarnate 'temple'. In one sense, Jesus purifies his Father's house; in another sense, he is himself the house in which the Father dwells (2:16-17). Thus by the end of the episode, Jesus has not only re-claimed the temple for his Father, but has also claimed it for his own. Its geographical terrain and his own body are mysteriously fused, to be vindicated in his bodily resurrection which will reveal his dominion over life and death. So that while in the first part, Jesus points to the Father, in the second he focuses on his own role in the Father's mission. The tension between these two dimensions expresses the complexity of John's theology at this point.[12]

The next reference to worship is the story of Jesus' meeting with the Samaritan woman which has, as its central scene, a conversation about worship (4:16-30). This is one of the few places in the Gospel where the language of worship becomes explicit.[13] Other related imagery is used in the Fourth Gospel, but the most significant is the congregating of 'worship' language in the one context. The woman is characterised in positive terms, especially as her spiritual understanding grows, and this underscores the significance of the story for the evangelist and particularly his depiction of the importance of worship. In the first scene of the narrative, the central symbol is that of water (4:7-15), but the woman at this early stage in the conversation has not reached an understanding of the giver or the gift (4:10). By the end of the scene she begins to comprehend something of what Jesus offers: she recognises Jesus as a water-giver and asks for the gift of water (4:15). Yet her comprehension remains on a material rather than symbolic or spiritual level: she is thinking of literal water (though perhaps magical in origins) that will save her considerable daily labour.

In the second scene, the attention moves explicitly to worship (4:16-30). Now the imagery shifts to that of sacred place (*topos*) and the true locus of worship, though the well remains the symbolic centre-piece. While the water points to the revelation that Jesus brings, it is also a symbol for the Spirit. Later in the Gospel, when Jesus calls people to come and quench their thirst in him, the evangelist explains: 'He said this concerning the Spirit which those believing in him were about to receive' (7:39). In the dialogue with the Samaritan woman, therefore, the shift from water to Spirit is very small: the one points symbolically to the other. Indeed, already in the Fourth Gospel, water has established itself as a core symbol, associated with revelation and the Spirit. As we saw in the previous chapter, this symbolism begins with the witness of John the Baptist testifying to Jesus as the one who, in contrast to John's baptizing in water (1:26), baptizes 'in the Holy Spirit' (1:33). It is also present in the symbol of birth 'from above' which is 'of water and the Spirit' (3:5) and in the baptizing work of Jesus' disciples (3:22-30; 4:1-2). Now in the story of the Samaritan woman, the symbol of water is developed further in terms of worship and the Spirit.

Scene two begins with Jesus asking the woman to return with her husband (4:16), and uncovering the reality of her life. Here Jesus is not so much pronouncing moral judgement against her but rather seeking to uncover the woman's 'thirst for life', seen in the restlessness and uncertainty of her relationships.[14] To this quest, the Johannine answer is found in the water of the well, which points to the revelation Jesus brings and his gift of the Spirit. Note that the revelation is as much about the woman and her life as it is about God; later she will say, with some hyperbole: 'Come, see a man who told me all I ever did' (4:29, 39). Her sense here is that Jesus has seen into her very being and disclosed her to herself, precisely in the process of demonstrating who he himself is.[15] Jesus' mission is to unveil human beings to themselves, as well as to disclose God. Indeed, the two aspects belong together: the knowledge of God and the knowledge of the self.[16] Authentic spirituality, according to John, concerns the awareness of who we are and who God is, the one in relation to the other.

As a consequence of her dawning insight, the woman raises the vexed theological question of the place of true worship, an issue that bitterly divides Jew and Samaritan (4:20). Her raising of the issue is not an attempt to divert attention from her personal life but rather the sign of increasing spiritual awareness: she perceives that the conversation is really about spirituality and the identity of Jesus (4:19; also 6:14, 9:17).[17] This enables Jesus to clarify the question of geographical location in the worship of God. Yet there are still a number of areas where the woman's knowledge is partial or mistaken. She does not understand that the scope of the salvation is at the same time specific ('of the Jews', 4:22) but also universal ('Saviour of the world', 4:42). Nor does she perceive the centrality of Jesus in the worship of God, and the association between Jesus and the Spirit. For the evangelist, the incarnation has radically re-shaped sacred geography and the end times.

Jesus responds to the woman's growing insight by pointing to a new spirituality in which worship of the Father is no longer dependent on geographical location. Rather it is to take place 'in spirit and truth'—which may have a secondary reference to the attitude ('spirit') of the worshipper,[18] but is more likely, in its primary orientation, to be a reference to the Holy Spirit (14:17; 15:26; 16:13; cf. 1 Jn 4:6), and better understood as 'the Spirit of truth' (4:23, 24).[19] Note how the two parallel phrases 'spirit and truth' frame the central explicit reference to God as Spirit:

the true worshippers will worship the Father *in spirit and truth* (v. 23)	**A**
God is *spirit* (v. 24a)	**B**
those who worship him must worship *in spirit and truth* (c. 24b)	**A¹**

The structure of these statements demonstrates the evangelist's meaning: that true worship has at its centre the divine Spirit who is the Spirit of truth, and that to know truly who God is to worship God, as the natural response to the divine nature and identity. The phrase

'Spirit of truth' is also rich in christological meaning. Elsewhere Jesus is 'the way, the truth and life', the means of access to the Father (14:6) and the one who leads disciples to the knowledge of liberating truth (8:32). The Johannine Spirit plays an essential role in the worship of the Father, paralleling that of Jesus. According to John, the Spirit lies at the core of spirituality, as we will see in the next chapter.

By the end of the narrative, Jesus is recognised as 'the Saviour of the world' (4:42), as the villagers come to their own appreciation of Jesus' saving role in the worship and adoration of God. The story is not a theological discourse on worship and the identity of Jesus. Rather, it is an unveiling of the spirituality of the evangelist in the experience of a group of Samaritan villagers, represented for the most part by the woman herself. Though considered heretical outsiders, they are drawn into the self-revealing of Jesus and brought to experience discipleship and worship. John's spirituality is grounded in a theocentric and incarnational understanding, addressed to the experience of real people. In the process these people discover themselves as much as they find God. There are four aspects to this Johannine understanding of worship:

- the Father as the object of worship, the One to whom authentic worship is directed
- the role of the Son as the true and ultimate Revealer of the Father (1:18)
- the Spirit as the one who inspires and directs authentic worship of God
- openness of the worshipper to the revelation of God and of the self.

The temple perspective on Jesus in the Fourth Gospel is particularly apparent in John 5-10, where the overarching theme is the feasts of Judaism. The rituals associated with these temple festivals are gathered up in the Word/Son who fulfils them in his own flesh. The Jewish feasts in these chapters (Sabbath, Passover, Tabernacles, and Dedication) are 'reinterpreted in the light of the Gospel's christological claim, that Jesus is the new Temple of God's dwelling'.[20] In each case, Jesus is 'the personification and the universalization' of the Old Testament feasts, bringing them to perfection and fullness of meaning.[21] As the ultimate temple, the Johannine Jesus in his divine humanity is thus the authentic 'place' where the Father is to be worshipped, bringing Israel's past to fruition. John underlines the theological significance through feast after feast, and the great symbols of these chapters—bread, water and light—all point in the same direction.

Thus Jesus' Sabbath work is not indicative of his indifference to the Law in John, but rather signifies that he, and he alone, shares the divine 'exemption' from the Sabbath: he carries out the uniquely divine work of giving life and judging. In the Passover, he is both the manna and the paschal lamb, the bread of life whose flesh and blood are the food and drink of eternal life. Similarly, the two main rituals of the Feast of Tabernacles are transformed in Jesus' person and ministry. The pouring of water each morning on the altar in the temple, taken from the Pool of Siloam is now, for John, symbolic of the one who offers the gift of living water (7:37-39, 9:7). Similarly, the lighting of the candelabra every evening in the temple so that it lights up the city points symbolically, for the evangelist, to Jesus who is 'the Light of the world' (8:12, 9:5). Finally, in the Feast of Dedication Jesus reveals himself as the one who, as the Good Shepherd, is fully and finally dedicated to God—in life, in death and in resurrection. In all these examples, the Johannine Jesus is the new temple of the last days: the dwelling of the radiance of God's glory, a radiance that is life-giving.

What all this amounts to in John's spiritual theology is that worship must pass through Jesus; he is 'the *means* of genuine worship' in this Gospel.[22] There is no other way to worship the Johannine Father except in the Johannine Son. As the locus of worship, the Jesus of the Fourth Gospel is the divinely-ordained temple in which prayer and the worship of God can flourish. By entering this 'sacred site', this divinely human presence, through prayer, human beings enter also their true identity, since his status as Son confers theirs as the re-born sons and daughters of God. The site of worship is the location, therefore, of authentic identity. Only this place gives access to true selfhood and thus, by extension, true worship in the Johannine world view.

The Farewell Discourse uses similar geographical imagery. Though John does not allude directly to the theme of worship, he uses closely-related imagery. Thus Jesus is the ultimate 'way' to the Father (14:6), the sole means by which access to God is attained. If the purpose of true belief is worship of the one God, then Jesus' role as the pathway to the Father's presence is a different, though related, symbol from that of sacred place: both are geographical images and both set the person of Jesus across the otherwise impassable gulf between divine and human. The bridge between earth and heaven is opened in the incarnation—the forging anew of the pathway from heaven to earth.

The language of abiding multiplies in this section of the Gospel, reaching a climax at 15:1-8.[23] Indeed these, and the verses which follow—with the theme of love and hate—form the centre-piece of Jesus' Last Meal, the whole framed by the Footwashing and Jesus' Great Prayer.[24] Jesus is pictured as the vine on which/whom the branches abide, tended by the Father as the vinedresser (15:1-8). The vine functions in this passage as an 'extended metaphor',[25] a kind of Johannine parable with allegorical elements. Here the attachment between Jesus and disciples stands at the centre of a relationship with God: affinity with Jesus means affinity with the God as source of life. The livelihood of the community of faith is dependent on this intimate affiliation. The vine is also a powerful symbol of the mutuality within the believing community, as well as the love between believers and Jesus. This theme becomes explicit in the verses which follow, with their reference to keeping the commandments (15:12, 17): for John, this means simply the love-command, 'love one another as I have loved you' (13:34). There is also an implication of worship in this language. The vine is a symbol not just of the Church (Israel) but is also suggestive of the eucharist. It 'has an inherent affinity with the eucharistic symbol of the wine' which 'reflects and evokes' the union of the believer with Christ.[26] In this radical new relationship, believers are conceived of as friends of Jesus (*philoi*, 15:15) because they are drawn into intimacy and knowledge. Through the revelation in the Johannine Jesus they have known the Father's will and have seen the Father's face. Note that this friendship does not rule out obedience, but it is the obedience of free adults rather than that of children or servants. In this Gospel, the true friends of Jesus offer love and adoration to the Father through him, a worship that produces life, growth and fruit; in return the Father and Son abide in them through the Spirit.

In John's spirituality, therefore, Jesus is the means of worship, the medium through which adoration is offered to the Father. Through his mediation, the Samaritan woman comes to understand the revelation about the nature and focus of true worship, as well as about herself. Later in the Farewell Discourse the disciples will understand that friendship with Jesus does not cancel out the rendering of worship and obedience (15:14), but rather sets it within the context of mutual love and intimacy. Jesus in this Gospel is the locus of worship, the 'sacred site' whose flesh, radiating divine glory, draws believers to authentic worship of the Father. In prayer, therefore, they place themselves within the 'site' of God's glory, which is Jesus Christ: he is the temple by means of whom they become present to God. For John, Jesus is both the *means of access* to God and the *place* where glorification of God takes place. His flesh is the outer court, the portico, the sanctuary, the altar, and the Holy of Holies. In him all the ceremonies and rituals, the festivals, prayers and sacrifices, find their meaning: the one to whom, as symbols, they each point, giving access to divine favour, truth and love. To worship God, for believers, is to stand within the selfhood of the Johannine Jesus and find there the dwelling-place at the heart of all reality, the temple which radiates light and pours forth water, giving guidance, illumination and life.

The Johannine Jesus as the Object of Worship

Secondly, as well as being the one who points to worship of the Father, the Johannine Jesus is also the *object* of worship.[27] We observed this double role in the Cleansing of the Temple where Jesus both purifies God's house yet is also himself God's abode. In John's Christology, the Father is the source of dominion and sovereignty, but the Son shares that same dominion bestowed by the Father. This dominion derives from the Son's role in creation—'all things came into being through him' (1:3)—and vibrantly present in the words and deeds of his ministry. Thus in the Shepherd Discourse, Jesus speaks of his own initiative in the resurrection (although elsewhere the New Testament speaks of God raising Jesus). Having divine power over life and death—a power that no ordinary mortal possesses—he is responsible for surrendering and re-claiming his own life in the Passion. It is a power that derives from the love and union he shares with the Father:

> For this reason the Father loves me because I lay down my life, in order that I may take it up again. No-one takes it from me, but I lay it down of myself. I have authority to lay down my life, and I have authority to take it up again. (10:17-18)

The same divine authority is present in the Raising of Lazarus where Jesus reveals himself to be 'the resurrection and the life' (11:25-26). In restoring Lazarus to life Jesus symbolically points to his own resurrection, and demonstrates his triumphant authority over death (5:21, 25) and over 'the ruler of this world' (12:31; 14:30; 16:11).

This authority over life and death which Jesus holds comes from his identity as Son. The imagery of sonship, first used in the Prologue, is developed most clearly in the discourse of John 5, following Jesus' healing of the disabled man by the pool. The issue of contention is the Sabbath which Jesus has supposedly broken by instructing the man to carry his pallet after the healing. Jesus' self-defence before the authorities centres around the question of work. According to John, Jesus' sabbath activity is far from being the sign of his contempt for the Law. On the contrary it is itself the sign of the unique nature of the work he has been sent to do. While God in one sense rests on the Sabbath, in another sense God's work continues even on the Sabbath, as is apparent from the fact that babies are born and people die on that Sabbath. In other words, God continues his work of giving life (birth) and making judgement (after death), even though God also observes the sabbatical rest. It is precisely this work that Jesus does in John's Gospel, the uniquely divine work of giving life and judging, the only 'work' that can be undertaken on the Sabbath and by God alone (5:17-31). All this underlies the role of Jesus as Word, Son and Life-giver in the Fourth Gospel.[28]

Although explicit language for worship is not present in John 5, the language is similar. The honour owed to the Father is to be offered also to the Son. The verb 'honour' (*timaô*) occurs four times in the one verse: 'so that everyone may *honour* the Son just as they *honour* the Father. The one not *honouring* the Son does not *honour* the Father who sent him' (5:23). This statement is connected to Jesus' role as Judge, where he has divine warrant to vindicate and to condemn (5:21-22, 24)—although in another sense the Johannine Jesus does not judge (8:15), but people judge themselves in their response to him (3:19-21). The imagery goes along with Jesus' own giving of honour to 'my Father' (8:49) in contrast to the opponents who 'dishonour' Jesus. By extension, the Father will honour those who serve or minister to Jesus (12:26). The relationship between the giving and receiving of honour shows that the imagery is close to the idea of glory (*doxa*).[29] The honour which belongs to the Father and the Son includes the faith recognition of the believing community and its worship. That which is owed the Father by right of creation—worship, honour, glory—is owed equally to the Son because, through his identity, he shares the unique work of the Father.[30]

The same Christology operates in John 17, which echoes the language of the Prologue, especially in the opening verses.[31] Jesus' stance is 'turned towards' or 'face-to-face with' God (1:1-2), as the eternal Son of the Father.[32] The mutual glorification of Father and Son, especially in the Passion narrative, points to their unity (17:1-4; 5:16b). Within the opening verses of John 17, framed by the prayer for glorification (17:1, 4-5), Jesus' claims for himself are unique. The authority he possesses is divine, an authority that extends over 'all flesh', a phrase that most likely incorporates creation and not just human beings (17:2). Moreover, eternal life is bound up with knowing not just the Father but also Jesus Christ as the 'Sent One' (17:3). This ties in with the life and light given to creation through the Word (1:3-4). As the only-begotten Son of the Father, Jesus holds God's own authority, an authority that is co-extensive with life itself.

On this basis, it makes sense that disciples in the Fourth Gospel offer worship also to Jesus. In John 9, for example, the man born blind sees his healer for the first time only at the end of the story: in his first encounter with Jesus he is blind and is told to go and wash in the Pool of Siloam. Only after he has been 'cast out' by the religious authorities does he come face-to-face with Jesus in the temple (9:34, 35). When Jesus finally reveals his identity—which has been in large part the subject of the interrogations in the previous scenes—the man responds by worshipping Jesus immediately (9:38b).[33] What the man born blind recognises is that Jesus is the Light of the world (8:12; 9:5). His believing response to Jesus leads appropriately to faith and worship.

The same may be said of Mary of Bethany's symbolic action in anointing Jesus' feet after the raising of Lazarus (12:1-8).[34] Mary's anointing is at one level an act of gratitude for the restoration of her brother. At another level, the anointing represents her response of faith to Jesus' gift of life, pointing forward to the Passion and the story of Jesus' own journey to death. As a true disciple, Mary responds to the costliness of Jesus' gift of life with the costliness of her own gift in an act of 'self-giving extravagance'.[35] The language of Mary's anointing comes close to that of worship. In the Gospel of Matthew, the two women disciples at the empty tomb—Mary Magdalene and the other Mary—fall at the feet of the risen Christ in an act of faith and worship (Matt 28:9); this is the same Jesus who proclaims, only a few verses later, that 'all authority in heaven and on earth has been given me' (Matt 28:18).[36] In a parallel way, the anointing of Jesus' feet in the Fourth Gospel becomes an act of worship, based on faith in Jesus as 'the resurrection and the life' even as he confronts his own death.[37]

The Easter narratives operate in a similar fashion (Jn 20-21). Once again, explicit language for worship is absent yet the imagery, in different ways, points in the same direction. Mary Magdalene's holding to Jesus may represent her misunderstanding, at one level, but in another sense it is her joyful recognition and homage to her Beloved (20:16-17). On the basis of worship she is commissioned to proclaim the resurrection (20:18). Thomas' confession to the risen Christ, 'my Lord and my God' (20:28), brings the narrative of the Gospel back in full circle to its beginning. Just as the Prologue reveals Jesus' divine identity (1:1-2, 18), so the Thomas story is an act of recognition of that identity. Once more the revelation is that of life. The tokens of death on the body of the risen Jesus—the scarred hands and feet, the wounded side—are paradoxically symbols of his sovereignty over life and death. Thomas' confession involves both recognition and worship: a confession of faith that is itself an act of adoration. It is also significant that Thomas' confession follows the giving of the Spirit in the previous scene (20:19-23). As a consequence of the Spirit's presence, he is able to make his faith confession. The Spirit of truth leads the unbelieving Thomas to one of the highest acts of worship in the Fourth Gospel. This act of worship is confirmed in the final scene where the seven disciples encounter the risen Christ on the beach. Worship and mission belong together in their response: in the beloved disciple's initial recognition and Simon Peter's headlong dive into the sea to reach the shore. Jesus' three-fold questioning of his love, though painful, is the rehabilitation of Peter's discipleship and leadership (21:15-17), drawing him to the ultimate act of worship in his martyrdom, as seen in the language of glorification: 'he [Jesus] indicated by what kind of death he [Peter] would glorify God' (21:19). This event lies beyond the narrative though clearly known to the readers of the Gospel. This time Peter will not deny his Lord, but accord him true worship and glory in following Jesus faithfully to death.[38]

    In John's spirituality, Jesus in his full identity is the object of the disciples' worship. As we saw with the Cleansing of the Temple, Jesus is not only the temple but also that to which the temple symbolically points. Just as the Father receives honour and glory, so too does the Son: both are the object of Christian worship. The flesh of Jesus is the canopy that covers true worshippers, but it is also the icon to which they offer not just veneration but also worship. The worship of God, for the Johannine community, while retaining its essential monotheism, is the worship of Father and Son—and also, by implication, of the Spirit. Johannine spirituality is not only made *through* Jesus but is also directed *to* him.

The Johannine Jesus as the true Worshipper

We have seen that, in John's spirituality, Jesus as Son is both the locus and object of worship. Yet there is a third dimension of worship: Jesus in this Gospel also stands before God as the one who offers worship to the Father—the true worshipper. The Synoptics are inclined to present Jesus in this way, as witnessed in his life of prayer and dependence on God (e.g. Lk 11:1-4; Mk 14:32-42/pars.; Matt 4:1-11/par.). This theme is particularly apparent in Luke, but all three Synoptic evangelists in their own way demonstrate Jesus' concern to uphold and model the worship of the one God.[39] In this sense, the focus at this point is on the human solidarity of Jesus, his sharing of human life and his offering of obedience and worship to God.

In the Johannine Son who renders his life as an act of obedience to God, Jesus can be understood as offering worship to the Father in his human solidarity. John 17 is perhaps the best example of this worship rendered by the divinely-human Son to the Father. Jesus' stance throughout this prayer on behalf of his disciples, present and future, is that of worship. His prayer for glorification (17:5, 24) is implicitly an act of worship. The language of John 17 is in this sense performative: it performs what it speaks. The prayer is a visualisation, an enactment of the relationship between Father and Son. It is a symbolic enactment of Jesus' death on the cross as the climax of Jesus' (and the Father's) glorification.[40] John 17 represents the ascent of the Son to the Father, in which Jesus enacts the exaltation of his life before God, already acting out, in prayer, the shape and direction of the crucifixion as worship. The prayer not only speaks of glory; it also performs that glorification which encapsulates the purpose and mission of the Son. Jesus' worship of the Father is at one and the same time unique and universal: the Son's returning of the Father's love is an act of worship as well as the expression of reciprocity. The cross signifies, then, not just the Father's love for the world (3:16) but also Jesus' love for the Father.

The imagery extends in a widening circle to include believers who are drawn into Jesus' act of oblation in his self-giving on the cross. All are called into the same relation, the same filial relationship, the perpetual return of love to the Father in prayer and worship. Believers in this Gospel become children of God and participate in the sonship of the Johannine Jesus.

The same theme is apparent in the prayers of the Gospel. While God only speaks directly on one occasion (12:28), Jesus is recorded as praying three times in John's Gospel. Jesus' identity shifts throughout the Gospel, back and forth, so that he is depicted not only as the object of worship—and thus by implication the receiver of prayer—but also as the worshipper, the Pray-er. On the first occasion, immediately before he summons Lazarus from the tomb, Jesus addresses the Father for the first time in the Gospel: 'Father, I thank you that you heard me. I know that you always hear me. But I have spoken for the sake of the crowd standing around, that they might believe you sent me' (11:41-42). In one sense, it is apparent from this that the Johannine Jesus has no need of prayer. The close bond of unity between Father and Son makes his petitions unnecessary. The harmony of will is so perfect that there is no interval between them, no need for Jesus to struggle to comprehend or obey the Father's will (as, for example, he does at Mk 14:14:32-42).[41] he only purpose of Jesus' explicit prayer is to deepen the faith of his hearers. His prayer thus becomes a form of revelation, another way in which he discloses his identity.

Twice more in the Gospel Jesus offers intercession to God, once more addressing God as 'Father'. Just after the coming of the Greeks, Jesus debates the form of prayer he should offer as he faces the distress of his Passion:

> Now my soul is troubled, and what am I to say? Father, save me from this hour? But for this reason, for this hour, I have come. Father, glorify your name! Then a voice came from heaven, I have glorified it and I will glorify it again. (12:28-29)

Not only is this the only time in the Fourth Gospel where Jesus soliloquises, it is also the occasion on the Father directly speaks (apart from the report of John the Baptist, 1:33). Here Jesus is choosing between two ways of responding to the prospect of death: either he can ask to be spared it, as he does at first in Mark's Gospel (where he prays that the 'cup' be taken from him, Mk 14:36/pars.), or he can accept his destiny without hesitation or struggle (though not without pain and distress!). His choice is for the second option in the Fourth Gospel, as is confirmed by the Father's response. Yet once again, Jesus' prayer is not strictly intercessory. As the crowd debates the significance of the voice they have heard—is it thunder? or an angel speaking?— Jesus discloses that the voice has come not for his own sake but for the crowd: 'Not for me did this voice occur but for you' (12:29-30). Once again Jesus' prayer is directed towards strengthening the faith of those present.

The same principle applies to John 17. The prayer, as we have seen, expresses the mutual glorification of Father and Son and the unity that binds them together—a unity into which believers, both present and future, are drawn. At the same time, the 'lifting up' or 'exalting' of Jesus on the cross (3:14; 8:28; 12:32, 34) is an act of prayer and worship, a returning of the Father's love by the Son, which is the inner meaning of the cross. As with the previous prayers, the petitions of John 17 (for the safe-guarding, sanctifying, unifying and mutual love of believers) exist for the sake of faith. Just as the 'signs' of the Fourth Gospel reveal Jesus' identity, so the prayer of John 17 attracts the readers to its hallowing power, so that their hearts are raised to God in truth and love, and they are enticed into the same perpetual return, the same circle of unity. The prayer of John 17 acts as a magnet to move the reader towards Jesus' love of the Father, into his sacrificial self-giving death, into his glorification of the Father and thus to worship. In this way, the primary mission of the Johannine Jesus, which is to find true worshippers for the Father who seeks them (4:23), is fulfilled.

In this sense, Jesus' prayers in the Fourth Gospel are more concerned with revelation than intercession. Yet they are still forms of prayer—prayer understand not primarily as a list of petitions but as the expression of mutual love and presence. The prayers express the abiding of Father and Son, the love and unity that binds them. They articulate, in other words, that divine indwelling into which believers are drawn. It would be inaccurate, therefore, to conclude that the Johannine Jesus does not need to pray. On the contrary, from the beginning to the end of the Gospel, Jesus' life and death is one of prayer: lived out before the face of the Father. His entire relationship is one of prayerful communion and mutual dependence. While petitions are needful for human beings, because they lack that intense and undivided unity and communion with God, Jesus does not need to intercede because his thoughts and desires are an open book before the Father and his will perfectly united with God's. In this sense, Jesus is the true and authentic worshipper of the Father in this Gospel.

Unlike the Synoptic Gospels (and especially the Gospel of Luke), John's Gospel has no particular focus on Jesus as a model of prayer and worship. In being the authentic worshipper of the Father, the Johannine Jesus is not set up as an example to be imitated. Rather he unites believers to himself in his prayer and worship. As a consequence, the community of faith is gathered into *his* prayer, *his* worship of the Father, *his* communion with God. That has the most profound implications for John's understanding of prayer. In the end, prayer is not about human effort; it is first and foremost an entry into the hallowing prayer of Jesus. This means that, when human efforts flounder, the words dry up, and the capacity for listening fails—especially in times of difficulty and suffering—the prayer remains: surrounding believers, gathering them in, blessing them in their frailty and weakness. It is Jesus' prayer that sustains them: his worship of the Father which, according to John, becomes theirs and on which their salvation rests.

It is for this reason that the Johannine Jesus assures the desolate disciples, 'Whatever you ask me in my name, this I will do, so that the Father may be glorified in the Son. If you ask anything of me in my name, I myself will do it' (14:13-14). The context and emphasis here is on the relationship of Father and Son, and the glorification of both in the life of disciples. Jesus' assurance is not the promise that disciples

will receive whatever they choose or imagine they need. Rather, their
unity with Christ will enable them to pray in accordance with the glory
of God. Later in the same long address, Jesus concludes his discourse
with the rather confusing promise: 'In that day you will not pray
(*erôtaô*) to me for anything. Truly, truly I tell you, whatever you ask
(*aiteô*) the Father in my name I myself will give you. Until now you
have asked for nothing in my name; ask and you will receive, so that
your joy may be fulfilled' (16:23-24). The initial reference to 'that day'
is most likely a reference to God's future. At the end of the age, when
disciples are fully and perfectly united with their Lord, they will not
need to pray for anything because 'their joy will be full'; their union
will be complete. In the meantime, they can and must pray, and do so
with the assurance of being heard and receiving their heart's desire.
Once again the 'whatever' is set within the context of divine glory.
Disciples are to pray in union with the Father and Son which itself
guides their prayer and gives them confidence that what they request
will be granted, in fulfilment of that godly will and glory.

Conclusion

The Johannine Jesus plays a pivotal and complex role in worship,
a role that is tied in the closest way to the centrality of God in the
Fourth Gospel. The focus is on God and on the worship of the one,
true God, which is precisely the mission and purpose of Jesus in this
Gospel. As Thompson has pointed out, 'The Gospel's theocentricity
can encompass its christocentricity, but it *cannot* work the other way.'[42]
It is not Jesus who is the centre of the Gospel of John, but God—in
whose being Jesus himself shares. The Johannine Jesus is the locus and
object of worship, the source of worship and the true worshipper, the
bridge between heaven and earth, mortal and vulnerable yet possessing
authority over 'all flesh'. Worship and prayer are to be offered *through*
him but also, since he is the visible manifestation of God, *to* him.[43] In
his flesh the prayer he offers the Father is the symbolic expression of
divine self-offering and mutual glorification, the source of believers'
hallowed life and worship.

At the same time, the worship of God in John's Gospel does not bypass the Spirit's place in worship. The mutuality within the Father-Son relationship includes, by extension, the 'Spirit of truth' who, in the absence of Jesus, leads believers 'into all truth' (16:13). We will see more of this in the following chapter. It is through the Spirit, operating in the life and death of Jesus, that human beings are able to offer authentic worship to the Father. True worship is possible only in the power of the Spirit who gives birth to believers, making them 'children of God' (1:12-13; 3:5) and 'friends' of Jesus (15:15), so that they share in Jesus' intimacy with the Father.

In this sense, it is possible to speak of John's theology as, in some sense, 'trinitarian'. Admittedly, such a description has the danger of anachronism, an understanding of the relationship between Father, Son and Spirit which comes from generations beyond that of the Fourth Gospel or any other New Testament text. Yet, if we set aside some of the technical terminology of the fourth and fifth centuries, it is not hard to recognise the Gospel of John as the source of subsequent developments.[44] Perhaps the theme of worship most clearly delineates this complexity of relationship within the Johannine God. The formulations of the Fourth Gospel 'provide the basis for what Christians came to understand as the Trinity.'[45]

At its core, John's spirituality arises from a theology of worship in and through Jesus, with the enabling presence of the indwelling Spirit. In John's spirituality, therefore, prayer is not ultimately a task, still less an achievement on the part of believers. Rather disciples allow themselves, through Jesus, to be gathered into a divine circle of love, the place where they find their true selves in worship of the one who is the source of life and love.

End Notes

[1.] The point is made by Jerome H. Neyrey in his two-part study of worship in John 14-17 ('Worship in the Fourth Gospel: A Cultural Interpretation of John 14-17' *BTB* 36 [2006], 107-17, 155-63); Neyrey examines worship theologically in the Fourth Gospel, and also within the cultural categories of the ancient world—particularly the relationship between patron-broker-client.

2. Parts of this chapter originated in Dorothy Lee, '"In the Spirit of Truth": Worship and Prayer in the Gospel of John and the Early Fathers' *Vigilianae Christianae* 58 (2004), 227-297.

3. 'The Prologue of the Gospel as the Key to Christological Truth' in R. Bauckham & C. Mosser (eds.), *The Gospel of John and Christian Theology* (Grand Rapids: Eerdmans, 2008), 292.

4. See C.K. Barrett, 'Christocentric or Theocentric? Observations on the Theological Method of the Fourth Gospel' in *Essays on John* (London: SPCK, 1982), 1-18.

5. On the importance of this description of Jesus, see P. Anderson, 'The Having-Sent-Me Father: Aspects of Agency, Encounter, and Irony in the Johannine Father-Son Relationship' *Semeia* 85 (1999), 33-57.

6. M.M. Thompson has written extensively on the portrait of the Johannine God in relation to Jesus; see esp. *The God of the Gospel of John* (Grand Rapids: Eerdmans, 2001); also Craig R. Koester, *The Word of Life: A Theology of John's Gospel* (Grand Rapids: Eerdmans, 2008), 25-52.

7. Further on this theme, see Craig R. Koester, *The Dwelling of God. The Tabernacle in the Old Testament, Intertestamental Jewish Literature, and the New Testament* (Washington:Catholic Biblical Association of America, 1989) 102-104, M. Coloe, *God Dwells with Us: Temple Symbolism in the Fourth Gospel* (Collegeville:Liturgical Press, 2001) 23-27, 31-63, and A. Kerr, *The Temple of Jesus' Body. The Temple Theme in the Gospel of John* (JSNTSup 220; London & New York: Sheffield Academic Press, 2002).

8. See Thompson, *God of the Gospel of John*, 213.

9. Further on 'flesh' in the Fourth Gospel, see Lee, *Flesh and Glory*, 30-50.

10. See Coloe, *God Dwells With Us*, 65-84.

11. Further on the paschal Lamb in John, see Dorothy A. Lee, 'Paschal Imagery in the Gospel of John: A Narrative and Symbolic Reading', *Pacifica* 24 (2011), 13-28.

12. See Dorothy Lee, 'John', in B.R. Gaventa & D. Petersen (eds.), *The New Interpreter's One Volume Commentary on the Bible* (Nashville: Abingdon, 2010), 715-6.

13. Thompson, *God of the Gospel of John*, 220-222.

14. On the structure of the narrative, and the stages of faith it delineates, see Dorothy Lee, *The Symbolic Narratives of the Fourth Gospel. The Interplay of Form and Meaning* (Sheffield: Sheffield Academic Press, 1994), 64-97

15. R. Bultmann, *The Gospel of John: A Commentary* (ET Oxford: Blackwell, 1971) 188; also C.M. Conway, *Men and Women in the Fourth Gospel. Gender and Johannine Characterization* (Atlanta: SBL, 1999) 116-

119. Note that women in the Old Testament world were unable to initiate divorce.

16. Some assume the woman's faith to be partial at this point; e.g. Francis J. Moloney, *The Gospel of John* (Collegeville: Liturgical Press, 1998) 29, and R.G. Maccini, *Her Testimony. Women as Witnesses According to John* (Sheffield: Sheffield Academic Press, 1996) 140- 42. For a more positive view, see T. Okure, *The Johannine Approach to Mission. A Contextual Study of John 4:1-42* (Tübingen: J.C.B. Mohr, 1988) 174-175, and Lee, *Symbolic Narratives*, 83-86.

17. Calvin asserts this duality; see J.T. McNeill (ed.), *Calvin: Institutes of the Christian Religion* (Philadelphia: Westminster, 1960), I.1.1 & 2.

18. R. Schnackenburg, *The Gospel According to St. John* (New York: Seabury, 1980) 1.434, and Conway, *Men and Women*, 119. For a different view, see B. Witherington, *John's Wisdom. A Commentary on the Fourth Gospel* (Cambridge: Lutterworth Press, 1995) 120-121.

19. See, e.g., J. Ashton, *The Interpretation of John* (2nd ed.; Oxford: Oxford University Press, 2007) 465, and Andreas J. Köstenberger & Scott R. Swain, *Father, Son and Spirit. The Trinity and John's Gospel* (NSBT 24. Downers Grove: InterVarsity Press, 2008), 94.

20. So R.E. Brown, *The Gospel According to John* (New York: Doubleday, 1966) 1.172, 180-181. In this Gospel the term mostly does refer to the divine Spirit (1:32, 33; 3:6, 8; 3:34; 4:24; 6:63; 7:39; 14:17, 26; 15:26; 16:13; 20:22). See esp Benny Thettayil, *In Spirit and Truth. An Exegetical Study of 4:19-26 and a Theological Investigation of the Replacement Theme in the Fourth Gospel* (Leuven: Peeters, 2007), 131-139).

21. Coloe, *God Dwells With Us*, 115.

22. F.J. Moloney, *Signs and Shadows. Reading John 5-12* (Minneapolis, 1996), 205.

23. Thompson, 'Worship in John', 276.

24. Further on this theme, see below, chapter 5.

25. See Moloney, *John*, 370-371, 477-479, and W. Brouwer, *The Literary Development of John 13-17. A Chiastic Reading* (Atlanta, 2000), especially 9-10, 117-118. Further on this, see chapter 5, below.

26. F.F. Segovia, *The Farewell of the Word. The Johannine Call to Abide* (Minneapolis:Fortress, 1991), 123-35.

27. T.L. Brodie, The Gospel According to John: A Literary and Theological Commentary (Oxford: Oxford University Press, 1993,) 482.

28. See Thompson, *God of the Gospel of John*, 223-226.

29. On the narrative structure of John 5, see Lee, *Symbolic Narratives*, 98-

125. This passage is central to understanding John's Father-Son theology.

30. In Classical Greek, *doxa* meant 'opinion'; in the Greek Old Testament (the Septuagint, LXX), it comes to mean 'good opinion', from which 'glory' comes. Later in the same chapter, Jesus speaks of *doxa* in a slightly different sense, as meaning 'honour, good opinion, status' (5:44).

31. C.H. Dodd sees this discussion as reflecting the practice of apprenticeship in the ancient world, where the son learns the family trade in his father's workshop, imitating him and being given a share in his father's life ('A Hidden Parable in the Fourth Gospel', in *More New Testament Studies* [Manchester: Manchester University Press, 1968], 30-40).

32. Pheme Perkins, 'The Gospel According to John', in R.E. Brown et al (eds.), *The New Jerome Biblical Commentary* (New Jersey: Prentice-Hall, 1990), 198.

33. For this translation of the preposition *pros* (usually translated as 'with'), see F.J. Moloney, "'In the Bosom of' or 'Turned towards' the Father?" *AusBR* 31 (1983), 63-71. See above, chapter 1.

34. While there is textual dispute over these verses, the weight of evidence supports their inclusion; see Schnackenburg, *St. John*, 2.254, 499.

35. This episode makes most sense as part of the Lazarus story, rather than an addition or response to it; see Lee, *Symbolic Narratives*, 191-197.

36. Craig R. Koester, *Symbolism in the Fourth Gospel: Meaning, Mystery, Community* (2nd ed.; Minneapolis, 2003) 114. See B. Byrne, *Lazarus: A Contemporary Reading of John* 11:1-46 (Collegeville: Liturgical Press, 1991), 59-60, and Lee, *Flesh and Glory*, 197-211.

37. In Luke's Gospel, several of the characters—disciples or suppliants—find themselves at Jesus' feet as an act of faith and recognition (e.g. Luke 5:8; 7:38, 44-46; 8:35; 10:39; 17:16).

38. The Johannine version of the anointing is distinct from the other Gospels, although it shares with them a sense of recognition that is close to worship. In the Markan version, the unnamed woman proclaims the gospel in her prophetic recognition of Jesus' kingship through death (Mk 14:3-9/Matt 26:6-13). In the Lukan story, the penitent woman's tears and anointing express more than gratitude for forgiveness; the anointing is an act of hospitality showing awareness of who Jesus really is (Lk 7:36-50). On the parallels with the anointing of the other Gospels, see Craig S. Keener, *The Gospel of John: A Commentary* (2 vols.; Peabody: Hendrickson, 2003), 2.859-861.

39. Further on imagery of following, in terms of Johannine spirituality, see below, chapter 5.

40. For example, in Matthew's temptation narrative Jesus' rendering of true

worship and obedience is a replaying of Israel's past, presenting it whole before God (Matt 4:1-12).

[41.] C.H. Dodd, *The Interpretation of the Fourth Gospel* (Cambridge: Cambridge University Press, 1953), 419-420. Dorothy Lee, 'The Prologue and Jesus' Final Prayer,' in *What We Have Heard from the Beginning: The Past, Present, and Future of Johannine Studies*, ed. T. Thatcher (Waco: Baylor University Press, 2007), 229-31.

[42.] Bultmann, *John*, 408.

[43.] Thompson, 'Worship in John', 277.

[44.] Thompson, *God of the Gospel of John*, 224-225.

[45.] See Andreas J. Köstenberger & Scott R. Swain, *Father, Son and Spirit. The Trinity and John's Gospel* (Downers Grove: InterVarsity Press, 2008), 19-22.

[46.] Thompson, 'Worship in John', 276. See especially Köstenberger & Swain, *Father, Son and Spirit*, 165-86.

Chapter 3
Spirituality and the Spirit-Paraclete

It is impossible to discuss John's spirituality without examining the work of the Holy Spirit in this Gospel. In Johannine theology, the Spirit signifies the immanence of God, born from the death of Jesus, the gift of both Father and Son; the one who is intimately close to believers, who knows and inhabits them, who prays with them and for them, who lifts them when they fall, and who makes effective in their hearts divine love and forgiveness.[1] John's Gospel has a particular theological outlook and significant emphases on the Spirit's presence and power within the community of faith; indeed the Spirit is given more attention in this Gospel than in the Synoptic Gospels.[2] Three times in the Fourth Gospel the Spirit is referred to as 'holy' (1:33; 14:26; 20:22), emphasising that the Spirit belongs to the divine realm. The various roles of the Spirit extend from beginning to end of the Gospel,[3] commencing with the testimony of John the Baptist and concluding with the appearance of the risen Jesus to the disciples on Easter Day. The majority of instances occur in the Farewell Discourse where the Spirit is mentioned in five different contexts: as the Paraclete (14:16, 26; 15:26; 16:7), the Spirit of truth (14:17; 15:26; 16:13) and the Holy Spirit (14:26). While the first half of the Gospel focuses on the relationship between Father and Son, the second half gives greater prominence to the Spirit, particularly in light of Jesus' departure.[4]

There are several aspects to John's portrayal of the Spirit throughout the Gospel narrative, each instance expressing one dimension of an intricate role. These are diverse but 'the various Spirit passages are interconnected and create a web of meaning.'[5] John speaks as much by implication as by utterance: having outlined the work and function of the Spirit, much is then assumed without direct reference to the Spirit. The Prayer of John 17, for example, makes no direct mention of the Spirit, but it is hard to avoid the impression of the Spirit's ubiquitous presence at its heart.[6]

The Spirit in the Ministry of Jesus

Before the Farewell Discourse, to which we will soon turn, the Spirit makes an appearance in four passages in the Fourth Gospel; following the Discourse, there are one or two further references. There is no direct allusion to the Spirit in the Prologue but, for those who have read the Gospel, the echoes of the Spirit's presence are strong: in the references to creation (1:3-4) and in the theme of birth (1:12-13). Readers familiar with the Synoptic Gospels expect the presence of the Spirit from the beginning: whether at the baptism of Jesus, as in Mark's Gospel (Mk 1:9-11), or in his miraculous conception in the other Synoptics (Matt 1:18, 20; Lk 1:35). By contrast, John implies but does not state the Spirit's presence in the opening verses of his Gospel, nor is there any appearance of angels acclaiming him; but later in the Fourth Gospel John tells us explicitly that the Spirit is the life-giver, while the flesh is useless (6:63). The ineffectiveness of flesh is already indicated in the Prologue by the inability of human beings to become children of God without divine authority: 'who, not of blood nor of the will of flesh nor of the will of a man, but of God were born' (1:13). The flesh of Jesus suffers no such limitations; on the contrary, it is the revelation of glory. It is surely not incidental that the first reference to the incarnation follows immediately the words 'but of God were born',[7] suggesting that Jesus' own birth, implied in the next verse, is above all and uniquely of God. In Jesus, and Jesus alone, flesh and Spirit are perfectly united, making his flesh, not only *not* useless, but the source and medium of salvation. John 1:14 suggests the efficacy and presence of the Spirit, even though John tells no tale of angelic annunciation or Spirit-inspired pregnancy.

Not only the Spirit but also Mary is absent from the opening sequence of the Gospel, though both make early appearances. It is not Mary who is the first Christian in this Gospel (unlike the Gospel of Luke) but John the Baptist. Yet, like the Baptist, she plays an important role in the gathering of the first disciples around Jesus; her titles of 'mother' and 'woman' in the Cana story indicate her role in this Gospel, as well as pointing forward to the cross where that role is fulfilled in the founding of the community (19:25-27). The evangelist presupposes her faith at the wedding at Cana. The lack of birth narratives in John means that there is no story of her coming to Christian faith as there is, for example, in Luke (Lk 1:26-38), where she is closely associated with the Holy Spirit who 'overshadows' her and who is the source of her miraculous pregnancy. John emphasises her role as mother of Jesus by only ever using that title, although her faith is crucially important for John (as it is also for Luke).

In the first appearance of the Spirit in John's Gospel, the testimony of John the Baptist confirms the Spirit's descent upon Jesus. Significantly, the voice of the Baptist (*phônê*, 1:23), which first introduces the Spirit, has already been heard in the Prologue. The Baptist has already spoken, bearing witness to Jesus: 'John testified to him and cried out, *This was he of whom I said, He who comes after me ranks ahead of me because he was before me*' (1:15). John the Baptist's voice comes into its own in the first narrative when he sees Jesus coming towards him, repeating the testimony we have already heard in the Prologue:

> The next day he saw Jesus coming toward him and declared, Behold the Lamb of God who takes away the sin of the world! *This is he of whom I said, After me comes a man who ranks ahead of me because he was before me*. I myself did not know him; but I came baptizing with water for this reason, that he might be revealed to Israel (1:29-31).

There is no direct meeting recorded between Jesus and the John the Baptist in this Gospel. The latter never addresses Jesus but only speaks of him in the third person. His recognition of Jesus as the Lamb of God is, as he himself confesses, not of his own intuition but comes from the self-revealing God who has appointed him to baptize. John's baptism, according to the Fourth Gospel, is fundamentally christological, its sole purpose being to point to the revelation of God in Christ. Thus the connection yet distinction between Jesus' and the Baptist's ministry and identity is preserved: one is the voice in the wilderness pointing to the other, the eternal Word made flesh; one baptizes in water in order to reveal the other, who baptizes in the Spirit; one retreats, the other advances; one recognises the advent of the Spirit in the other and his identity as Son of God.

Significantly, John the Baptist's vision attests not only to Jesus but also, and equally, to the Spirit. The same verb is employed in the Prologue, indicating a subjective experience that has its grounds in objective reality: 'we saw ... I saw ' (*etheasametha*, 1:14; *tetheamai*, 1:32). John the Baptist is the first of the believing community to behold the glory in the flesh. For the evangelist, Jesus' pre-eminence —his unique identity and mission—is intricately tied to the abiding presence of the Spirit. Just as 1:14 speaks of the union of flesh and glory in Jesus, so the baptism of Jesus, which in this Gospel is not in water but in the Spirit, signifies the union of flesh and Spirit in Jesus. It would be a mistake to read this in an 'adoptionist' way, as if it were the moment when Jesus takes on some kind of divine status. The Prologue makes clear that that identity pre-exists Jesus' earthly life. The Spirit's descent signals rather the beginning of Jesus' ministry, just as it does in the Synoptic accounts of Jesus' baptism. John the Baptist's report of his visionary experience in the Fourth Gospel reveals that Jesus' identity is defined, not only in terms of the eternal Word, but also as the abiding-place of the Spirit (1:32-34). As Craig Koester points out, the first thing the Spirit does in the Fourth Gospel is to reveal the identity Jesus possesses, not to raise him to a higher level.

What does the descent of the Spirit on Jesus signify in John's Gospel? Mark's version is more dramatic, with the motif of Jesus' descent into the waters of the Jordan, the descending dove which Jesus alone sees, and the divine voice acclaiming him (Mk 1:9-11). The identity of the Markan Jesus as the beloved, well-pleasing Son is revealed at this point, with the Spirit as the driving force behind Jesus' ministry. John's account is less dramatic and more interior, as we have observed: the dove descends, though without mention of Jesus' descent into the waters, and the Father speaks, but to the Baptist alone, acclaiming Jesus' essential connection to the Spirit. The language of baptism thus becomes metaphorical. In the Johannine baptism Jesus' intimate relationship with the Spirit is manifest, just as the Prologue has established his intimacy with the Father from 'before the foundation of the world' (17:24). The baptism presents Jesus as the recipient, the bearer and future bestower of the Spirit. The climactic affirmation of the baptism—'this is the Son of God' (1:34)—which is spoken by John the Baptist in John's Gospel rather than the Father, confirms Jesus' divine sonship on the basis, not just of his relationship with God, but also of his attachment to the Spirit. John the Baptist thus plays a crucial role in the opening chapter of the Fourth Gospel, testifying to the identity of Jesus in relation to the Father and the Spirit. This testimony will be the bridge leading to the formation of the believing community (1:35-42). The Fourth Gospel's account of the baptism, therefore, places great stress on the Spirit and the Spirit's connection to Jesus and his ministry. This link will again arise in the Farewell Discourse which will unfold the Spirit's parallel role for the community of faith precisely in relation to Jesus.

In the following chapters, the Spirit is central to the creative and re-creative work of God in the mission and ministry of Jesus. Now the Spirit is revealed to be as significant for the life of believers as for Jesus. The dialogue between Jesus and Nicodemus concerns the Spirit who alone gives birth to believers; it is 'a comprehensive new creation'. Birth 'from above' means birth from the Spirit, this being the only way to enter the new order brought about by, and embodied in, Jesus (3:1-10; cf. 1:12-13). The association of the Spirit with water underlines the point:

> Jesus answered, Very truly, I tell you, no one can enter the kingdom of God without being born of water and Spirit [*pneuma*]. What is born of the flesh is flesh, and what is born of the Spirit is spirit. Do not be astonished that I said to you, You must be born from above. The wind [*pneuma*] blows where it chooses, and you hear the sound of it, but you do not know where it comes from or where it goes. So it is with everyone who is born of the Spirit. (3:5-8).

Illustration 3: Giotto Di Bondone, Scenes from the Life of Christ: Baptism of Christ, 1304-06 Fresco, 200 x 185 cm. Cappella Scrovegni (Arena Chapel), Padua[8]

Giotto's painting of the baptism of Jesus above owes something to both the Synoptics and the Gospel of John. Along with two of his disciples, John the Baptist is on the right baptizing Jesus, who stands naked in the translucent waters of the Jordan River. On the left are angels waiting to assist Jesus from the water and holding garments in their outstretched arms. Above Jesus' head is the divine being, hand reaching down to touch Jesus, indicating both the Spirit and the voice of the Father. In different ways, John and the Synoptics contain similar elements, as depicted here: the essential role played by John the Baptist, the descent of the dove, the Father's voice, and the testimony to Jesus as the Son of God. Only the Fourth Gospel makes mentions of angels ('descending and ascending on the Son of Man', 1:51), although not until later in this narrative when the first group of disciples is formed. In Orthodox theology, this event is a 'theophany', a divine revelation not just of Jesus' identity but also of the Father and the Spirit.

The reference to water shows that, unlike the Baptist's water baptism—which is important but yet 'of the earth' (3:31)—the 'baptism' associated with Jesus is both of water and Spirit. Here the Spirit plays a maternal role in giving birth to believers, water suggesting childbirth as well as the baptismal link. Yet the Spirit's origins and workings are mysterious, like the wind itself, and the re-birth is also a mystery, a mystical movement of the Spirit within the spirit of the believer. Note that this is not a question of the earthly against the heavenly—human birth versus divine birth—but rather, as in the incarnation, the coming together of both. Physical birth, which has positive theological meaning in itself (and already the domain of the quickening Spirit), becomes the symbol for spiritual birth (also the work of the Spirit). The Spirit is the life-giver in this Gospel (see 6:63), the one who vivifies human flesh so that it regains its identity as God's offspring. The imagery echoes the making of Adam in the second creation account, where God breathes into his nostrils the breath of life (ruach, Gen 2:7). Just as God breathed life into the flesh of Adam, so in John's Gospel God breathes life into fallen flesh. The birth of believers takes place in the same way as ordinary human birth, the same vivifying and inspiring Spirit lying behind both.

In the following chapter, the Spirit is also associated with the faith journey of the Samaritans (4:1-42). On the basis of John 3, we know that the Spirit is present in the Samaritan woman's story, mysteriously at work in the unfolding development of the woman's — and later the villagers'—faith. The Spirit who abides on the Johannine Jesus draws believers to the Son as the divine yet human site of worship of the Father. We have already noted, in an earlier chapter,[9] that there are probably three direct allusions to the Spirit in the story of the Samaritan woman, associated with the theme of worship:

> But the hour is coming, and is now here, when
> the true worshippers will worship the Father in
> spirit and truth,
> for the Father seeks such as these to worship
> him.
> God is Spirit,

and those who worship him must worship in
spirit and truth (4:23-24).

As we saw then, the most likely reference of the phrase 'in spirit and
truth' is to the Spirit of God, since the phrase occurs twice, on either
side of the statement 'God is spirit (Spirit)' [10].Its meaning would then
be, in effect, 'the Spirit of truth'. As well as setting the Spirit at the
centre of worship, along with Jesus and the Father, the Johannine
structure of these verses also places truth at the heart of worship. The
language of truth is closely linked to that of revelation. Jesus, as we
have seen, reveals to the woman the truth about God and the truth
about herself. Worship is concerned with truth-telling, revealing the
one who is himself the Truth (8:32; 14:6; cf. 18:38), and in loving
relationship with whom, through the dynamic presence of the Spirit,
truth unfolds itself. Yet there may also be a secondary sense to the
phrase 'in spirit and truth' which relates to the human spirit, the spirit
of the believer. Once again the two terms go together for the fourth
evangelist: 'in a spirit of truth' is probably the sense, meaning that the
worshipper too must approach in a spirit of sincerity and the desire for
truth, with a truthful spirit.

The Spirit also plays an essential role in John's temple
Christology, developed particularly through John 5 to 10. The most
important text in these chapters is Jesus' invitation to discipleship in the
Tabernacles Discourse (7:37-39), a passage that John clearly interprets
as being about the Spirit, not yet given to the community. There is
some difficulty over the translation of this text. The original Greek
simply says, 'Out of *his* heart shall flow rivers of living water'. From
whose heart does the living water flow: the believer's or Jesus'? On the
one hand, Jesus speaks to the Samaritan woman about water springing
up to eternal life within the one who believes in him (4:14). With this
text in mind, the reference to 'his' would be the believer's heart. This
is the view taken by the translators of the NRSV:[11]

On the last day of the festival, the great day,
while Jesus was standing there, he cried out, Let
anyone who is thirsty come to me, and let the

> one who believes in me drink. As the scripture
> has said, *Out of the believer's heart* shall flow
> rivers of living water. Now he said this about the
> Spirit, which believers in him were to receive;
> for as yet there was no Spirit, because Jesus was
> not yet glorified (7:37-39).

On the other hand, living water has its source in the Johannine Jesus who is the giver of the Spirit. The Old Testament foresees streams of water, in the last days, springing miraculously from the temple in Jerusalem (Ezek 47:1-12; Zech 14:8; cf. Isa 12:3). This coheres with John's temple Christology, and especially the blood and water flowing from the side of the crucified Jesus (19:34). The NJB offers this translation, retaining the ambiguity of the Greek while using slightly different punctuation: [12]

> On the last day, the great day of the festival,
> Jesus stood and cried out: Let anyone who is
> thirsty come to me! Let anyone who believes in
> me come and drink! As scripture says, From his
> heart shall flow streams of living water (7:37-
> 38).

It may be that both meanings have a place here, the one referring to Jesus' wounded side and the other to the inner life of the believer. If so, the christological meaning should have priority. What is notable in 4:1-42 and 7:37-39 is that these two passages in John, where the theme of mission to the world is most explicit, both have the gift of the Spirit at their centre. The principal source of living water must, therefore, be Jesus himself, ironically through his death; he is the one from whose 'belly' or 'side' living water flows (19:34). Believers, who share in his saving death, will also be given the same Spirit; from their side too living water will flow to nourish the world around them. John's temple Christology is confirmed in this typology, as well as the centrality of the Spirit. It is the Spirit who fulfils the promise of water in the last days, as it flows from the temple of Jesus' body, offered to those who believe in the here-and-now so that they might become a source of living water for others.

The Paraclete in the Farewell Discourse

A particular and unique manifestation of the role of the Holy Spirit in the Fourth Gospel is that of 'Paraclete', an unusual title confined mostly in the New Testament to John's Farewell Discourse (*paraklêtos*).[13] It occurs only in John's Gospel in relation to the Spirit. How to render it in English has been a perpetual problem for translators, the options ranging from 'Comforter' (KJV) to 'Advocate' (NRSV, NEB, JB), 'Counsellor' (NIV) and 'Helper' (GNB, ESV). There are also Wisdom overtones in the language John uses for the Spirit, as of the Johannine Jesus. In fact, all these meanings are present in John's construction— which makes the task of selecting one translation a difficult one. With its forensic overtones, the most popular these days is 'Advocate', which connects to the trial motif throughout the Fourth Gospel. However, on balance, the NJB is probably right to retain the original 'Paraclete', explaining in a footnote at 14:16 something of the variety of meanings that this rich term connotes. As Raymond Brown points out,

> No one translation of *parklêtos* captures the complexity of the functions, forensic and otherwise, that this figure has. ... We would probably be wise also in modern times to settle for 'Paraclete', a near-transliteration that preserves the uniqueness of the title and does not emphasize one of the functions to the detriment of others.[14]

However we translate it, the core meaning of 'Paraclete' has to do with theology and Christology, as well as the life of discipleship. The Spirit, in this sense—as elsewhere in John—is both theological and ecclesial, connected on one side to God through Christ and, on the other side, to the life of the faith community.[15] In their study of the trinity in the Fourth Gospel, Köstenberger and Swain capture well this dual dynamic, the parallelism of procession from Father to Son to believing community:

the Spirit 'descends from the Father upon the Son that he might flow through the Son to all who believe, bringing forgiveness and renewal, life and light.'[16]

While the Paraclete has continuity with the role of the Spirit elsewhere in the Fourth Gospel, the meaning in the chapters leading up to Jesus' arrest is quite specific; indeed, it represents an enlarged understanding of the Spirit in this Gospel.[17] The basic theme and context of the Farewell Discourse is the departure of Jesus, a departure that, chiefly because of the coming of the Spirit, will turn out to be for the disciples' 'wellbeing and benefit' (16:7).[18] In this context the title 'Paraclete' finds meaning in its four occurrences in these chapters (14:15-17, 25; 15:26; 16:7-11); a fifth passage is closely connected to the others and usually grouped with them (16:13-15). In each case, the fourth evangelist emphasises the closest possible connection between the Spirit and Jesus, and the Spirit and the Father. The Spirit comes from both, though the gift comes ultimately from the Father, actualising Jesus' presence for the disciples in the context of his departure; just as the Son glorifies the Father, so the Spirit glorifies the Son. In this sense, the Spirit is both christological—the continuing revelation of Jesus— and theological: the donation of the Father who sends the Son and the Spirit. The pattern for the sending of the Son is repeated in the sending of the Spirit.

There are several roles which the Paraclete plays in the Farewell Discourse, creating a cluster of meaning that deepens and broadens our understanding of the Johannine Spirit. First and foremost, the Paraclete represents the *presence* of Jesus. In the first Paraclete-passage, John explicitly refers to the Spirit as *another* Paraclete (14:16), implying that Jesus himself is the first Paraclete.[19] This does not mean that Jesus' role is replaced, but rather that there is a close parallelism between the ministry of Jesus and that of the Spirit: the Spirit's function is to actualise the presence of Jesus in his absence, not replace it.[20] In other words, the Spirit, while not being identical to Jesus, is 'the *mediator* of Jesus' presence'.[21] Brown has famously described the Paraclete as 'the personal presence of Jesus with the Christian while Jesus is with the Father'.[22] This is a helpful definition, as far as it goes. But it is individualistic, unlike the Farewell Discourse in general which has as its focus the life of the community. The Paraclete indwells the community in the first place and, in an extended or consequent sense, the individual disciple. What Jesus has meant for the disciples, the Spirit will now maintain for them in every respect. That means, therefore, that the disciples are not bereft, not left 'orphaned' (14:18): the love and care Jesus has shown them will continue. Jesus' final return will be anticipated by the arrival of the Spirit, who will play the same nurturing, maternal role for the disciples that Jesus has done. Because of the Spirit, therefore, Jesus' departure will not be an abandonment of the faith community but a new way of being present to them. It is consolation in the deepest and truest sense—not a consolation prize for those who have missed out. The role of the Johannine Spirit is simply and surely to 'be in you' (14:17).

Secondly, as the 'Spirit of truth' (14:17; 16:13), the Paraclete is the teacher and interpreter, the one who instructs believers in, and reminds them of, Jesus' teaching, so guiding them into 'all truth' (14:26; 16:13). This parallels the role of the Johannine Jesus as Light of the world, the one who illuminates those who believe so that they do not 'walk in darkness' (8:12); truth also lies at the basis of God's nature (5:32; 7:28; 8:26).[23] As with Jesus, the encounter with truth is not so much a sudden blinding flash of insight as a gradual movement, a movement that may also involve misunderstanding and mistaken turnings. Yet the Spirit assures disciples that the goal will be attained, that they will come to know, that their minds and hearts will be illuminated more and more as they travel on the path of the Spirit's guidance and companionship. This teaching has a cerebral element, but it concerns the whole person: the whole of one's being enlightened by the Johannine Jesus whose light continues to shine in the leading of the Spirit, who strengthens disciples in their search for truth.

Thirdly, the Paraclete has a forensic role, as reflected in the translation 'Advocate'. Lying behind this imagery is that of a trial scene, which begins with the testimony of John the Baptist against the religious leaders who interrogate him (1:19-34). Jesus, in particular, is the target of animosity, the world placing him on trial—and eventually condemning him—but ironically the tables are overturned and the world itself is placed on trial before Jesus, the Judge and Light of the world. At the crucifixion, the world is exposed, whether Jew or Gentile, for its injustice and treachery even at the highest levels, while the Son of Man is vindicated, not only as innocent, but also as the fount of all goodness, truth and justice. The Johannine Jesus also warns his disciples that the same treatment will be meted out to them: like their Lord and Master, they too will be placed on trial, persecuted, condemned and hounded out of their communities. Here, in a context of injustice and persecution, the Paraclete plays a key role. The Spirit is the defendant and advocate, testifying on behalf of Jesus, defending and protecting the disciples so that they too are empowered to bear witness (15:26-27). At the same time, the Paraclete is the vigorous and victorious prosecutor of Jesus' and the disciples' enemies, playing out that final judgement which, in John, has already taken place in and through the cross (16:8-11).

This portrait of the Paraclete in the three functions of presence, guidance and witness are both retrospective and prospective. Looking back over the ministry of the Johannine Jesus, we gain a sense of what the Paraclete does in being present with the disciples, in shining the light with which they are illuminated, and in bearing witness to the Father. John assumes the reader's knowledge of all this. Similarly, we hold the same picture as we continue reading, particularly in Jesus' great prayer which is the climax of this section of the Gospel, making actual all that Jesus has promised for his disciples. The prayer of John 17 is performative, as we have already observed, winding itself around the believer, drawing him or her into the bulwark of Jesus' presence, his prayerful union with the Father, his glory. This warding is made effective through the Spirit's presence, guidance and witness, making real day-after-day the same prayer, the perpetual ascent of the Son to the Father in which believers are joined, binding them in love to the divine, trinitarian life. They take the Paraclete with them as they make the journey, always surrounding them in that protective and loving prayer, always enmeshing them in its embrace, even in adversity and pain. The Spirit-Paraclete acts as presence and comforter, as witness to the heart giving it boldness, and as guide, leading it to where it needs to go. The function is hermeneutical, the Spirit interpreting for believers the meaning of the gospel, guiding them in their future life together,[24] and drawing them into the orbit of Father and Son.

The Spirit in the Passion and Resurrection Narratives

The final chapters of the Fourth Gospel move in a different direction (Jn 18-21): into the public arena, at first, where Jesus is exposed to the darkness of his enemies; and then back to the private arena of Jesus' relationship with his disciples. In this context, there are far fewer references to the Spirit, but one at least is of great importance in the Fourth Gospel and the other is an interpretation of an ambiguous text. Once again, as with John 17, we know that, through the events of the Passion, the Spirit who abides on Jesus does not abandon him but holds him in unity with the Father right till the end, re-gathering the disciples in Easter faith following the resurrection. We recall that, during the Feast of Tabernacles, John has already linked the bestowal of the Spirit to Jesus' glorification: 'Now he said this about the Spirit, which believers in him were to receive; *for as yet there was no Spirit, because Jesus was not yet glorified*' (7:39). The sense here is not that the Spirit does not yet exist—that would contradict the abiding of the Spirit on the Johannine Jesus since the baptism—but that the Spirit as the Paraclete, *the Spirit of Jesus*, has not yet been given to the disciples.

In the Passion narrative, there are two implicit references to the Spirit. John uses ambiguous language to describe the death of Jesus: 'When Jesus had received the wine, he said, It is accomplished (*tetelestai*). Then he bowed his head and gave up his spirit' (19:30). Another possible translation is: 'Then he bowed his head and *handed over his Spirit.*'[25] Ambiguity is not uncommon in the Fourth Gospel and, as elsewhere, the most likely scenario is that the text contains both meanings. This is Jesus' last mortal breath. It is also the self-surrender of his life: 'no-one takes it from me but I give it up of my own accord' (10:18). This statement, therefore, in describing Jesus' death—with the emphasis on Jesus giving up his life and no-one taking it from him[26]— also anticipates his conferral of the Holy Spirit which issues from his death.[27] One problem with this view is that Jesus does not formally confer the Spirit on the disciples until after the resurrection. But the same could be said of the ascension: John speaks of the crucifixion as the 'ascension' of Jesus, his lifting up and glorification on the cross, even though Jesus tells Mary Magdalene after the resurrection that he has 'not yet ascended' (20:17). The point for the evangelist is theological rather than chronological: the events of cross, resurrection, ascension, and giving of the Spirit are essentially one, even if they seem divided in time.[28]

The impression of ambiguity at 19:30 is confirmed in the final scene of the crucifixion, where Jesus' side is pierced, and blood and water flow out. The *crurifragium* is the climax of the Johannine Passion story and has no Synoptic parallel.[29] Throughout the Fourth Gospel, water has been mostly associated with the Holy Spirit, as is clear in the context of Tabernacles, with Jesus' call to the thirsty to come and drink: 'Now he said this about the Spirit, which believers in him were to receive' (7:39a). The same link is implied in the dialogue between Jesus and the Samaritan woman in its movement from living water (scene 1, 4:7-15) to worship in the Spirit (scene 2, 4:16-30). 'Living water' flows from the cross of Christ, the giving of life from death. And Jesus' departure, as the Farewell Discourse has made plain, means the arrival of the Spirit, the Spirit of the Johannine Jesus, giving water to the thirsty and filling them with life in abundance. Here the Spirit inaugurates the new covenant, shed by the sacrificial Lamb of God.[30] Here too the Spirit's role is sacramental, the water suggesting the waters of baptism (new birth) and the blood pointing to the wine of the eucharist (new life). John's point here is that, on the cross, an event that spells destruction and death paradoxically transformed into an experience of life, through the donation of the Spirit. The Holy Spirit plays the same role as in John 3, giving life to believers; not simply in a moment of conversion but in the ongoing conversion of life that is sustained within the believing community.

Last of all, the Johannine Jesus gives the Spirit to the disciples on the evening of Easter Day, in his first appearance to the gathered community (20:19-23). This can be seen as the central episode of John

20, the appearances to Mary Magdalene and Thomas bounding the
narrative on either side (20:1-18, 20:24-29).[31] Those who are blessed
for not having seen yet believed (20:29b) are blessed because they are
given the gift of the Spirit. Note that the context of Jesus' first appearing
to the disciples is their fear and unbelief, symbolised by the fact that
the doors are locked 'for fear of the Jews' (20:19a). The risen Jesus
is no more constrained by locked doors than he is by a heavy stone
against the mouth of the tomb; he enters them with the same authority
he enters and exits death. Twice he offers the disciples the gift of peace
(20:19b, 21a), showing them his wounds as joyful signs of his identity
and the efficacy of his saving death (20:20), and sending them on the
same mission which the Father has sent him (20:21b). Only then, once
the disciples come to Easter faith and are given the peace of the risen
Jesus and the Father's mission, does Jesus breath on them, bestowing
on them the promised Spirit, his own Spirit (20:22), and empowering
them for their task.

Perhaps unexpectedly, the disciples are also given the gift of
reconciliation, the authority to release and retain sins: 'If you forgive
the sins of any, they are forgiven them; if you retain the sins of any,
they are retained' (20:23). Forgiveness has not been an explicit theme
of the Fourth Gospel and might escape the attention of the modern
reader, but it is implied in the references to cleansing at the Last
Supper (13:10-11, 15:2-3). John the Baptist's use of the title 'Lamb
of God' has also, in Johannine usage, a reference to sin (1:29. 36),
even though sin is not part of the original paschal symbolism; yet the
fourth evangelist has integrated this concept into his understanding
of Passover, bringing together other Old Testament allusions.[32] The
same theme is apparent in the resurrection narratives. As Jesus has
offered cleansing from sin in his sacrificial death, so the disciples are
empowered to offer forgiveness and reconciliation in their mission.
The idea of 'retaining' sins is much more difficult to interpret than that
of forgiving. But, as Koester points out, in terms of the Fourth Gospel,
it means 'exposing sin, identifying sin, and holding people to account
for sin';[33] its purpose is not to drive people away from the good news
but rather to challenge them to repentance. Thus the power to 'release

and retain' is a divine gift, its purpose life-giving and redemptive. It represents an aspect of the Spirit not hitherto alluded to in the Fourth Gospel but expanding the reader's understanding of the Spirit's place in the life of the believing community.

These points demonstrate the strongly ecclesial focus of these verses, the so-called 'Johannine Pentecost'.[34] The gift of peace, the commissioning, and the authority for reconciliation indicate the ongoing life and mission of the believing community. The role of the Spirit continues the promise of the Paraclete's presence with the community of faith. As Sandra Schneiders has pointed out, John 20:19-23 functions as

> a narrative-theological synthesis of Johannine ecclesiology in which the Church appears as the body of the Risen Lord who is in its midst as the glory of God and which is commissioned to be in the world the presence of the post-Easter Jesus as the pre-Easter Jesus had been the presence of God in the world.'[35]

Johannine Symbolism of the Spirit

Throughout this complex presentation, a number of symbols for the Spirit stand out in the Fourth Gospel. First is the symbol of water. This imagery begins in the baptism of Jesus where the Spirit descends and abides on Jesus, enabling John the Baptist to recognise him as the one who will baptize with the Holy Spirit—a baptism to which the Baptist's own baptism in water symbolically points (1:31-33). Water baptism is a symbol, therefore, of baptism in the Spirit. In the next chapters, the Spirit is associated with new life, birth and worship. The water at the wedding in Cana is transformed to become the symbol of the new in Jesus, the union of heaven and earth, the marriage of human flesh and divine glory—'you have kept the good wine until now' (2:10)—a union that can only be effected by the divine Spirit. In John 4:1-42, water signifies the new spiritual birth 'from above' required for entry into the kingdom of God; whereas in John 3, water becomes the primary symbol of the Johannine Spirit which, given by Jesus, quenches the thirst for life. Water is also associated with the temple and the feast of Tabernacles, symbolism that is deeply christological and points to the Johannine Jesus as the temple of God, the 'place where your glory abides' (Ps 26:8), and the place also whence living waters flow (Zech 14:18). What is unique about the Spirit in the Fourth Gospel is the portrayal of the Paraclete, who gives disciples the same sense of presence, witness and guidance they have received from Jesus himself, who comes ultimately from the Father. The christological aspect of the Spirit is emphasised in the crucifixion: the one whose last breath is the giving up of *pneuma* is the one from whose wounded side the living waters of *pneuma* flow.

The second symbol of the Spirit is the dove, as testified in the vision of John the Baptist: 'I saw the Spirit descending from heaven like a dove, and it remained on him' (1:32). The dove takes on symbolic value once the Baptist recognises it for what it is. He himself confesses his lack of recognition until the divine voice speaks, assuring him that the one on whom the dove settles is the baptizer in the Spirit and Son of God (1:33-34). It is hard to know why the evangelist— as also the Synoptic evangelists—associates the Spirit with a dove in relation to Jesus' baptism. There are several biblical allusions to doves which may provide some kind of background: a dove is associated with the covenant at the end of the flood story (Gen 8:8-12); doves are considered attractive and beloved creatures (Ps 74:19; Song 2:12, 14; 5:2; 6:9); they care for their mates and their young, regurgitating their food to feed them (2 Esr 2:15); unlike many other birds, they are ritually clean and particularly appropriate for sacrifice (Gen 15:9; Lev 12:6; Lk 2:24); they come to be associated with purity and peace (Matt 10:16); and as wild creatures in flight, they are also seen as elusive (Ps 55:6). In what ways, then, is the Spirit in John the Baptist's vision 'like a dove'? The evangelist does not draw out the symbolism explicitly but, in the mind of the biblically literate reader, the dove suggests beauty, purity, peace, care, swiftness, elusiveness, and mystery.

The third symbol of the Spirit in John's Gospel is that of the wind, apparent in the dialogue with Nicodemus: 'The wind (*pneuma*) blows (*pneô*) where it chooses, and you hear the sound of it (*phonê*, voice), but you do not know where it comes from or where it goes' (3:8). The noun used, *pneuma*, can mean 'wind' or 'spirit' ('Spirit').[36] In the Old Testament, the wind is associated with creation—'a wind from God swept over the face of the waters' (Gen 1:2 NRSV; see Job 26:13; Amos 4:13)[37]—with the subsiding of the waters by God after the flood (Gen 8:1), and with God's dividing of the waters at the Red Sea (Exod 14:21); it can also signify God's wrath and judgement (Pss 1:4; 35:5). The winds are God's messengers and the vehicle on which God rides (Ps 104:3-4). The wind is even described as winged (2 Sam 22:11; Pss 18:10, 104:3; also Zech 5:9), like a bird or an angel flying through the air. In the Fourth Gospel, the wind as symbol of the Spirit picks up Old Testament themes of creation, salvation and the immanence of God. But, for John, it also describes something of the inscrutability of the Spirit, whose origins and destiny are equally mysterious and beyond human capacity to calculate.

The fourth symbol for the Spirit in this Gospel is that of breath, which is closely related to the image of the wind. In the creation account, it is God's breath that vivifies Adam: 'then the Lord God formed man from the dust of the ground, and breathed into his nostrils the breath of life; and the man became a living being' (Gen 2:7 NRSV; 2 Esdr 3:5).[38] The same link between 'spirit' and 'breath' is found elsewhere in the Old Testament, the two terms used synonymously. Job, for example, says of God (amidst his suffering): 'The spirit of God has made me, and the breath of the Almighty gives me life' (Job 33:4; cf. Isa 42:5); death is God taking back that spirit and that breath (Job 34:14; Ps 104:29; Eccl 12:7). Indeed, all of creation comes from the breath of God (Ps 33:6), so that God's re-creation is the restoring of flesh and blood and breath (Ezek 37:5-10). God's breath is powerful, not only giving life but also executing judgement (Isa 11:4; cf 2 Thess 2:8). And idols are worthless, false gods an illusion, for they have no breath: no power to create or withhold life (Jer 10:14, 51:17). Even more significantly, Wisdom is described as 'a breath of the power of God, and a pure emanation of the glory of the Almighty' (Wisd 7:25 NRSV; the word for 'breath' here is *atmis*, 'vapour').

Jesus' breathing the Holy Spirit on the disciples on Easter Sunday is probably the most powerful metaphor for the Spirit in the Fourth Gospel (20:22). As we have seen the image coheres with Jesus' expiration on the cross, his last breath the sign of his self-giving love— loving his disciples 'to the end' (13:1). The same symbolism is linked also to the image of the wind. What does it mean to say that the Spirit is the *breath* of Jesus? Breath is what gives and sustains life; if we stop breathing we die. The Spirit in John is the expiration of Jesus: that which he breathes out and leaves behind, his parting gift which is life-giving. Yet there is a sense that this is not a one-off event, as in the Lukan Pentecost (Acts 2), but rather the experience of the community Sunday-by-Sunday as they celebrate the resurrection. John thus ties the coming of the Spirit to the events of Jesus' death and resurrection, and also to the worship life of the community, in the closest possible way.

The imagery of wind and breath emphasises three things about the Spirit in the Fourth Gospel: first, the dynamic power to create and re-create, the source of life for the whole creation, physical and spiritual; secondly, mysterious origins, nature and presence; thirdly, the most proximate association with Jesus himself—that which empowers his ministry, sustaining and giving him life, and that which he confers on the community to keep alive his presence. The Spirit is given formally on Easter Day because of the importance of resurrection as the archetypal symbol of new life, re-created life, life that transcends death, just as wind and spirit are associated with the creation of the world and humankind. The intimacy between God and Jesus, between Father and Son, is a major feature of this Gospel, but the imagery of breath—the Spirit as the breath of Jesus—is just as intimate. The term 'spirit' refers also to human beings, their innermost being, which is closely tied to breath. The Spirit is the breath of new life, just as the Spirit also gives lives to mortal bodies. Perhaps that is why modern meditation techniques often use breathing to enable the sense of being centred. We use the phrase 'closer to us than our own breathing' to make the point about the intimacy of our breath to us, which enters and exits our body every day, every minute, every second, waking or sleeping, conscious or unconscious, whatever our mood or feeling.

Breath becomes part of us, in one sense belonging to us (we speak of '*my* breath') yet not identical to us. Indeed the way we breath can reflect our physical and emotional state. The Spirit leaves the body of Jesus, crucified and risen, and enters the mortal bodies of disciples so that they inhale what the Johannine Jesus exhales, breathing his life, his love, his authority, his triumph over death and darkness.

John has a complex understanding of the Holy Spirit which he unfolds throughout the Fourth Gospel. The Spirit is the Spirit of Jesus, who comes ultimately from the Father, Jesus' parting gift to his community, the source of his ongoing presence with them and the guarantee of their relationship with the Father. The Spirit is the one who enables understanding of the relationship between Father and Son, making that relationship both intelligible and actual: 'It is pneumatology that first enables the Johannine understanding of the relation of Father and Son to become a comprehensive systematic whole.'[39] As the Spirit 'rests and remains' on Jesus, sent by the Father, so too the Spirit will 'rest and remain' on believers,[40] donated by the Father, and energising them for their ministry in the world. As the Paraclete, the consoling Spirit makes real the presence of Jesus, witnesses to Jesus as the Light of the world amid hostility and persecution, and guides the community in its pilgrimage towards the fullness of life and truth. The symbols of the Johannine Spirit are water, with its sacramental overtones, the dove, the wind and breath, each pointing to the mystery and beauty of the Spirit, the intimacy of the Spirit's presence, and the profound reconciliation that is engendered, making actual Jesus' victory in his death and resurrection, and confirming his propinquity in the ongoing life of the believing community.

End Notes

[1.] That the Spirit is personal in the Fourth Gospel and not an impersonal force is clear from the parallels with the Johannine Jesus; see Rudolf Schnackenburg, *The Gospel According to St John* (3 vols.; New York: Seabury & Crossroad, 1980 & 1982), 3.149-50, and Craig S. Keener, *The Gospel of John: A Commentary* (2 vols.; Peabody, MS: Hendrickson, 2003), 962-71.

[2.] Gary M. Burge, *The Anointed Community. The Holy Spirit in the*

Johannine Tradition (Grand Rapids: Eerdmans, 1987), 41-43.

3. For a succinct summary of the Spirit's role in the Gospel of John, see R. Bieringer, "'Greater than Our Hearts" (1 John 3:20): The Spirit in the Gospel of John' *BToday* 45 (2007) 305-9, and Andreas J. Köstenberger & Scott R. Swain, *Father, Son and Spirit. The Trinity and John's Gospel* (Downers Grove: InterVarsity Press, 2008), 93-103, 135-48.

4. Köstenberger & Swain, *Father, Son and Spirit*, 93-6.

5. Craig R. Koester, *The Word of Life. A Theology of John's Gospel* (Grand Rapids: Eerdmans, 2008), 134.

6. So Köstenberger & Swain, *Father, Son and Spirit*, 177-9.

7. The instinct connecting the two verses is perhaps the reason for the (later) textual variant 'who was born' at 1:13, referring to Jesus himself. This variant reads the singular rather than the plural, referring to Jesus and the virgin birth: '*he* was born, not of blood … but of God'. No Greek text contains this version but it is found in some old Latin witnesses and Tertullian strongly supported it. The evidence is in favour of the plural, as in modern translations; Bruce M. Metzger, *A Textual Commentary on the Greek New Testament* (3rd ed.; London & New York: United Bible Societies, 1975), 196-197. See Schnackenburg, *St John*, 1.264-265; also George R. Beasley-Murray, *John* (WBC; Waco: Waco Books, 1987), 2, who more or less supports the plural but thinks the issue is more complex than is generally admitted.

8. http://www.giottodibondone.org/No.-23-Scenes-from-the-Life-of-Christ--7.-Baptism-of-Christ-1304-06.html.

9. See above, chapter 2, p. 60.

10. Benny Thettayil argues that, of the three possible meanings of *pneuma* here—the human spirit, the spirit as against the law, the divine Spirit—'the Holy Spirit' is most Johannine, and possesses the closest association with truth (*In Spirit and Truth. An Exegetical Study of 4:19-26 and a Theological Investigation of the Replacement Theme in the Fourth Gospel* [Leuven: Peeters, 2007], 131-139).

11. For the view that Jesus is referring to the believer, cf. C.K. Barrett, *The Gospel According to St. John* (end ed.; London: SPCK, 1978), 326-327, Ernst Haenchen, *A Commentary on the Gospel of John* (ET: Philadelphia, 1984). 2.17, Barnabas Lindars, *The Gospel of John* (Grand Rapids, 1981), 299-300, and Köstenberger & Swain, *Father, Son and Spirit*, 95.

12. So Raymond E. Brown, *The Gospel According to John* (AB 29; New York: Doubleday), 1.320-321, Francis J. Moloney, *The Gospel of John* (SP 4; Collegeville: Liturgical Press, 1998), 256, and Schnackenburg, *St. John*, 2.153-154; also Lee, *Flesh and Glory*, 41-42, and Koester, *Word of Life*,

145-146.

[13.] See Dorothy Lee, 'John, 'in B.R. Gaventa & D. Petersen (eds.), *The New Interpreter's One Volume Commentary on the Bible* (Nashville: Abingdon, 2010), 725-7.

[14.] 'The Paraclete', Appendix V in *John*, 2.1137.

[15.] For a lucid and comprehensive discussion of *Paraklêtos* in the Farewell Discourse, see especially, Keener, *Gospel of John*, 2.953-982.

[16.] Köstenberger & Swain, *Father, Son and Spirit,* 148.

[17.] D.M. Tolmie, *Jesus' Farewell to the Disciples. John 13:1-17:26 in Narratological Perspective* (BIS 12; Leiden: Brill, 1995), 133-135.

[18.] See below, chapter 4.

[19.] In the Johannine epistles, Jesus is once referred to as Paraclete, in the context of forgiveness of sins (1 Jn 2:1). See further, chapter 7 below.

[20.] The point is made by Koester, *Word of Life*, 147-149; also Marianne Meye Thompson, *The God of the Gospel of John* (Grand Rapids: Eerdmans, 2001), 181-182. See Thettayil, *In Spirit and Truth*, 143-146, and George L. Parsenios, *Departure and Consolation. The Johannine Farewell Discourses in Light of Greco-Roman Literature* (SNT 117; Leiden: Brill, 2005), 78-84. Parsenios relates the role of the Paraclete to that of tokens of a lost love's presence that will ameliorate the absence in ancient literature: e.g. Admetus' loss of his beloved Alcestis in Euripides' play of that name (102-109), where Admetus uses dreams, memory, and a simulacrum of his wife to render her present.

[21.] Ruth Sheridan, 'The Paraclete and Jesus in the Johannine Farewell Discourse' *Pacifica* 20 (2007), 127.

[22.] 'Paraclete', *John*, 2.1139. For a list of the parallels between Jesus and the Spirit in John, see Thettayil, *In Spirit and Truth*, 148.

[23.] Koester, *Word of Life*, 155-156

[24.] Schnelle, 'Johannine Theology', 706-8.

[25.] The verb used here, *paradidômi*, can mean to give up/surrender or hand over/down; it is a stronger term than the Synoptic equivalents (*exepneusen*, Mk 15:37/Lk 23:46; *aphêken to pneuma*, Matt 27:50). This view, that Jesus is handing over the Spirit, goes back to E.C. Hoskyns, *The Fourth Gospel* (2 vols.; London: Faber & Faber, 1939), 2.633-4. Against this, cf. David Crump who argues that Jesus is here sending the Spirit back to the Father ('Who Gets What? God or Disciples, Human Spirit or Holy Spirit in John 19:30' *NovT* 51 [2009], 78-89).

[26.] Schnackenburg, *St John*, 3.284-285.

[27.] So Brown, *John*, 2.927-931, and Keener, *Gospel of John*, 1148-1149;

against this, cf. Beasley-Murray, *John*, 353.

28. Luke's chronology is very different from John's, spreading these events over fifty days, yet there are parallels: 'this scene fulfils the promise of the farewell discourse, just as the scene of Pentecost, in Acts, fulfils the promise made at the end of Luke's Gospel' (John Ashton, *Understanding the Fourth Gospel* [Oxford: Clarendon, 1991], 425). Theologically, cross, resurrection, ascension, and giving of the Spirit are inseparable, each flowing from the others and constituting the one 'moment' of revelation.

29. However, a Roman soldier does play an important role in the Synoptics: following the death of Jesus, the centurion utters words of faith ('truly this was God's Son, Mk 15:39/Matt 27:54 [with his companions]; 'indeed this man was righteous/innocent', Lk 23:47). There is a textual addition at Matt 27:49—'another, having taken a spear, pierced his side, and there came forth water and blood'—but it is unlikely to be original; see Metzger, *Textual Commentary*, 71.

30. Hoskyns sees a parallel with Heb 9:19-20 where the new covenant is inaugurated with blood, water and hyssop (*Fourth Gospel*, 634-635).

31. Further on this see Dorothy Lee, 'Partnership in Easter Faith: The Role of Mary Magdalene and Thomas in John 20' *JSNT* 58 (1995), 37-49.

32. See Dorothy Lee, 'Paschal Imagery in the Gospel of John: A Narrative and Symbolic Reading' *Pacifica* 24 (2011), 13-28.

33. Koester, *Word of Life*, 159 (159-160).

34. Against this, Köstenberger & Swain argue that Jn 20:19-23 'represents a symbolic promise of the soon-to-be-given gift of the Spirit, not the actual giving of him fifty days later at Pentecost' (*Father, Son and Spirit*, 101-102).

35. 'The Raising of the New Temple: John 20,19-23 and Johannine Ecclesiology' *NTS* 52 (2006), 338-9.

36. The more common noun for 'wind' in Greek is *anemos* (e.g. 6:18).

37. Other translations read 'the Spirit of God' (e.g. KJB, RSV, ESV, NIV; LXX *pneuma theou*).

38. The noun used in the LXX for 'breath' is *pnoê*, a cognate of *pneuma*.

39. Schnelle, 'Johannine Theology', 712.

40. The language is that of Köstenberber & Swain, *Father, Son and Spirit*, 135-48.

Chapter 4
Spirituality and Absence

The emphasis of John's theology is on the radiant presence of love, joy, peace and union within the believing community. Its spirituality has a strongly optimistic vision, an uplifting focus on all that disciples gain now in Jesus. In technical terms, John's eschatology—his understanding of ultimate reality and the last days—is present-oriented; though it points to God's redeeming future, it stresses that much of that future is already articulated in the Christ-event. Where the Synoptic Gospels and Paul tend to have a more future-oriented understanding of salvation (though that statement requires considerable nuance), of all New Testament theology John's Gospel gives greatest weight to the present as the locale of God's transforming activity. Note that all the New Testament sees the future as already anticipated in the life, death and resurrection of Jesus, and in the life of the household of faith. But whereas the other Gospels promise the future coming of the Son of Man in glory (e.g. Mk 8:38; 13:26; 14:62), in John that glorious coming defines primarily the incarnation as both the place and time of God's advent. At the same time, we need to acknowledge that John's spirituality is not simply a theology of presence, fullness and joy:[1] there is more to be said than that. This chapter explores symbols of loss and absence, and the spirituality that emerges from John's presentation of such symbolism.

Absence in Mark or John?

Perhaps such a claim for the Gospel of John may be seen to contradict the tenor of John's theology, and to import a more Synoptic perspective into the Fourth Gospel. Certainly the theme of divine absence is more commonly associated with the Gospel of Mark than of John. Mark's crucifixion narrative, with its portrayal of an 'utterly forlorn Jesus' immediately before his death[2]—'My God, my God, why have you abandoned me?' (Mk 15:33)—depicts the anguish of the beloved Son as the experience of divine absence.[3] Yet the Markan God enters the depths of suffering, the experience of divine absence, in order to redeem it. That theme is already prefigured in the baptism, the descent of Jesus into the watery depths (Mk 1:9),[4] and is suggested also by Jesus' intermittent injunctions to silence. The same imagery of absence appears again in the resurrection story, where the Markan Jesus is never actually encountered.[5]

By contrast, the major symbols of John's theology at first glance intimate only the presence of love, joy, peace and union within the community, as a given of believing existence. In a real sense, salvation has been achieved in the world of the fourth evangelist: in the incarnation where the gulf between Creator and creation is bridged and, by extension, on the cross where 'the ruler of the world' is overthrown (12:31; also 14:30, 16:11). John's account of the Passion appears, at first, to stress only the presence of glory in the crucifixion, in the fulfilment of the Father's will. Here John seems more concerned to depict plenitude and presence than desolation and absence. Jesus' last utterance on the cross ('it is accomplished', *tetelestai*, 19:30) is, for the evangelist, a cry of salvation and manifestation of divine glory, suffusing human flesh—crucified flesh that, ironically, symbolises not death and decay but life and hope (19:34). The incarnation, leading inexorably to the cross, is the transformation of flesh to radiate glory in the Son's ascent to the Father. Henceforth, categories of 'above' and 'below' stand (admittedly, somewhat uneasily) alongside the temporal axis (the old age and the new age), with its tension between present and future. John is not just contrasting the present with the future: the fullness of the present means that he can also speak of the earthly and the heavenly, and the contrast between them. The stress on 'above' and 'below' emphasises the ingathering of creation—all that is encompassed by 'flesh' (*sarx*)—into the divine embrace. It gives a strong sense of presence to the Johannine narrative.

Yet, despite appearances, there is a discernible juxtaposition of presence and absence in both Mark and John, although this dynamic is articulated in different ways. It is simplistic to think of the Markan crucifixion as characterised only by suffering and absence, while John is represented by glory and presence. The tearing of the temple veil and the centurion's confession of faith—'truly this man was God's

Son' (Mk 15:39)[6]— indicate that, for Mark, there is a sense of divine presence on the cross even in its seeming absence.[7] Along with the angelic presence and the promise of a future meeting, the emptiness of the tomb on Easter Sunday stands as a Markan symbol, ironically, of the paradoxical and mysterious proximity of God (Mk 16:5-6).[8] Similarly, quite apart from the major theme of departure and loss, John's Passion story does not lack indications of suffering, particularly in the intimations of Jesus' distress—in the events leading up to the Passion (12:27), and in Jesus' thirst on the cross which leads him to accept the sponge of sour wine offered him (19:28-29).[9] Even a cursory examination of the Johannine narrative illustrates that the question of absence is very much to the fore in John's spirituality—may, indeed, be part of the theological impetus behind the writing of the Fourth Gospel. Mark and John cannot be so neatly divided. As we will see, there is room for a theology of absence in John's theology, just as there is of presence in Mark. John's theology is not all love and roses. The sun has unquestionably arisen, but there are dark clouds that obscure it. This point of obscurity is where we need to make room for a Johannine theology of absence, despite the focus on presence—a theology that portrays absence as inevitable and, ultimately, beneficial for the life of the community.

Absence and Conflict

Apart from anything else, the Gospel presents considerable conflict throughout the narrative. Indeed, one way of viewing the story as a whole is a trial scene:[10] where the *kosmos* (the fallen world) attempts to put Jesus on trial.[11] This imagery explains, in literary terms, much of the conflict of the Gospel. The trial which begins with John the Baptist and the questioning by the authorities (1:19-28) continues throughout the ministry of Jesus. Ironically, the *kosmos* finds itself instead under the penetrating and searing judgement of the Son of Man, the Light of the world: the tables are turned and the trial is directed against those who condemn Jesus. Note that at the end of the dramatic trial before Pilate, the Roman governor is said to 'seat himself' on the throne of judgement before passing sentence; yet the Greek verb has an ambiguity and could mean that Pilate sat *Jesus* on the judgement-seat (19:13). Of course, we are not to take this literally: it is indubitably Pilate who pronounces judgement on Jesus, despite being convinced of his innocence. Yet in a deeper and ironical sense, Pilate is being judged—is judging himself—in performing such an act of injustice and placing political expediency above truth.

Moreover, according to John, the trial with all its conflict is to extend to the life of the believing community. The Farewell Discourse, even at its very centre where it rhapsodies over love and abiding, sternly warns of the inevitability of persecution and suffering from the forces of evil: significantly, the two passages are set against each other back-to-back (15:1-17; 15:18-16:4a). Similarly, the story of the man born blind is not only about conversion but also the persecution which inevitably accompanies it—a tale that, according to some, gives a glimpse into the post-Easter life of believers. While the community may be a place of light—although John continuously reminds the reader throughout the Gospel of the treachery of Judas Iscariot within the intimate circle of believers[12]—it is also surrounded by darkness. The death of Lazarus and the grief of his sisters, although happily resolved, nonetheless points to the continuation and inevitability of death, even for believers, along with its anguish and grief (11:1-12:11).

So, while much is realised in the spiritual life of the Johannine community—through the presence of the Spirit-Paraclete who actualises 'the resurrection and the life' in the experience of believers—much also is left unrealised, unresolved, awaiting the final consummation. For John, it is a question of making present the triumph already effected by the cross. In a real sense, salvation has been achieved: both in the incarnation where the gulf between Creator and creation has been bridged, and on the cross where 'the prince of this world' has been defeated (12:31; 14:30; 16:11). But that reality is still to be grasped through faith (1:12-13). In the meantime, conflict with the *kosmos* points to what is still unrealised in the life of the community in the post-Easter context.

Johannine Indications of Absence

If John has indeed space for a theology of absence, we would expect to find it clearly denoted in the narrative dynamics of the Gospel. In fact, there are several different kinds of absence in the Fourth Gospel and different ways in which it functions, deriving fundamentally from the absence of Jesus. In the first place, and most obviously, Jesus' power manifests itself in physical absence. At the beginning of his ministry, Jesus miraculously perceives Nathaniel sitting under the fig tree, recognising him as 'an Israelite in whom there is no guile' (1:47). Here Jesus' literal absence is compensated for by powers of discernment that transcend geographical limitations. The story of the healing of the royal official's son, at the end of the Cana-to-Cana narrative cycle, exhibits the same kind of power (4:46-54). In this narrative, the life-giving speech of the divine Word is not limited by distance or absence: Jesus assures the official that his son will live and the man departs in faith and obedience, to have the word confirmed on his way home (4:51-52). The absence of Jesus presents no problem in this situation; there is no impediment, geographical or otherwise, to the utterance of his healing word and its effectiveness. Here the royal official parallels the mother of Jesus at the wedding at Cana (2:1-11) as a model of faith and trust. There is an inscrutable presence in both cases that defies geographical, and any other, limits.

In a development of the same idea, the evangelist can depict faith as developing without Jesus' proximity or intervention. This absence is particularly noteworthy in the story of the man born blind. Even the healing itself, in a sense, is performed at a distance (9:6-7), not directly by the word of Jesus but through the clay and the waters of Siloam, with their richly symbolic overtones.[13] In this case, the healing takes place through the making of a paste from clay and Jesus' instructions to the man to wash in the Pool of Siloam (9:6). Both actions have christological meaning. Just as Adam was made from the dust of the earth (Gen 2:7), so the man's eyes are created from dust by the same creative, divine energy; and the Pool itself, according to the evangelist's etymology, means 'sent', pointing symbolically to Jesus as the 'Sent One' (9:7).

The irony of the narrative is that the man born blind, having been healed physically by Jesus at the beginning, moves towards faith in the absence of Jesus under questioning by the authorities. In the middle sections, where Jesus is missing from the narrative, the man associates himself more and more closely with his healer, through the increasingly hostile interrogations to which he is subjected (9:13-17, 24-34). The more the authorities attempt to coerce him into defaming Jesus, the more he supports him, denying vehemently that Jesus is a sinner (9:31-33). The material point is that the man's movement to faith occurs in Jesus' absence and in the context of hostility and persecution.[14] Most significantly, the man does not physically *see* his healer until the end of the story, after the authorities have ejected him from their presence—and, it may be, from the synagogue (9:34b). Only at this point does Jesus seek the man out (9:35-39). Significantly, the meeting takes place in the temple, reinforcing the festal imagery of this section of the Gospel, including the feast of Tabernacles (7:1-9:41), where Jesus is depicted as the object of worship, the new and living temple where God's glory abides. By this stage the man born blind is ready to make an explicit confession of faith, having defended his healer so passionately under interrogation.[15]

Note the heavy irony of the last verses (9:39-41). Where we would expect to find the illuminating presence of God—in the religious authorities—we find instead only blindness, or rather the illusion of sight. In the end, it is they who are the sinners, not the man born blind (whose disability is not the result of sin, 9:2-3), and not Jesus himself (9:31-33); the sabbath healing is an indication not of sin but of Jesus' true identity. In this narrative, therefore, absence functions ironically, and is surrounded by indications of presence. The material point is that the man's movement to faith, though begun and ended with Jesus, takes place in the context of Jesus' absence. What we begin to realize in this narrative is that absence can function paradoxically to elicit faith, even in the pain of misunderstanding and rejection.[16]

Through the narrative John indicates that the absence of Jesus is a real factor in believing existence. The community has to deal with that absence and the persecution which is a concomitant of discipleship. Suffering at the hands of the *kosmos* is exacerbated by Jesus' absence: one gains an increasing sense of the man born blind's vulnerability, especially in the interview with his parents who are completely cowed by the authorities (9:18-23). But John also perceives that such persecution need not be interpreted as ultimately negative. On the contrary, in the experience of the man born blind, it is Jesus' absence, along with hostile questioning by the Pharisees, that compels him to think through the implications of his healing and the identity of his healer. In the end, he makes a stand for the absent Jesus and suffers as a consequence. Note that, on this point, the man born blind contrasts markedly with the disabled man in John 5. Both healings take place on a Sabbath and both involve a meeting with Jesus in the temple, but in the first case there is no indication of faith on the part of the healed man and, far from defending Jesus, he betrays his identity to the authorities (5:15). Nor, ironically, is there the same feature of an absent Jesus. Thus in the story of the man born blind, absence functions powerfully to elicit faith, despite the pain of persecution and misunderstanding. John reflects also the experience of the community bereft of the physical presence of Jesus, yet committed to faith in him, a faith that suffering has the potential to intensify.

In this first type of absence, Jesus' lack of appearance on the Johannine scene is not a sufficient barrier to the 'signs' and works of his ministry. These still operate even where his presence is lacking. This is not a principle of the Gospel, as such, since it operates in one context (the healing of the royal official's son) but not in others (the possibility of Lazarus being healed, 11:6). But it does illustrate that absence is not an impediment to Jesus' mission. At the same time, faith in Jesus can grow and develop to a considerable extent without his physical nearness. In both cases, the power that attends the Johannine Jesus is not only located in bodily proximity but also in his word that transcends spatial limits, and in the experience of hostility and misunderstanding, where Jesus himself is absent.

Absence and Suffering

The second dimension of absence in the Fourth Gospel is closely connected, though more puzzling. Jesus' absence can seem strange at points, almost contrived, without any reason given. Whether literally absent or not, Jesus' unwillingness to respond, initially at least, aggravates rather than alleviates suffering. This riddle is hinted at in the two Cana stories, where Jesus is at first reluctant to perform the 'sign' and seems to dismiss the one who requests it (2:3-4, 4:48). Here it is more the absence of Jesus' characteristic graciousness than his physical absence. The dismissal is summarised in the enigmatic question of Jesus to his mother ('What is that to you and to me, woman?' *ti emoi kai soi, gynai?* 2:4).[17] The request of the royal official is likewise set aside, in a critique of faith based on 'signs', directed not just at the suppliant but also at a wider, though unspecified, audience (2:48). In both cases, it is significant, first, that the 'sign' takes place following the assurance and/or command of Jesus (2:6, 4:50), and, secondly, that neither of these two exemplary characters is discouraged by Jesus' off-putting response (2:5, 4:49). On the contrary, their faith seems, if anything, strengthened by the rebuff.

The same motif of disinclination is apparent in the Lazarus story (11:1-12:11), where Jesus physically absents himself from Lazarus' sick-bed despite the urgent summons of Mary and Martha. The key sentence here is the narrator's own: 'When therefore he heard that he was ill, he remained there in the place where he was for two days' (11:6). This utterance appears as an editorial explanation, but it explains nothing—if anything, it adds to the enigma of Jesus' absence. Yet we know that the healing could be performed at a distance. The problem of Jesus' silence and absence in this story is exacerbated by the fact that the family are disciples of the Johannine Jesus, designated his 'friends' (*philos,* friend; *philein,* to love, 11:5, 11; cf. 15:15). It is captured later in the story by the objection of the mourners: 'Could not he who opened the eyes of the blind man have kept this man from dying?' (11:37). Admittedly, the timing of the Lazarus story is difficult and bewildering. Jesus announces Lazarus' death two days after receiving the message (11:11), and it is possible that Lazarus has already died by the time the message reaches him (11:3).[18] Yet, after receiving the message, Jesus speaks at once of Lazarus' 'illness' (*astheneia*), indicating that it is not an illness ('towards death', *pros thanaton*) but 'for the glory of God' (*hyper tês doxas tou theou*, 11:4). When he does decide to go to Judaea, two days later, Jesus now possess the knowledge that Lazarus is dead (11:11), a fact that astonishes the disciples who have heard no such rumour.

Perhaps the most disturbing feature of the Lazarus story, which also heightens the narrative tension, is that Jesus' absence is itself a source of anguish for the sisters, already agonised by the death of their beloved brother. The point is sharply made by both women on their first meeting with Jesus—'Lord, if you had been here my brother would not have died' (11: 21, 32)—and even more vividly signified in Mary's throwing herself at Jesus' feet (11:32).[19] The absence of Jesus seems inexplicable and the sisters' reproaches comprehensible. In their opinion at least, Jesus could have done more and come sooner. While the tragedy is dramatically reversed at the open mouth of the tomb in the calling forth of Lazarus to life (11:43-44),[20] Jesus' presence comes very late—in human terms, too late—and his tardiness accentuates the sisters' suffering, not to mention that of their companions.[21] The reproaches stands alongside the revelation of divine glory which the 'sign' unfolds. In this sense, death and absence are intertwined. Indeed, death is closely linked here to the physical absence of Jesus: death in this story 'can only mean that Jesus is absent'.[22] The reproaches express a poignant sense of Jesus' absence that resonates beyond the ministry of Jesus into the post-Easter context. Here absence is a perplexing motif and even repellent to the reader. It is hard to gauge from such a narrative how absence might function constructively. In this Johannine scene the absence of Jesus seems inexplicable and the reproaches comprehensible.

By any standards, Jesus' absence here is a form of affliction, compounding the suffering of those already affected by illness and death. This form of absence is the most inexplicable in the Fourth Gospel, the most difficult to comprehend in light of the love which motivates the mission of the Johannine Jesus (3:16-17). It is also difficult to understand how such absence might function in a positive sense (quite apart from its value in creating dramatic tension), let alone how it might work symbolically. Reproach seems the only legitimate human response to this type of absence: so unfathomable and bizarre. Yet, for the evangelist, even this mode of absence has a vital part to play in the unfolding of meaning. Divine absence at its most incomprehensible, without necessarily any explication on the part of the evangelist, takes on a deeper significance, so that what seems most unconstructive becomes, in the hands of the fourth evangelist, the medium of life and love.

Absence and Jesus' Departure

The third way in which absence features in the narrative of the Fourth Gospel is in relation to Jesus' departure. This dimension of absence occupies most of the second half of the Gospel. The departure motif is the primary concern, as well as the theological and literary context, of the Johannine Last Supper (Jn 13:1-17:26).[23] While there is no account of the institution of the eucharist, as in the Synoptic Gospels (Mk 14:22-25/pars.), the evangelist instead narrates the footwashing (13:1-20), the announcement of the betrayer (13:21-30), and begins the long farewell speech (13:31-16:33), culminating in Jesus' final, great prayer (17:1-26). In these chapters, Jesus addresses his disciples in the context of his impending arrest, trial and death, but also takes as his primary theme that departure and its significance. In this respect, John goes much further than the other Gospels in addressing directly and at length the painful reality of Jesus' absence. In literary terms, John 13-17 prepare the reader for the Passion, much as the Apocalyptic Discourse does in Mark 13 (though it too points to the future beyond Easter). John goes further than the other Gospels in addressing directly and at length the painful reality of Jesus' absence, giving it a radically new meaning and helping the reader to perceive it, not only as an experience of grief and loss, but more fundamentally as the bearer of life. That there is to be a separation between the disciples and their Lord is plain: 'where I am going you cannot come' (13:33; also 13:36). Later in the same discourse Jesus speaks of the disciples' sorrow (16:6, 20-22), implying that their dismay at his departure is not illusory but

Illustration 4: Duccio di Buoninsegna. Maestà (back, predella), The Raising of
Lazarus.
1308-11. Tempera on wood panel. Kimbell Art Museum, Fort Worth, TX, USA.

Duccio's painting of the Raising of Lazarus above depicts Jesus'
conversation with Martha whose face wears an anxious expression,
suggestive of grief, misunderstanding and reproach. At his feet
crouches Mary, her pose representing grief and abjection, yet
also pointing forward to the anointing. Out of the darkness of the
tomb Lazarus emerges awkwardly, still bound, unable to walk by
himself, Jesus' hand (representing his creative word) compelling
him forth while directing Martha towards him. To one side, a man
covers his nose against the stench of death. The painting captures
John's theme that out of death—the absence of life—comes life,
summoned by Jesus' word.

real—real enough for the Johannine Jesus to address it at some length.
The parabolic metaphor of the woman in childbirth responds to the
anguish of the disciples at what they perceive to be, in every sense, a

death (16:21), but which, on the contrary, turns out to be otherwise—a death that, as Jesus endeavours to explain, is life-giving, as the imagery of birth indicates.[24] Jesus' concluding prayer, which signifies the ascent of the Son to the Father, is addressed precisely to a context of bereavement and loss.

The same is apparent in the Passion and resurrection narratives (18:1-21:25). As well as the high point of the incarnation, the cross is the ladder of ascent by which the Son returns to the Father. It is the means and instrument of his departure. Yet it is also closely allied to Jesus' taking on of the powers of darkness, which is 'an encounter between Jesus (the one sent by the Father from the world above) and Satan (the ruler of the world below), and an encounter that will result in Jesus' departure from this world'.[25] In Johannine terms, '[t]he crucifixion is the central symbolic action in the Fourth Gospel, fusing and conveying several levels of meaning simultaneously'.[26] Absence and departure, via the cross, are filled with emblematic meaning. They stand at the climax of the Gospel and its portrayal of the incarnation, as well as the place where the paradox of absence and presence is mostly sharply delineated.

After the crucifixion, the meeting between Jesus and Mary Magdalene in the Easter garden gives a new perspective on the cross as image of departure, this time in light of the resurrection (20:1-18).[27] While death is the ultimate image of Jesus' departure, resurrection suggests the opposite; yet the post-Easter situation proves more complex. Initially, Mary confronts the absence of Jesus' body in the tomb and misunderstands it (20:2, 13, 15), as is clear from her encounter with the two angels. They do not disclose the message of the resurrection, unlike the angel (or angels) in the Synoptic Gospels (Mark 16:6-7/pars.), and only say a few words—'Woman, why are you weeping?' (20:13)—but it is their stance which is of real significance. Like the cherubim on the ark of the covenant, they are located at either end of the stone slab on which the body of Jesus was laid, a mystical symbol of divine presence (Exod 25:18-22, Hebr 9:4-5), precisely in the context of a manifest absence.[28] As with the ark, there is an absence and a presence in this symbolism. That presence is elusive, veiled, mysterious, and its workings are profoundly symbolic and paradoxical, but that is the nature of divine revelation in this Gospel. When Mary Magdalene subsequently meets the Risen One (20:14-17), she fails at first to recognise him and then, when she does realise his identity, she tries to clutch hold of him (20:16-17a). In other words, she mistakes his self-manifestation for presence and so has to confront a new kind of absence—the ascension[29]—which is very different from the stark emptiness of the tomb. One form of absence is replaced by another more ominous and painful. Thus the message she now proclaims to her fellow-disciples is not only the resurrection but also paradoxically the loss of Jesus in what is, for her, a new sense of absence: his return to 'my Father and your Father, and my God and your God' (20:17).[30]

In these different ways, the Fourth Gospel portrays the impact of Jesus' absence and departure. The persecution which is to be the disciples' lot in the world arises from the ongoing reality of the *kosmos*. Though in one sense overcome, the *kosmos* continues in its hostility and falsehood. John speaks of the *kosmos* as the realm of darkness, with its hatred, unfreedom, deceit, betrayal, sin and death. Its existence is of penultimate rather than ultimate significance, yet it still has enough sting in its tail to cause grief and pain to the disciples, highlighting for them the divine absence. The Johannine community is directed, nonetheless, to continue in faith, love, abiding, prayer, witness, and keeping the commandments. No weight of absence alters the importance of the mission to which they are called.

This brief survey of the Johannine narrative reveals something of the complex way in which absence functions within the plot of the Gospel. It is a significant theological theme, as well as a literary device to heighten the tension and drama. At first glance, it seems to raise more questions than it resolves, even though at points the evangelist takes some pains to unfold its significance for the post-Easter life of the community of faith. Absence is a theological theme as well as a mechanism of the narrative, and it appears in many contexts of the Fourth Gospel, until in the final chapters it hardly leaves the stage. So vital a motif needs to be understood, and can only be grasped, within the symbolic framework of the Gospel as a whole.

Absence as Johannine Symbol

What happens with images of absence is that, through the unfolding narrative of the Fourth Gospel, they take on distinctive symbolic meaning. Though absence seems negative, at each level we encounter it in the Gospel, it becomes a momentous symbolic force. But how can absence function as a symbol in this Gospel? In order to answer this question, we need to compare the way absence functions in relation to other, better known and more widely acknowledged Johannine symbols. Within the Johannine symbolic universe, these images require two levels of understanding, the literal and the symbolic, in which the literal is used as the raw material for the symbolism of the Gospel. In the storyteller's hands, the literal or material becomes symbolic of the spiritual, conveying the reader from one plane of reality to another: from the familiar to the unfamiliar, from the material to the spiritual, from the human to the divine.[31] Significantly, the core symbols and metaphors of the Gospel are generally taken from ordinary human experience: bread, wine, water, light, shepherds, gates, paths.[32] These are familiar aspects of created reality, many of which, though arising from a specific cultural experience, nonetheless have universal appeal. They are the expressions of human need, that which is necessary for human life to thrive and to become the medium for revelation in this Gospel.

Extraordinary as it may seem, something similar is true for images of absence in the Fourth Gospel. Unlike the great, recognisable Johannine symbols, the import of absence seems at first glance decidedly negative and painful, not life-giving at all, still less obviously metaphorical or symbolic (as in the case of bread or water, for example, which are much more self-evident). Yet absence too comes to take on figurative meaning in its various manifestations throughout the Gospel, as outlined above. Absence, as we have seen, reaches its climax in the Easter events with the dominant motif of Jesus' departure, where the symbolic value is most intense, most focused and most paradoxical.

Since they operate at two levels, symbol and metaphor require what has been called 'stereoscopic vision' to enable them to be grasped.[33] The reader needs both to hold to, yet in a sense relinquish, the literal meaning in order for the second-order meaning to emerge. It is not a question of 'moving on': leaving behind the literal in order to grasp the figurative. Form is not orange-peel to be discarded for the 'fruit' of meaning to emerge. The evangelist's central understanding of the incarnation does not permit such a move. Flesh and glory coalesce in this portrait of revelation, the one giving rise to the other, without rejection. Form and content belong together.[34] Both hands are needed to grasp properly the symbol, the literal as well as the metaphorical, the material as well as the spiritual, for the simple reason that, in John's understanding, 'God can no longer be conceived apart from the incarnation of the Logos'.[35] The incarnation as the basis for all Johannine symbolism has vital implications for all the images of the Gospel, including that of absence.

For this reason the evangelist has a number of ways in which he makes plain that the void created by Jesus' absence is real. In this way, he establishes the literal before unfolding the figurative. The literal level is captured in certain evocative statements of the Gospel: 'What is that to me and to you?' (2:4); 'Lord, if you had been here' (11:21, 32); 'you will grieve … in the world you will have affliction' (16:33); 'do not hold onto me' (20:17). Whatever else they find, the disciples and friends of Jesus know the experience of his absence, an absence that will continue beyond Easter. The crucifixion is itself the high symbol of that absence, especially in the image of the pierced side which the evangelist highlights both by the witness of the beloved disciple and by the Scriptures used to underline it (19:35-37). Strangely enough, it is this same symbol of death that is presented to Thomas in order to lead him to faith in the risen Jesus (20:27). The wounds signifying absence and death are offered to him as symbols of presence and life.

But there is also a contrast with the way other symbols operate in the Fourth Gospel. The movement from 'light', meaning the sun, to a metaphorical and symbolic understanding of Jesus as life-giver and guide (8:12, 9:5), is a linear movement from the material to the spiritual. The same is true of other symbols in the Gospel. With absence, however, a significant change is involved in the movement from material to spiritual, since in this case the material meaning contradicts the spiritual. The symbolic move from Jesus' departure and absence becomes symbolic of its opposite. In taking on symbolic value, the images suggesting darkness and emptiness become symbols evoking fullness and light.[36] The most potent indication of this transformation is the gift of the Spirit-Paraclete who occupies the void formed by Jesus' departure until his final return. The void is real, as is the pain of departure, and though the sorrow of the disciples will turn to joy it is still sorrow and they are not condemned for experiencing it. What happens instead is that, as with the tomb, emptiness paradoxically becomes symbolic of plenitude and meaning.[37]

The same is true for the affliction of disciples in the world. Again it too is transformed into an experience of joy, just as for the man born blind it is the hostility of the authorities which leads him to discover Jesus as the light of the world. In a similar way, throughout the Fourth Gospel, the hostility of the religious leaders towards Jesus leads to greater revelation: not to a dimming of the light but to its radiance. The same pattern is repeated in the Bread of Life narrative (6:1-71), the Tabernacles Discourse (7:1-52, 8:12-59) and, of course, the cross itself. Overturning its intentions, persecution effects its opposite: the strengthening of faith, the deepening of insight, and the flourishing of revelation. Absence become symbolic of presence, the void a symbol of plenitude.

A much later parallel to this motif is the poem 'Valediction' by the English Jacobean poet, John Donne, which deals with the theme of absence, in this case between two lovers about to part. In the poem, absence too functions paradoxically and constructively, though to the untrained eye (the 'dull sublunary' mind), it is an experience of unmitigated and unalleviated pain. Yet absence functions, for Donne, to reveal presence and a deeper, more refined level of love between the lovers:

> Our two souls, therefore, which are one,
> Though I must go, endure not yet
> A breach, but an expansion,
> Like gold to airy thinness beat.[38]

The notion of 'airy' expansion—which Donne develops in his famous image of the pair of compasses—provides a parallel to the motif of absence in the Fourth Gospel, though in an entirely different medium, century and culture. To this extent, though anachronistic in the literal sense, it assists in comprehending the experience of the Johannine disciples.

Perhaps we can take this a step further. Absence and departure are concepts that have to do with space and place, as Donne's poem makes plain. Although the movement of distance leads to painful absence, the making of space can also operate constructively, as it does for Donne's lovers. In a literary sense, the clearing of imaginative space creates possibilities for something new and different to emerge. In John's Gospel, the absence caused by the incarnation in the celestial realm, the space that opens between Father and Son, is the very place believers are invited to inhabit. Similarly, the place of Jesus' absence becomes the place of the Spirit's presence. Absence creates loss but also possibilities for new life in the Johannine worldview ('it is for your benefit that I go away', 16:7).[39] It allows space and creates a place for believers to enter into the life of God—as if the embrace of Father and Son formed an ever-expanding circle, making space for those who are 'children of God'.

Implications of John's Spirituality

The Fourth Gospel gives substantial consolation to the disciples, precisely in and through absence. Most importantly, the disciples are given the gift of the Spirit, as we saw in the last chapter, the divine presence which has rested on Jesus himself and is now to signify his presence-in-absence (14:16). So positively does Jesus speak of the Spirit's advent— subsequently fulfilled in the events of his death and resurrection (19:30b; 20:19-23)—that his departure is not interpreted as loss but gain (16:7). In the same way, in the resurrection narrative, Jesus commends future believers who will enter into the fullness of faith, through the Spirit, even though they have not had Thomas' experience (20:29). The Spirit as the Paraclete replays the role of Jesus

in the life of disciples.[40] With Jesus' departure they are not orphaned
(14:18), for the Spirit will give them the comfort, love, peace, teaching
and guidance that Jesus himself has given them. The divine speech,
uttered in Jesus the Word made flesh, will not fall silent. Most
importantly, the central task of glorification—which lies at the core of
John's understanding of salvation—will not cease, precisely because
of the presence of the Paraclete (16:14).

The absence of the Johannine Jesus has itself significant
theological meaning. Apart from anything else, the destination is as
significant as the journey. Jesus leaves the disciples in order to return
to the Father. In this Gospel, the cross is the means and medium of that
return and, from the standpoint of the celestial world, represents his
entry into his eternal home. The fact that Jesus is now with the Father,
and has bestowed the Spirit on the disciples, is the primary source of
consolation for those who grieve his absence. They are not, after all,
to be cut off from the divine circle of love; on the contrary, even with
Jesus' absence, the lines stand firm, and the circle, though it may have
revolved alarmingly on its axis, remains secure.

The departure and thus absence of the Johannine Jesus is
described throughout the Farewell Discourse as temporary. At three
points, Jesus uses the phrase 'a little while' (13:33; 14:19; 16:16-19),
which, to the listening disciples, is more bewildering than anything
else in these chapters. Jesus compares their sorrow to that of a woman
in labour, for whom the pangs of childbirth are but the prelude to the
joy of producing a child. For modern commentators, the bewilderment
remains: Is Jesus speaking of his own future return or of the advent
of the Spirit? The answer cannot simply be the Spirit. If the central
salvific event of this Gospel is the incarnation, it is not enough for
incarnate flesh to be replaced by an intangible Spirit. Nor is Jesus
speaking only of his future return, since the 'hour' in this Gospel has
already arrived in the events of the cross: 'the hour is coming and now
is' (4:23; 5:25; 16:23; cf. 12:27; 13:1, 17:1). Yet John invites us to see
the complexity *sub specie eternitatis*—from the standpoint of God and
the future. Just as a mountain range on the horizon obscures the actual
distance between one peak and another, so the return of the Son of

Man—the 'little while'—is fulfilled in *both* the advent of the Paraclete *and* the future return of Jesus in flesh. From this divine vantage-point the interval between departure and return, between presence and absence—no matter how long it seems to the waiting disciples—is but short: no more than the duration of labour-pains. In the meantime, the advent of the Spirit is, as we have already seen, central to the realising of God's future in this Gospel. The Johannine Paraclete is given to the orphaned, grieving disciples to fill the void created by Jesus' departure until his return, and to effect the realisation of that future in every moment of their lives.

This brief survey illustrates something of the dynamic between presence and absence within which the Gospel of John operates. It is true that the evangelist's spirituality has its focus on the fullness of love and joy which incarnation and cross bring for those who have become 'children of God' and intimate 'friends of Jesus'. Yet John is also aware of the painful consequences of Jesus' departure. The longest discourse in the Gospel is concerned with that departure and its implications for the life of the community. Given that John's Gospel reflects a post-Easter context, the Farewell Discourse is not just about the past situation of the disciples on the night before Jesus' arrest. John uses that original context to speak of the absence of Jesus for the life of the community in the here-and-now. The fact that Jesus in John 17 prays explicitly for future believers (17:20-26)—as well as the beatitude he pronounces on future disciples to Thomas (20:29b)—shows that it is very much to the forefront in the evangelist's thinking. John's Gospel, for all its plenitude, is deeply concerned with the problem of Jesus' absence and has much to say on the subject which seeks to recognise and, as much as possible, resolve the dilemma in which believers find themselves: profoundly attached to an absent Lord.

So how can that which is not—absence—function as that which is—presence? And how is it possible to claim that, in the spirituality of the Fourth Gospel, material elements such as bread and water, which can be touched, seen, tasted, operate in the same way as something that is, by definition, untouched, unseen, untasted? Certainly it is true that the absence of a loved one can seem tangible, creating a void, pushing other things aside to form the outlines of a space that is literally empty. However, something further is happening here; we are approaching a 'negative theology' (*via negativa*) within the Fourth Gospel.[41] That may seem an odd claim for a Gospel based on the Word, God's self-communication in flesh and matter. Yet it is not irrelevant to the world of the fourth evangelist. It reflects the same dynamic as the last verse of the Prologue, where God cannot be seen but is revealed in Jesus Christ (1:18).[42] Revelation and hiddenness belong together in this Gospel. Johannine figurative language and representation can deal with this paradox, because it does not attempt to define or capture God. The unseen God who is seen, the silent deity whose voice is resoundingly heard, the spirit which becomes matter, the absence which becomes a means of presence: all this is held together in John's symbolism which has the capacity to name the unnameable, conceive the inconceivable, and be simultaneously present in absence.

Absence is a real, if complex, phenomenon in the world of the Fourth Gospel. On the one hand, it is painful, an aspect of the unfinality of the world, the experience of desolation and death. On the other hand, absence is bounded by presence on every side, reassuring the Johannine reader that its tenure is temporary and not without joy or consolation. For all its ambiguity, the interval in which the church now lives reverberates with the sound of Jesus' last, most triumphant utterance in the farewell discourse, just before the great Prayer (16:33b): 'Fear not, for I have overcome the world.' It is true that the reproachful words of Martha and Mary, when confronted by the tragic death of their brother and the absence of their Lord, still resound across grief and loss: 'Lord, if you had been here …' (11:21, 32). The Johannine answer, while acknowledging the poignancy of the reproach, reveals Jesus as the one whose presence already communicates resurrection and life, even where God seems most painfully absent and silent. A victory has been effected, in John's understanding, that no weight of suffering, evil, anguish or death can undo. Despite absence, it is presence that has the last word in the spirituality of this Gospel: in the advent of the Paraclete making present the Father and the Son in the orphaned heart of the believer, in the ongoing life of the believing community, and in the resounding Johannine promise of Jesus' return.

End Notes

1. For some, the point has more weight if the Johannine epistles were written after the Gospel, where there are signs of conflict within the community and a possible split; see, e.g., J. Painter, Culpepper R.A. & Segovia, F.F., ed. *Word, Theology, and Community in John* (St Louis, MO: Chalice,2002), 1-26.

2. Raymond E. Brown, *The Death of the Messiah. From Gethsemane to the Grave. A Commentary on the Passion Narratives in the Four Gospels* (2 vols.; London: Geoffrey Chapman, 1994), 2.1051.

3. Jesus' cry is the literal expression of his experience at this point, rather than evoking the whole of Psalm 22 as argued, e.g., by Dennis E. Nineham, *The Gospel of St Mark*, Penguin Gospel Commentaries (Hammondsworth, Middlesex: Penguin, 1963), 428-29, and Donald Senior, *The Passion of Jesus in the Gospel of John*, The Passion Series 4 (Collegeville, MN: Liturgical Press, 1991), 123-24. Francis J. Moloney, *The Gospel of Mark: A Commentary* (Peabody: Hendrickson, 2002), 325-28, makes this point well, warning of the danger of softening the starkness of Mark's Gospel at this moment; so also R.T. France, *The Gospel of Mark: A Commentary on the Greek Text*, The New International Greek Testament Commentary (Grand Rapids: Eerdmans, 2002), 652-53.

4. Like the Markan baptism (Mk 1:9-11); see Dorothy Lee, *Transfiguration* (London/New York: Continuum, 2004), 25-27.

5. Assuming, with the majority of scholars, that Mark's Gospel originally ended at 16:8.

6. Unlike Matthew's account, with its earthquake and other apocalyptic signs denoting clearly the divine presence (Matt 27:51-54).

7. R.H. Lightfoot, *The Gospel Message of St Mark* (Oxford: Clarendon, 1950), 55-58.

8. Even in Luke's Gospel, the disciples on the road to Emmaus never recognise the Stranger and, when they at last do at the supper in Emmaus, they see him as he truly is only for the second it takes him to disappear (Luke 24:13-32).

9. This point does not rule out a symbolic meaning for Jesus' thirst and drink—his readiness to take the cup held out to him by the Father—but John's Passion operates also as irony.

10. See Andrew T. Lincoln, *Truth on Trial: The Lawsuit Motif in the Fourth*

Gospel (Peabody, MA: Hendrickson, 2000), esp. 21-35, 57-138.

[11.] The term 'world' is ambiguous in John's Gospel and, in each instance, needs to be carefully interpreted within its context. In some places, 'world' is a neutral and even positive term. In other places, it refers to the realm of death and darkness and is not co-extensive with the material world. In these latter contexts, I have chosen to use the Greek *kosmos* to emphasise the distinction. Further on this, see Dorothy Lee, *Flesh and Glory: Symbol, Gender and Theology in the Gospel of John* (New York: Crossroad, 2002), 182-84.

[12.] See Jn 6:64, 71; 12:4; 13:2, 11, 21, 26; 18:2-3, 5.

[13.] On the creation parallels, see especially Irenaeus: 'Notice here too how the Lord spit on the earth, and made clay and smeared it on his eyes, showing how the ancient creation was made', in Joel C. Elowsky, ed. *John 1-10*, Ancient Christian Commentary on Scripture: New Testament Iva (Downers Grove, Il: InterVarsity Press,2006), 324.

[14.] John 9 has been seen as providing a paradigm for the effects of persecution on the later Johannine community (cf. 16:1-4a); so J. Louis Martyn, *The Gospel of John in Christian History* (New York: Paulist, 1978). More recently, there has been criticism of this view as offering a simplistic picture of the relationship between text and context. See Warren Carter, *John and Empire: Initial Explorations* (New York/London: T & T Clark, 2008), 20-25; also Tobias Hägerland, 'John's Gospel: A Two-Level Drama?' *JSNT* 25 (2003), 309-22.

[15.] Assuming, as against Raymond E. Brown, *The Gospel According to John*, 2 vols., Anchor Bible 29-29a (Garden City, New York: Doubleday, 1966), 375, that 9:38-39a is part of the Johannine text.

[16.] A further irony is the absence of theological perception among the religious authorities in whom we would expect to find it, as summarised in Jesus' closing judgement (9:39-41).

[17.] On the ambiguity of the phrase, see the summary in Brown, *John*, 1.99.

[18.] George R. Beasley-Murray, *John* (WBC; Waco: Waco Books), 188.

[19.] Further on this, see Lee, *Flesh and Glory*, 207-08.

[20.] It was popularly believed in Jewish circles that the soul only departed three days after death; see C.K. Barrett, *The Gospel According to St John. An Introduction with Commentary and Notes on the Greek Text* (2nd ed.; London: SPCK, 1978), 401.

[21.] Sandra M. Schneiders, *'Written That You May Believe'. Encountering Jesus in the Fourth Gospel* (2nd ed.; New York: Crossroad, 2003), 149-61, sees the narrative as dealing with the question of death in the believing community—death, she argues, being transformed without being 'denatured'.

22. Ibid., 153.

23. For a literary study of the Farewell Discourse, which explores the significance for discipleship, see D.F. Tolmie, *Jesus' Farewell to the Disciples. John 13:1-17:26 in Narratological Perspective*, ed. R.A. Culpepper & R. Rendtorff, Biblical Interpretation Series 12 (Leiden/New York/Köln: Brill, 1995), esp 145-80.

24. Further on this parabolic metaphor, see Lee, *Flesh and Glory*, 151-52; also Judith Lieu, 'Scripture and the Feminine in John', in A. Brenner (ed.), *A Feminist Companion to the Hebrew Bible in the New Testament* (Sheffield: Sheffield Academic Press, 1996), 225-40.

25. Fernando F. Segovia, *The Farewell of the Word. The Johannine Call to Abide* (Minneapolis: Fortress, 1991), 113-14.

26. Craig Koester, *Symbolism in the Fourth Gospel: Meaning, Mystery, Community* (2nd ed.; Minneapolis: Fortress, 2003), 218.

27. Lee, *Flesh and Glory*, 220-32.

28. B.F. Westcott, *The Gospel According to St John. The Authorised Version with Introduction and Notes* (London: John Murray, 1882), 291, and Rowan Williams, *On Christian Theology*, ed. G. Jones & L. Ayres, Challenges in Contemporary Theology (Oxford: Blackwell, 2000), 186-87.

29. Most commentators nowadays prefer 'Do not hold on/cling to me' to translate *mê mou haptou*—literally, 'do not touch me'.

30. Note the careful nuance of the language; see Lee, *Flesh and Glory*, 122. On the covenantal nature of the language here, see Schneiders, *'Written That You May Believe'*, 199-200.

31. Lee, *Flesh and Glory*, 9-28.

32. R. Alan Culpepper, *Anatomy of the Fourth Gospel: A Study in Literary Design* (Philadelphia: Fortress, 1983), 190-98, identifies light, water and bread as the three core symbols of John's Gospel.

33. Lee, *Flesh and Glory*, 27-35.

34. Ibid., 9-28.

35. H. Weder, "Deus Incarnatus: On the Hermeneutics of Christology in the Johannine Writings," in *Exploring the Gospel of John: In Honor of D. Moody Smith*, ed. R.A. Culpepper & C.C. Black (Westminster: John Knox, 1996), 331.

36. For an outline of how light and dark operate in the Johannine narrative, see Koester, *Symbolism*, 123-54.; on the different dimensions of darkness, see Craig Koester, "What Does It Mean to Be Human? Imagery and the Human Condition in John's Gospel," in *Imagery in the Gospel of John*.

Terms, Forms, Themes, and Theology of Johannine Figurative Language, ed. J. Frey, Van der Watt, J.G., Zimmermann, R. (Tübingen: Mohr Siebeck, 2006), 414-16.

[37.] On the presence-in-absence theme of the Farewell Discourse, and the role of the Paraclete, see especially Ruth Sheridan, 'The Paraclete and Jesus in the Johannine Farewell Discourse' *Pacifica* 20 (2007), 125-41.

[38.] J. Donne, 'A Valediction: forbidding mourning' in Helen Gardner, ed. *The Metaphysical Poets*, 2 ed. (Middlesex: Penguin,1966), 73-74. The poem was said to be written by Donne to his wife, Anne More, when he left on a journey to France in 1611.

[39.] Commenting on the 'dwelling-places' at 14:3, Augustine explains the metaphor in similar terms: 'The meaning is that in order that those mansions may be prepared, the just must live by faith … and if you *see*, there is no faith … Let Christ go away then so that he is not seen. Let him remain concealed that faith may be exercised. Then a place is prepared if you live by faith': Joel C. Elowsky, *John 11-21*, ed. R.C. Oden, *Ancient Christian Commentary on Scripture: New Testament* IV B (Downers Grove, Il: InterVarsity Press, 2007), 122.

[40.] Further on this, see above, chapter 3.

[41.] The early Fathers, influenced by Neoplatonism, speak of this perspective as 'apophasis', where God's hiddenness and otherness are as significant for Christian faith, within trinitarian theology as God's self-revelation in Christ.

[42.] Paul Fiddes, 'The Quest for a Place Which Is "Not-a-Place": The Hiddness of God and the Presence of God', in O. Davies & D. Turner (eds.), *Silence and the Word: Negative Theology and Incarnation* (Cambridge: Cambridge University Press, 2002), 60.

Chapter 5
Spirituality and Discipleship

Spirituality and discipleship are, in one sense, overlapping if not synonymous terms in the world of the fourth evangelist. In John's spiritual theology, the true disciple is by definition a contemplative, one who gazes upon (contemplates) the divine glory revealed in Jesus (1:14). To speak of Johannine spirituality, therefore, means also to speak of discipleship. There are a number of symbolic expressions for that life which enrich the overall picture of Johannine theology. These images express the core meaning of spirituality and discipleship in ways that parallel the Synoptic Gospels, while retaining their unique perspective. The fourth evangelist's presentation of discipleship is a complex one, the images seemingly diverse and unconnected, even at points contradictory. Yet the diversity can be deceptive: John's symbolism may seem disconnected but each image provides a vital dimension to the whole, the several aspects held together within the framework of John's Christology.[1]

Discipleship, according to John, is not individualistic, each person in his or her private relationship with God through Christ.[2] John's spirituality manifests itself in the life of the community. Although obscured in English translation, the pronouns in the Farewell Discourse are plural, denoting the believing community as a whole. Unlike other parts of the New Testament, John's Gospel does not use explicit language of 'church' (*ekklêsia*), although the word does occur in the third Johannine epistle (3 Jn 6, 9).[3] Yet ecclesial images are present in the Fourth Gospel: in symbols of sheep and fold (10:1-18), vine and branches (15:1-17), fish and nets (21:1-14), as well as in the orientation of discipleship towards love of others in the community. Those who are disciples of the Johannine Jesus, who believe, learn, follow, abide, love, and obey, do so in the context of community. Discipleship is first and foremost an ecclesial reality in this Gospel.[4]

At the end of the Farewell Discourse, Jesus prays on behalf of his gathered disciples: 'Hallow them in the truth' (17:11). A few verses later he adds: 'And for their sake I hallow myself, so that they too may be hallowed in truth' (17:19). The verb used here, *hagiazô*, is a cognate of the adjective *hagios*, 'holy', used three times in the Gospel of the Spirit (1:33; 14:26; 20:22), once of Jesus (6:69; 10:36), and once in Jesus' address to God in prayer ('Holy Father', 17:11). From this it is apparent that the notion of holiness belongs to the divine realm, denoting God's otherness and goodness. It also signifies the consecration of Jesus' life to God for the sake of 'his own'.[5] While Judaism in this Gospel has its rites of 'purification' to enable the people of God to enter that divine, hallowed space (2:6; 11:55; 18:28), these rites are fulfilled in the Johannine Jesus, in whom they gain definitive meaning. He is the means of access to the holy place; indeed, as we have already seen, he is himself the holy place. To be a disciple of Jesus—to belong within the divine family—means to be hallowed, made holy, consecrated, in him and by him. In the Footwashing, Jesus declares the disciples, with the exception of Judas Iscariot, to be ritually 'clean' (*katharos*) because of their union with him, an intimacy, unity and cleansing symbolised in the washing of their feet (13:10-11);[6] elsewhere they are said to be made clean by 'the word' of Jesus (15:3). To be 'hallowed in truth' is synonymous with being cleansed by Jesus' word.[7] Both convey a sense of belonging to the divine realm, a sharing in the divine goodness disclosed in the Johannine Jesus. In this way, disciples are enticed into the life of heaven—drawn into that eternal truth, love, and beauty which is characteristically divine, and in which Father, Son and Spirit dwell.

There are a number of Johannine images that are particularly pertinent to understanding what it means to be hallowed in God's truth and love. John's theology of discipleship employs several distinct motifs that outline the shape of this spiritual vision of holiness, and enable entry into the community which Jesus represents, both divine and human. In particular, we focus on six Johannine images for discipleship that recur throughout the Gospel and which John enlarges in the narrative: believing, following, gazing, abiding, loving, obeying. These are not necessarily unique to the Fourth Gospel, but their combination and development is, giving the idea of discipleship a different flavour to that of the Synoptic Gospels. At the same time,

John's imagery is not easily separable, and one image tends to fold over into another.

Believing

It is impossible to explore the breadth and depth of John's spirituality without coming up against the matter of faith. To believe, and go on believing, despite adversity and discouragement, is intrinsic to Johannine spirituality, and expresses something of the purpose of the Gospel (20:30-31).[8] Faith and theology are not divisible in this equation, as each feeds, nurtures, and directs the other. In John's Gospel, believing is one of the major themes of the narrative. Repeatedly, the Gospel emphasises faith as the reason for Jesus' coming and the purpose of his every word and action. Indeed, the Gospel frequently displays a division between those who find faith and those who reject it—the latter often including those who consider themselves most religious.[9] Nevertheless, for John, the test of faith lies in the response to the Johannine Jesus who is the embodiment of God and the focus of believing existence.

In John's understanding, believing is the only legitimate response to revelation. The Fourth Gospel invariably uses the verbal form 'believe' (*pisteuô*) which occurs often throughout the Gospel.[10] In the overwhelming majority of cases, the word has to do with believing in Jesus.[11] However, in Johannine terms, to believe in Jesus means to believe in God: 'the one who believes in me believes not in me but in the one who sent me' (12:44); 'believe in God, believe also in me' (14:1). In John's Christology, faith in Jesus the Son is faith in God the Father. Jesus is the human face of God. Thus believing is the only appropriate rejoinder to Jesus' identity, and indeed the ministry of the Johannine Jesus is geared towards eliciting such response, as the beginning and end of the Gospel make plain. In the Prologue John the Baptist comes 'as a witness to testify to the light, so that all might *believe* through him' (1:7), and the first part of the resurrection narrative closes with the summary words: 'these are written that you may come to *believe* that Jesus is the Christ, the Son of God' (20:31). The in-between narratives portray different responses to Jesus, both believing and unbelieving.

John understands faith as a spectrum rather than a dualistic either-or; many of the characters of the Gospel stand somewhere in the middle, their faith capable of moving forwards or backwards as the revelation unfolds.[12]

In John's Gospel believing leads above all else to life, eternal life, a life that swells the present moment yet perdures to eternity: a present possession and a future hope, overcoming all that is meant by 'death', both spiritual and physical. It is contiguous with creation itself—the life of the natural world—yet possesses a dimension beyond the present dispensation, one that ultimately transcends its limitations and its mortality. Thus it is a gift in the here-and-now, as creation is a gift, while containing the seeds of resurrection which, both now and at the end, will overcome evil, suffering, and death. This life is abundant, bountiful, rich, and fulfilling, giving safety and nurture—as the sheep are protected in the fold at night and taken to pasture by day (10:9-10)—illuminating the darkness of ignorance and sin, liberating from all that binds and constricts (8:32-36), and opening blind eyes to goodness and truth. The source of this life is the Johannine Jesus, the Word who is the source of creation and who reveals himself, in the flesh, as the resurrection and the life (11:25-26), making his own journey—an archetypal one—from life to death and death to life, the seed that falls into the ground and dies, blossoming from earth to produce much fruit (12:24).

John describes faith as the fundamental, and indeed only, 'work' (*ergon*) required by God of human beings: 'This is the work of God,' explains Jesus to the crowds after the feeding when they ask what works [*erga,* pl.] they are required to do, 'that you believe in him whom he [God] has sent' (6:29). Nothing else is required but believing and yet believing itself must be discerned, since not all that claims itself as faith is true faith. True believing, in this Gospel, represents an 'unreserved openness to God; an 'unreserved readiness to accept the truth,' and an 'unqualified loyalty to reality as one experiences it', which is in fact 'the condition of receiving divine revelation.'[13] Such faith issues in worship and in love, a love that derives from God and ripples out from the believing community as a sign to the unbelieving world (13:35). Indeed, such love authenticates faith. The work of faith, seemingly passive, is nonetheless so dynamic and creative that it restores to human beings their lost status as children of God, re-born not of flesh but of the Spirit (1:12-13; 3:3-8).

To believe means to open the heart to a double revelation, according to the fourth evangelist: the revelation of God in Jesus, on the one hand, and the revelation of the self, on the other.[14] The story of the Samaritan woman is perhaps the most explicit example. The woman's faith grows as the revelation deepens, a revelation as much of her own self ('Come, see a man who told me all that I ever did', 4:29) as of Jesus' identity ('I who speak to you am the one', 4:26). The same is true throughout the Gospel, from Peter at the beginning whom Jesus recognises and re-names (1:42), to Nathanael whose guileless heart Jesus at once discerns (1:47), to the mother of Jesus and the royal official who, at Cana, show exemplary faith (2:1-11, 4:46-54), and again to Peter at the end of the Gospel, whose love for Jesus is revealed as the basis of his future destiny (21:15-19). In his own person, the Johannine Jesus reveals what it means to be divine and human, since—as we saw in a previous chapter—he is both the object of faith in union with the Father and the one who displays authentic faith in the Father.

This means that faith has cognitive content, and is not simply experiential and intuitive. John's spirituality is grounded in teaching. Again and again Jesus speaks of the necessity for believing in who he is: the Son sent by the Father, the Messiah/Christ and Son of God, the Son of Man, the Saviour of the world. Whatever their origins in Judaism, these titles in their Johannine framework show Jesus as the ultimate revelation of God, the one who exists in intimate union with God, sharing God's being and God's unique work. To believe is to acknowledge that identity not just with the lips but with the heart, a belief that leads to life and sharing in Jesus' own glory: 'And this is eternal life, that they may know you, the only true God, and Jesus Christ whom you have sent' (17:2). Elsewhere, John speaks in similar terms of believing in the name of Jesus (2:23; 3:18; 14:13-14; 15:16, 21; 16:23-24; 20:31), which is closely allied to the name of God (5:43; 10:25; 12:13, 28; 17:6. 11-12, 26). God's unique self-naming is the revelation of self-giving love and glory into which believers are enticed, to receive thereby the authority of their true identity: 'But to all who received him, who believed in his name, he gave power to become children of God' (1:12).

Believing in Jesus presents the reader with a number of equations in the Fourth Gospel. The most important is that to believe in God means to believe in Jesus, and vice versa. The necessity of holding the two together in faith is explicated in the imagery of Father and Son, which itself assumes a *sine qua non* status: it is impossible, in Johannine symbolic terms, to have the one without the other. The point is further stressed in the theme of unity between Father and Son, a unity in which believers share (17:20-23). This is not the only equation. To believe in the Johannine Jesus as the revelation of the Father is to believe in the God of the Old Testament, the God of Moses in particular (5:45-47), but also the God of Jacob, Abraham, Isaiah (4:12; 8:52-58, 12:38-41). Moreover, as a corollary to this, believing in the words of Jesus is tantamount to believing in Scripture, the two being closely equated (e.g. 2:22). To believe in God, therefore, means believing in Jesus, in Moses and in the Old Testament Scriptures. That is why, in this Gospel, all the feasts and rites associated with the temple fall within the Johannine christological vision. All that belongs to the temple belongs to the Johannine Jesus, since the temple itself—like the Old Testament in general—finds its primary value in pointing figuratively to him.

In John's Gospel, believing can also be ambiguous. The most ferocious section of the Gospel outside the Passion narrative is the dialogue between Jesus and 'the Jews' in the Tabernacles' Discourse (7:1-8:59), where those who initially come to faith reject Jesus' challenge and end up abusing him and hurling stones at him (8:59). In the previous narrative, many of those who believed in Jesus are so scandalised by his words that they lose faith and cease following him (6:66), until he is left only with the Twelve. Faith can be premature and shallow, easily quenched. Jesus himself does not always respond positively to those who claim belief: his 'attitude towards those who believe is not one of unqualified approval'.[15] To the royal official who approaches him (4:48), Jesus says, 'Unless you see signs and wonders you [pl.] will not believe'. Faith based only on 'signs' is impoverished and inadequate, unless it can see through the 'signs', as through a window, to the divine glory they reveal. Like icons, they point beyond themselves, windows on the eternal, unveilings of Jesus' identity. On a purely material level, however miraculous and amazing, the faith they produce is superficial and temporary, according to John; unable to grasp revelation in its fullness.

Unbelief is characteristic of Jesus' opponents, that group which is called figuratively 'the Jews'.[16] They reject Jesus' claims for himself and his ministry, considering them heretical and demonic (8:48, 52), sinful (9:24), dangerously seditious (11:48), and blasphemous (5:18; 19:7). Despite the claim to be disciples of Moses, and therefore of God (5:45-46; 8:39, 41; 9:28-29), in Johannine terms they reject the one whom God sent and of whom Moses spoke (1:45).[17] Their unbelief undermines their identity. For John, they are not true leaders of God's people, but irresponsible shepherds engulfed in sin (9:41). The opponents' response to the Johannine Jesus reveals the nature of unbelief as 'a deep perversion of the spirit that makes a person incapable of accepting the truth because of an idolatrous commitment to something other than God.'[18] In this case, that 'something other than God' is the honour (*doxa*) they seek for themselves and derive from one another (5:44).[19]

Even in the best disciples, believing can be partial and in need of development and growth. This is true, for example, of Martha who, while making the core Christian confession (made by Peter in the Synoptic Gospels, Mk 8:29/pars.), 'I believe you are the Christ' (11:27), recoils at the open mouth of the tomb, her faith wavering. Indeed the whole group of disciples needs to come to Easter faith after the resurrection, despite Jesus' earlier declarations of his departure (10:17-18; 12:23-33; 13:31-33; 14:28; 16:16-22). In such contexts, John's Jesus shows a very different response from those who are genuinely struggling with faith, as against those who reject it outright or feign a feeble belief. Indeed, by its definition faith in this Gospel is something that needs to grow through experience, as the implications of the revelation dawn. The Spirit is the one responsible for this nurturing in faith, this calling to mind, this ongoing teaching in the life of the church (16:13). John's is a spirituality of growth in faith, increasing understanding of the mystery of God and the mystery of the self. In those who struggle to believe, the attitude of the Johannine Jesus is patient and understanding, leading the believer to a deeper faith and a deeper apprehension of its meaning.

Learning

The word 'disciple' (*mathêtês*) is linked to the Greek verb to 'learn' (*manthanô*) and literally means *one who learns*.[20] In all the Gospels, disciples are primarily those who learn of Jesus, a status they never relinquish: discipleship is always an educative journey, a gradual process of conversion, of being lead from one reality to another, one level to another. Although Matthew is generally regarded as the teaching Gospel, John also has a concern for this theme and presents Jesus in the role of Teacher,[21] his teaching involving prophetic sign, symbol and dialogue. The conversation partner is invited into a relationship and learns through misunderstanding and mistaken turnings. The pattern is repeated in many of the meetings between Jesus and significant characters in the Fourth Gospel. Their initial inability to understand and their groping towards truth is never presented negatively in John. On the contrary, the negative characters in this Gospel are those who assume they have no need to learn and lack openness to Jesus' teaching (e.g. 9:39-41).[22] Those who struggle and misunderstand are treated kindly by the Johannine Jesus, who leads them to a fuller understanding.

The motif of misunderstanding leading to understanding is present, as we have already observed, in the dialogue between Jesus and the Samaritan woman, but it is apparent elsewhere in the Fourth Gospel: in the experience of the man born blind (paradoxically in Jesus' absence), in the stories of Martha, Peter, Mary Magdalene and Thomas. Even a character such as Nicodemus, whom Jesus reproaches as one who should know—'Are you a [lit. *the*] teacher of Israel and yet you do not understand these things?' (3:10)—ends up making his own way to Jesus, if slowly; by the end of the Gospel he has learned enough to risk his faith by coming into the open in the burial of Jesus (7:50-52; 19:38-42). In each story, Jesus leads people to a richer understanding of the gift of life, an understanding that is intuitive and transformative. The readers, like the characters of the drama, are beguiled by the dynamics of the symbolism. In being appropriated, the symbols offer a lens by which the viewer can see him or herself, as well as God. Mostly in John's Gospel this means moving from a literal or material understanding to one that is spiritual and symbolic. Misunderstanding is inevitable on this journey. Indeed, it could be seen as necessary, since the symbolism only reveals itself as the reader grasps the literal meaning—mistakenly—while groping towards the metaphorical, perceiving at last the symbolic in the literal, the spiritual in the material. To move from one plane of learning to another is always, in John's Gospel, a movement that involves taking the first step, however dimly understood, in order to progress to a higher level.

In John's Gospel, to learn has also a cognitive dimension, as we have seen, and is not simply about subjective intuition and experience. The Johannine symbols and metaphors have cognitive content, and are not decorative embellishments, educative tools to make the lesson palatable. On the contrary, the theological content of faith gives it a centre, a broad terrain of understanding into which disciples venture further and further. In Johannine terms, to learn is to discover something of who Jesus is, as Son of God, as divine revelation, as Word made flesh. Such cognition works alongside intuition to teach disciples what it means to have faith. Who is the object of faith? is a vital question in Johannine spirituality and far from peripheral to spiritual experience. The content itself creates a space in which believing identity can flourish.

John speaks of this kind of discipleship as 'knowing', a knowing that is closely associated with the theme of eternal life (17:3).[23] Knowing is relational, depending not just on affectivity but also on communication and intelligible understanding.[24] In a theological sense, such knowing is the product of divine revelation, graciously given to those whose hearts are open (1:31, 33). Knowing issues from the divine realm, based on the mutuality of Father and Son (10:15). The Johannine Jesus knows the Father intimately (7:29), as well as the human realm (1:48; 2:22-23; 18:4; 21:17); believers are given a share in this knowledge, so that they too can know the Father, through Jesus, and know themselves before God (17:6). A major characteristic of true discipleship in the Fourth Gospel is precisely this knowledge (6:69; 10:4, 14), however partial it may be (4:25; 9:25; 10:38; 11:24, 14:5); not knowing is a tragic sign of disbelief (1:10; 6:42; 8:14, 19, 55; 16:3). The knowledge which derives from faith is also an effective sign to the unbelieving world (17:25).

Learning and knowledge are both concerned with truth, another key Johannine conception that weaves its way in and out of the text, associated with Jesus himself and also the Spirit (1:14, 17; 14:16, 17; 15:26; 16:13). John's Gospel employs a number of expressions for this concept: 'knowing the truth' (8:32; 17:8), 'speaking the truth' (8:40, 45-46; 16:7; 19:35), 'bearing witness to the truth' (5:33; 18:37), 'doing the truth' (3:21), 'being of the truth' (18:37), 'worshipping in truth' (4:23-24), and 'being told/hearing the truth' (8:40).[25] Truth is linked to the witness imagery in the Fourth Gospel: to bear witness is to proclaim courageously what has been revealed as true. The Gospel begins and ends with this note of truthful testimony, in John the Baptist and the beloved disciple, both of whom, humanly speaking, are the source of faith for future disciples (1:6-8, 17; 19, 32-34; 21:24). The community testifies to the truth received, a truth that is christological (note the 'we' language at 1:14; 21:24). However, the real witness in this Gospel is Jesus himself, who attests to the truth and embodies it, a role continued after his departure by the Holy Spirit, the 'Spirit of truth' (14:17; 15:26; 16:13; cf. 4:23-24). In embodying the truth, 'God's reality becomes manifest in him, manifest as will and power to save.'[26]

In John's Gospel, as we have already seen, learning means an openness to the truth of revelation. Jesus embodies this revelation in his identity as well as his words; as the Teacher from God, he teaches both self-knowledge and the knowledge of God. More than that: as the Word made flesh, he is the fulfilment of his own teaching, representing both divine and human within himself—divulging God's glory in his humanity. To be taught by the Johannine Jesus, therefore, is to move along a spiritual path from blindness to sight, from the darkness of ignorance to the light of faith and knowledge. To be a disciple, a learner, is to become a true child of God, a beloved friend and brother or sister of Jesus. As Jesus proclaims in the middle of the bread of life narrative, just as the conflict is escalating:

> No one can come to me unless drawn by the Father who sent me; and I will raise that person up on the last day. It is said in the prophets, 'And they shall all be taught by God' [Isa 51:13]. Everyone who has heard and learned from the Father comes to me. Not that anyone has seen the Father except the one who is from God; he has seen the Father (6:45-46).

There is a distinctly sapiential tone to this declaration. Jesus teaches about God just as Wisdom does in offering her teaching to the one who craves it: 'She will nourish him with the bread of understanding, and give him the water of learning to drink' (Sir 15:3).[27] To be taught by the Johannine Jesus, who is both holy Wisdom and the Bread of heaven, is to be taught by the Father, a teaching that is life-giving, both now and in the future. John's understanding of discipleship as learning, therefore, involves intimate relationship and intelligent knowing within the lived experience of disciples.

Abiding

In this Gospel, believing and learning are set in the context of disciples' abiding on Jesus. The image of abiding is a unique term for discipleship in the Fourth Gospel.[28] The verb *menô* ('abide') occurs about forty times throughout the narrative. Sometimes its usage is mundane, as in the English 'stay' or 'remain', but more often John conveys a deeper meaning, sometimes concealed in translation.[29] At the beginning of the Gospel narrative, the two disciples of John the Baptist approach Jesus on the basis of the Baptist's testimony to the 'Lamb of God' (1:29, 35), and ask the question: 'Rabbi ... where are you staying (*abiding*)?' (1:38).[30] The conversation works at two levels, the obvious level of polite interest and a second, metaphorical level where everything is really about the meaning of discipleship. Jesus' reply, 'Come and see'

(1:39), is more than a temporary invitation to inspect his dwelling-place or even to receive temporal hospitality. The invitation, like the initial question, is pregnant with meaning; likewise, the conclusion—'they remained (*abided*) with him that day' (1:39). Perhaps at this stage, these two levels are not immediately obvious to the reader, but in the light of what ensues, the brief dialogue is charged with symbolic meaning.

The first occurrences of the verb 'abide' are in relation to the Spirit. The Fourth Gospel does not explicitly relate the Synoptic story of Jesus' baptism (Mk 1:9-11/pars.); instead, John the Baptist, in the course of his own baptizing, has a vision in which he sees the Spirit descend on Jesus, and 'it remained (*abided*) on him' (1:32). The vision is authenticated by the Baptist's report of the confirming word of God addressed to him.[31] For the fourth evangelist, Jesus is the one on whom the Spirit abides, an abiding that will transfer to his disciples at his departure. The language suggests that the dialogue with the two disciples, a few verses later, has greater significance than is initially apparent: it is really about the desire for discipleship and Jesus' hospitality. Note that the first half of the Gospel will end with Gentiles wishing to 'see' Jesus (12:20). To 'abide' with Jesus, to 'come and see', in other words, is metaphorical for discipleship. The one on whom the Spirit abides draws disciples to abide with him.

Several other usages of 'abide' yield a similar meaning. For example, the Samaritan villagers approach Jesus after the Samaritan woman's testimony (4:29, 39)—they are the fields 'white for harvest' (4:35)—and Jesus remains (*abides*) with them for two days (4:40). This too has a straightforward, ordinary meaning: Jesus breaks his journey and accepts their hospitality for two days, thumbing his nose at Jewish convention that sees Samaritans as unclean and thus outside the bounds of hospitality. But, in Johannine terms, the expression suggests something theologically more significant, more symbolic.[32] Jesus makes more than a literal, two-day stay with these people. His whole person has come to 'inhabit' them in a way that points to their conversion, their acceptance of him as the Saviour of the world, as the permanent centre of their hearts and lives. They have become his disciples, just like the woman herself.

No such ambiguity exists in the Bread of Life narrative where, towards the end of the dialogue, Jesus turns to the subject of consuming his flesh and blood (6:51-59). In addition to the strongly sapiential nature of the imagery,[33] the language becomes overtly eucharistic, although the latter has been at least implied throughout; the feeding narrative, with Jesus as host, and the addition of the reference to thirst at 6:35 make that plain.[34] Here the language of abiding is unambiguously symbolic. Sharing in the eucharist by faith forms and fosters a reciprocal bond of *abiding* between the Johannine Jesus and disciples: 'Those who eat my flesh and drink my blood abide in me, and I in them' (6:56). This bond, which is essential for discipleship ('unless you eat...', 6:53), parallels the abiding that exists between the Father and Jesus (6:57); indeed, they are one and the same thing, since Jesus draws disciples into *his* affiliation with the Father. In this passage abiding is explicitly relational, describing symbolically the mutuality of the life which flows between Jesus and his disciples, a life that originates with the Father. There is intimacy in this relationship, mutuality, and affection, the one giving freely to the other in such a way that even death is trumped and cannot undo the cords of love binding them. To be bound in abiding-love to the Johannine Jesus is to be bound to God, the Father of unending life.

The majority of occurrences of the verb 'to abide' are clustered in the Farewell Discourse. Here we find the only appearances of the noun equivalent, *monê*, which means literally an 'abiding-place' ('dwelling places', 14:2; 'home', 14:23).[35] This imagery operates in two seemingly contradictory ways. On the one hand, and foundationally, the Father and Son will make their 'abiding-place' in the heart of the believer, through the presence of the Spirit-Paraclete: 'we will come to them and make our *home* with them' (14:23). Although the Fourth Gospel never speaks of believers as the 'temple' of the Spirit, as Paul does (1 Cor 3:16-17), this image is the Johannine equivalent. The believer—and, indeed, the believing community as a whole[36]—becomes the 'home' of God, Father, Son and Paraclete, the place where they abide. At the same time, near the beginning of the Farewell Discourse, Jesus comforts the disciples in view of his departure with the promise that his purpose in going is to 'prepare a place' for them with the Father who has 'many dwelling places' (14:2). So, while the Father comes to dwell within believers, with the Son and through the Spirit, so believers come to dwell with the Father as the end of their journey, a journey that is taken on the path which is Jesus himself (14:6). The destination which lies at the end of the journey—to break the metaphor—is nonetheless inaugurated in the life of the community. The goal is also the means, just as the path is also its end. What John describes, therefore, is a two-way path, in which God journeys to us and we journey to God, the bridge between the two—the road itself—being the Johannine Jesus and, after his departure, the Johannine Spirit.

At the narrative centre of the Last Meal is the symbol of the vine and the branches (15:1-17). Just as the image of following comes into its own, pictorially speaking, in the 'parable' of the sheep and the shepherd, where it blazes into colour (10:1-18), so with abiding and the imagery of the vine and the branches.[37] The full display of abiding manifests itself in the rich imagery which, in retrospect, underlines all previous usage. [38] Significantly, in both cases, we find characteristic Old Testament symbols for Israel—flock and vineyard—where images of desolation and devastation are metaphorical either for Israel's breach of the covenant or the failure of its leaders (e.g. Isa 5:1-7; Jer 2:21; 23:1-6; Ezek 19:10-14; 34: 1-16; Pss 23, 80). The Johannine Jesus now places himself at the centre of both images, transforming them from desolating symbols of destruction and loss within the community of faith to life-giving and life-affirming symbols of joy and hope. Not only is Jesus the Shepherd of the flock who gives abundant life to the sheep, but he is also the Vine who carries sap to the branches, enabling them to flourish and produce plentiful grapes for the harvest. In each case, the abiding of disciples on Jesus is undergirded by the Son's abiding in the Father, and the Father's abiding in the Son—an abiding in which the Spirit also takes part (1:32-33, 15:10).

Other language in John parallels the imagery of abiding. In the Prologue, John sets out the tragedy of the Word coming to 'his own', and 'his own' rejecting him (*ta idia:* 'what was his own'; *hoi idioi,* 'his own people', 1:11). Whether the Prologue is referring to Israel or, more generally, to the world created through the Word, is immaterial here.

Illustration 5: Greek Orthodox Icon of Christ the Vine[39]

The icon pictured above is the Greek Orthodox representation of Christ the Vine (*hê ampelos*). Christ sits enthroned in the centre, the lower part of his body replaced by the tree-like trunk of the vine. His arms are open to embrace those on either side of him and also the viewer. The book which faces the viewer is the Book of the Gospels and contains the words, 'I am the vine, you are the branches, and my Father is the vine-grower. The one who abides in me, and I in them, bears much fruit.' Twirled within the branches are the twelve apostles, representing the community of faith, the church, of which the vine is a key Johannine symbol. The faces of the apostles are turned towards Jesus, the centre, the one whose life gives them life, whose presence holds the vine in being. The icon represents visually the Johannine imagery of the vine as the abiding-place of the church, and the believer, the source from which they draw life.

What is important is that John uses the expression 'his own' on at least two other occasions in ways that parallel the abiding language. John introduces the second major division of the Gospel with a kind of 'mini-prologue' (13:1-3) that serves to introduce the themes of this new section, as well as the Footwashing itself. The following chapters will consist of Jesus alone with his intimate disciples (including Judas the betrayer) and the evangelist refers to them as 'his own' (*hoi idioi*): 'having loved his own who were in the world, he loved them to the end' (13:1b). Later in the discourse, Jesus warns the disciples that, at his arrest, they will leave him, 'each one to his own home' (*ta idia*, 16:32). The language of 'his own' is the language of home, of belonging. The disciples belong to Jesus, they are his 'home'—even though they will abandon him and scatter. Most significantly, at the foot of the cross, Jesus gives his mother and the beloved disciple to one another, with the result that, 'from that hour the disciple took her into his own home' (*ta idia*, 19:27).[40] The rejection indicated in the Prologue is overturned in this highly symbolic scene. Jesus does find 'his own' and, even with his departure, that sense of home and abiding does not cease. It continues with the presence of the Spirit and the birth of the Christian community. The family relationship between disciples provides a true home, a sense of abiding, given by the Father and where the Father dwells. In John's Gospel, disciples find their true home in God and God finds a true home in them.

The Johannine picture of abiding may seem an oddly inactive image of discipleship, particularly in comparison with the Synoptic Gospels. In John's Gospel, discipleship is not primarily about effort and achievement, although the evangelist describes it as both fruitful and dynamic. Rather, the priority is on rest and homecoming, and mutual love within the fold. It calls disciples into a familiarity of relationship where 'Jesus' self-revelation is his ongoing and progressive opening to his disciples of his own inner life, the life of divine filiation, which is infinite in its depth and breadth and richness.'[42] Indeed, the imagery of abiding and home-coming, in this Gospel, is one way of outlining the incarnation. The Son enters radically into human life, making his home, his abiding-place, with human beings and inviting them in turn to find a home with the Father through him. He represents, therefore, both God's abiding with believers and believers' abiding with God. Without him, according to John, no such abiding, no sense of home, can exist. The Johannine Jesus holds together the two threads, just as he holds in being the vine, giving life, fecundity and joy to those who know how to abide in his presence.[41]

Loving

Abiding is closely allied to the language of love, a further Johannine image of discipleship. Images of love and friendship are frequent in the Gospel of John. The first appearance of the verb 'love' sets the tone for its usage later on: 'God so *loved* the world that he gave his only Son' (3:16). A more literal translation is: 'God loved the world *in this way* that he gave his Son'.[42] In other words, this much-quoted verse is as much about the way in which God loves as it is about the extent of God's love. The Johannine Jesus is referring here to his own death, his 'lifting up' on the cross like the bronze serpent in the wilderness (3:14-15), an exaltation that will paradoxically bring life and healing, just as the serpent did. The crucifixion is itself primarily the sign of the incarnation in this Gospel. John sees the initiative for the incarnation in the divine love for the world God has created, a love that, far from being dominating and coercive, is self-giving and open to rejection. The gift of the Johannine Jesus in the flesh is the gift of God's self, motivated by love. What the incarnation is about—the ministry of Jesus, the cross, the resurrection—is purely and simply the restorative love of God.

More foundational than God's love for the world is the Father's love for the Son, and the Son's for the Father (3:35, 5:20, 10:17, 14:31, 15:9, 17:23-24, 26). This is the basis of love in the Fourth Gospel. At the centre of all reality exists an archetypal love, out of which the world is born and by which it is redeemed. The crucifixion is the sign of God's love for the world, but it is also—and essentially—the symbol of the Son's love for the Father, a self-offering of love and glory that brings about salvation. The Father's glorification of the Son is likewise the expression of divine love, the one for the other. From one angle, the Jesus-event in this Gospel provides a glimpse into the life of God, which articulates itself in love of the world. That love is the enticing of the world into the divine orbit, so that within the being of God—within the love of Father and Son—the world finds its place, gathered into the Son's devotion to the Father and participating in the Father's love for the Son. The Spirit is the one who enables this love, who channels it, both within the divine being and between the world and God.

The inner relationship between Father and Son, through the agency of the Spirit, is archetypal also for discipleship. God's love comes first and human love is given in response. Indeed, the sign of one's true love of God, according to John, is seen in one's response to Jesus (8:42), since to love the Father is to recognise and love the Son. In finding this love disciples regain a lost identity as 'children of God', through the birthing of the Spirit (3:3, 5). In entering the mutuality of the divine relation, they become not only children but also friends of God.[43] In the Johannine language for love, friendship is also a part, though the term 'friend' in English can sometimes seem weak. In the ancient world, friendship was highly valued, even in a society organised around the family; personal friends were seen as members of one's household, part of the family.[44] This strong connection between love and friendship is already hinted at in the last words John the Baptist utters in the Fourth Gospel: 'The friend of the bridegroom, who stands and hears him, rejoices greatly at the bridegroom's voice' (3:29). John the Baptist is that 'friend' because he responds to divine love with his own love and friendship, which is so strong and sure that he is able to step aside when the Johannine Jesus comes onto the scene, allowing himself and all he stands for to give way before the 'bridegroom'.

The members of the Bethany family are also depicted as friends of Jesus, those loved by him (11:3, 5). For John, this is not primarily an indication of natural human ties, but rather the language of discipleship. Jesus proves his friendship for Lazarus ('see how he loved him', 11:35) by raising him from the dead, an act that places Jesus himself in danger of his life, and leads directly to the cross in this Gospel. Martha and Mary are also 'friends' of Jesus, disciples whose faith is challenged to grow beyond their imaginings. Both women respond positively to Jesus' love and friendship, though Martha's faith—which enables her to recognise Jesus as 'the resurrection and the life' (11:25-26)— wavers at the mouth of the tomb, as we have already seen, the stench of death signifying its devastation and irreversibility (11:39). But perhaps Mary expresses mostly completely the authentic response of true friendship in her anointing of Jesus' feet (12:1-8). Hers is an act of unparalleled generosity in the Fourth Gospel, expressing the mutuality of the relationship between disciples and their Lord. She responds to the costliness of Jesus' gift—his life given to bring Lazarus from death—with the costliness of her own gift, the lavish expenditure of the perfumed oil. The mutuality of this friendship is itself the perfume which pervades the house, overcoming the nauseous stench of death with life.[45] Friendship with Jesus is life-giving for disciples, calling them into a union of mutual love. Barrett sums it up: 'Love seems to be, for John, a reciprocal relation. The Father loves the Son ... and the Son loves the Father ... Jesus loves his own ... and his own love, or should, one another ... They must also love him.'[46]

The image of abiding for discipleship, which we noted above, is closely tied to that of love and friendship. The most explicit discussion of this theme follows immediately from the vine and the branches (15:1-17). Jesus uses the language of friendship to paraphrase and explain the viticultural imagery. Abiding is really about friendship, a friendship that begins with Jesus himself and his love for disciples, manifest especially in his death. At this point, the Johannine Jesus dissolves the imagery of slavery and servitude, replacing it with that of friendship and love: 'I do not call you slaves any longer, because the slave does not know what the master is doing; but I have called you friends, because I have made known to you everything that I have heard from my Father' (*douloi, philoi,* 15:15).

The friends of Jesus are called not only into friendship with Jesus (and, through him, with God), but also with one another. One of Jesus' parting gifts is the love-command: 'I give you a new commandment, that you love one another. Just as I have loved you, you also should love one another' (13:34). What is 'new' about this command is not the love aspect, because that too is part of the life of Israel and the covenant (Lev 19:18), but rather the concessive clause, 'as I have loved you'. The command is new because the Johannine Jesus has lived it and bestowed the same love on disciples; they are held in it by his love, which is the love of the Father. That is the essential command/s in this Gospel (whether singular or plural). Those who are embraced by the Father's love for the Son belong in a mutual relation of love with God and with one another.

The footwashing plays an important role in confirming John's understanding of love and friendship in this Gospel. The story is not an easy one to interpret, despite the widespread interpretation of humble service to the world. Footwashing in the ancient world was about literal cleanliness and the offering of hospitality, but in the Jewish world it also included cultic aspects.[47] So, for example, those entering the temple had to do so with clean feet, a demand for ritual purity rather than physical cleanliness. That is the main sense in which the footwashing in used in John 13. The narrative context is all-important—its central place at the Last Supper, where it replaces the Synoptic institution of the eucharist (Mk 14:22-25/pars.), and the formal, almost liturgical language, giving it a quasi-ritual quality. Jesus' words to Peter make this explicit: 'unless I wash you, you have no share with me' (13:8). The footwashing, for John, is symbolic of the death of Jesus and its cleansing effects,[48] since everything in the opening verses points to Jesus' departure on the cross (13:1-3). Union with the Johannine Jesus in his self-giving death is the context here. For the disciples, the washing of the feet is fundamentally a preparation for that death, a ritual enactment of the sacrificial ministry of God in that death. The cross, for John, as we already seen is a glorification, an act of adoration—the ascent of the Son to the Father—the self-projection of the Father's true nature, extended in love for the world. Yet it is also an act of humble service on the part of Jesus: not just obedience to God, but also service to 'his own', those whom the Father has given him. The footwashing in that sense is a symbolic act, pointing to the death of Jesus, but it is also a symbolic act of preparation for the disciples: the means by which they are ritually 'cleansed' in order to be in union with Jesus, to enter the 'temple' of his body, crucified and risen.

Immediately after, John gives a more extended interpretation which seems to take the meaning in a different direction, a meaning that most readers have found easier to deal with (13:12-15). Here Jesus' washing of the feet becomes a model for disciples to imitate: 'if I, your Lord and Teacher, have washed your feet, you also ought to wash one another's feet' (13:14). Note that the emphasis is on disciples washing *each other's* feet; this is not a text about mission but about relations within the community of faith. In this interpretation, footwashing is a symbol of the love-command: 'love one another as I have loved you' (13:34). It is emblematic of the love which is to thrive among the community of friends, who are to love and serve one another in Christ-like ways. Yet this is not strictly a new or second interpretation of the footwashing.[50] Rather, it flows from the initial meaning, in the same sense that love for the brothers and sisters flows from the love of the Johannine Jesus. The point is not simply that of imitation, but a matter of being taken into a circle of love, close to others who belong in the same place. The closer disciples are to the divine centre of love, the closer they come to one another, like the spokes of a wheel. The footwashing is about participation in Jesus and in his saving death—it is about his act of humility, love, and service on the cross, and it is equally about the love and friendship which characterises the life of the community of faith as a consequence.

Two further passages deserve mention in relation to John's understanding of discipleship as love and friendship. Although the imagery shifts to familial language, the gift of the mother of Jesus and the beloved discile to one another at the foot of the cross—to which we have already alluded in relation to 'abiding'—is perhaps the primary symbol of love and friendship within the household of faith (19:25-27). John in any case moves easily between images of family and images of friendship, each expressing a different through related facet of the Johannine communion-in-love. The relationship of these two important figures in the Fourth Gospel, neither of whom is ever named, becomes archetypal for the whole community. Indeed, this moment in the Johannine Passion narrative is in one sense the birth of the church, centred around the familial and friendly affection between its members. It may also be, for John, that the acceptance of the mother of Jesus 'into his own home' (*eis ta idia*, 19:27) is a fundamental feature of discipleship, an invitation offered to all disciples who identity themselves with the beloved disciple. She is the first to show trust in the word of Jesus, thus from the beginning nurturing the faith of disciples (2:5).

The beloved disciple is the quintessential 'friend of Jesus' in this Gospel, his title indicating his revered place within the Johannine community. Here he stands not only as the foundational witness of the Gospel but also as the symbol of the relationship which flourishes between Jesus and his disciples. At the Last Supper, where he is first identified, he is reclining on the breast of Jesus—he holds the place of honour at the banquet—and John's language is carefully nuanced: just as Jesus in the Prologue is 'close to the Father's heart' (1:18), so the beloved disciple (like all true disciples) is close to Jesus' heart (13:21).[50] His posture means literally that his couch is next to Jesus, so positioned that he has easy access to private conversation with Jesus, but for John it is also symbolic: the same closeness is the style of friendship to which all disciples are called.

Finally, Jesus' conversation with Simon Peter after his risen appearance to the seven disciples on the beach in Galilee is also pertinent to our discussion of love and friendship (21:15-19). We will touch on this passage in relation to Peter's call to 'follow' Jesus even to martyrdom and death. But at the heart of following is love, and so Jesus asks Peter three times to declare his love, a love that exceeds all else.[51] In doing so, Jesus rehabilitates Peter after his threefold denial, re-establishing the love that once foundered but will now stand firm. It is also the commissioning of Peter as shepherd of the Good Shepherd's flock, but note that both following and shepherding are based on Peter's love for Jesus. That is to be the core of his vocation, the motivation that drives everything else, the centre of his being.[52] In other words, behind Peter's mission and commissioning lies a profound spirituality of love and friendship without which such vocation is impossible. For John, not only Peter but also disciples are called into the same love, the same filiation and friendship; called to be 'beloved disciples', to be the friends of Jesus and friends to one another even to the point of death. This Johannine model of friendship is one that demands all.

Following

At the same time, imagery of love and friendship do not cancel out the dependence of disciples on their Lord in the Fourth Gospel. Two images, in particular, express this sense of authority in relationship. The first of these of these is that of following. This image is not as frequent or as significant in the Gospel of John as it is in the Synoptic Gospels, where it is the main image of discipleship.[53] Mark presents the disciples on the long journey to Jerusalem literally walking behind Jesus (Mk 10:32), a statement that only makes sense at a metaphorical level: discipleship, for Mark, means following Jesus on the *via dolorosa*, the journey to suffering and death, which is paradoxically the road to life. Furthermore, in Mark, the image is placed at the beginning of Jesus' ministry in the calling of the first four disciples, where Jesus' imperious call, without preamble, incites Peter, Andrew, James and John to leave their fishing and follow him (Mk 1:16-20/Matt 4:18-22). This story, so early in Mark's Gospel, gives the image of following considerable prominence thereafter, metaphorically and theologically. As Jesus gathers disciples around himself to form his 'new family' (Mk 3:31-35/pars.), the imagery of following, along with that of fishing, is defined for Mark in terms of discipleship, ministry and mission.

John gives the imagery of following somewhat less status, though it still has a place within the narrative of the Fourth Gospel. The imagery of following is not prominent in the story of the first disciples. Jesus calls only one of the initial group, Philip (1:43), and his call is at variance with that of Peter, Andrew, the unnamed disciple (most likely, the beloved disciple), and Nathanael, stressing Jesus' authority.[54] Each is drawn to Jesus by virtue of the testimony of another: John the Baptist, in the first place, then Andrew, and finally Nathaniel through Philip. The pattern underscores the significance of witness in John's theology, giving it precedence over the Synoptic image of following in the opening sequences of Jesus' ministry.

Nonetheless, the Fourth Gospel begins and ends with imagery of following: the two disciples who 'come and see' at the beginning (1:38-39), and Peter who is called to follow at the end (21:22).[55] The first two disciples—disciples of John the Baptist—hearing the witness to Jesus as the Lamb of God, take the initiative and themselves 'follow' Jesus (1:37-38, 40). He accepts their allegiance and they remain with him as disciples, leaving behind, not their fishing nets and occupation, but their leader, John the Baptist. Perhaps the story of Philip being called directly by Jesus to 'follow' indicates that John has an awareness of the Synoptic tradition where the earliest group is called directly by Jesus. Or perhaps, more likely, it signals to the reader that, whatever the first disciples think they are doing in coming to Jesus of their own volition, it is Jesus' initiative that lies behind it, pulling them towards him like a magnet. Note that there is no indication of fishing within the Johannine story; on the contrary, the first two disciples are disciples of John the Baptist. Yet, significantly, fishing is linked both to mission and discipleship in the last chapter. Some of the same disciples are gathered in Galilee after the resurrection and set off on a fishing expedition where they meet the risen Christ (21:1-14). In an odd parallel with Luke's Gospel, who places this incident—or one very like it—near the beginning of Jesus' ministry (Lk 5:1-11), omitting the Markan story of the calling of the first four disciples, the fishermen in John's account obey Jesus' instructions and seize a miraculous catch of fish, which is symbolic of their new vocation and the authority which empowers it.

The image of following in relation to discipleship occurs a handful of times throughout the ministry of the Johannine Jesus. At the feast of Tabernacles, Jesus calls people to discipleship as the Light of the world, promising those who choose to *follow* him that their path will be illuminated (8:12). More significantly for the imagery, following is part of the allegorical parable of the shepherd and the sheep, where it develops vivid pictorial meaning. 'Following' is an image of the intimacy and trust which the sheep have for the Shepherd, their recognition of his beloved voice (10:4, 16, 27). His care for them goes so far as to die and rise again in order that they 'might have life, and have it abundantly' (10:10). The death and resurrection imagery recurs towards the end of Jesus' ministry where, in response to the coming of the Greeks as would-be disciples, Jesus teaches that following him means service, and service means losing one's life in order to 'keep it for eternal life' (12:25). The language of following is linked to the image of the seed that must 'die' in the soil, in order to sprout and grow into a living plant (12:24).

The same conception of following again appears as the story moves towards the Passion. Simon Peter, whose determination is to follow Jesus even to death, is warned that he will fail in that desire, at least for the present time (13:36-37). It is significant that the Farewell Discourse begins and ends with reference to the disciples' failure to remain with Jesus (16:32). Peter does make an attempt to follow, after Jesus' arrest (18:15), but the attempt fails dismally in his three-fold denial (18:15-18, 25-27). After the resurrection Jesus rehabilitates Peter with the three-fold question, 'Do you love me?' and the three-fold commissioning of him as shepherd of the Good Shepherd's flock (21:15-19).[56] Jesus completes his interrogation and commissioning— which Peter finds deeply painful—with the simple command, 'Follow me' (21:19), and the evangelist makes plain that this involves a summons to martyrdom.[57] The theme of following as martyrdom fits with Jesus' earlier assurance to Peter that, though he will fail in the near future, he will indeed one day succeed in following Jesus (13:37) and go where Jesus has gone: namely, to death. Peter is now to follow the risen Christ but, as the shepherd of Jesus' flock, the sheep in a sense will also follow Peter. Note the way in which John in this scene brings together the imagery of sheep, shepherd and following, immediately after the fishing incident and the miraculous catch of fish. There are links with Synoptic traditions, but also signs of John the evangelist going his own way and drawing on his own unique traditions. The imagery of following the shepherd has more significance for John.

Following, therefore, in John's Gospel is about personal attachment to Jesus based on love and trust, a love that is prepared to face martyrdom for his sake and for the sake of the flock. The bond between disciples and Jesus makes possible the following of him. The imagery is closely tied to the shepherd and the flock—

pastoral ministry—but also more widely, through the association of the fishing imagery, to mission. Yet, at the heart of following is love, the one motivating force in the relation between Jesus and the community of disciples: between the Good Shepherd and his flock. In terms of Johannine spirituality, following Jesus involves a close, intimate attachment to him—learning to discern his voice and trust him implicitly as the sheep do the shepherd. Just as Mary of Bethany gives a costly gift to Jesus in the anointing (12:1-8), so Johannine disciples are called to give themselves to him, body and soul, flesh and spirit. And like Mary Magdalene in the Easter garden, they learn to hear the Good Shepherd calling them by name, filling them with his love and presence, and sending them forth to proclaim his risen life (20:16-18).

Obeying

The other image expressing dependence and authority in the Fourth Gospel is that of obeying. For all its stress on intimacy, the Gospel's imagery of love and friendship does not rule out obedience. The Johannine Jesus goes so far as to define his friends as those who 'do what I command you' (15:14). As with following, obeying arises from the deep bond between Jesus and disciples. In the context of the vine, and the theme of abiding-in-love, obedience means the command to love, the one ethical imperative deriving from John's spirituality. To be a disciple, to abide on the vine, means to be drawn into a fellowship of love, a communion of affection and commitment. John does not lessen the paradox even in the radical shift from the language of slavery to that of friendship. Jesus remains their 'Teacher and Lord' (13:13-14); this is not a democratic union of equal persons but a mutual relationship in which those who are called to obey are, paradoxically and gratuitously, given the status of friends. The friends of Jesus receive knowledge and are not kept in the dark. This means that their obedience flows from an informed and intelligent love rather than from necessity and fear; it is the obedience rendered by free adults rather than that of children or slaves. Yet the divine priority remains in place: the initiative lies with the one who has chosen the disciples and appointed them 'to go and bear fruit, fruit that will last' (lit. *fruit that abides*, 15:16).

John's Gospel does not often use explicit language for obedience, preferring in most cases to use the imagery of keeping or guarding. The verb used here, *têreô*, can be used, for example, of keeping the Mosaic Law, and specifically the sabbath (7:19; 9:16). We have already seen something of the significance of this language in discussing Jesus as the Word.[58] To keep Jesus' word or his commandment/s is a way of speaking of obedience, yet the connotations are richer. To keep suggests guarding and treasuring something of value. The archetype of this cherishing is Jesus himself who keeps the Father's word (e.g. 8:55) and summons disciples to do likewise with his (8:51; 14:15, 21, 23-24; 15:10). Yet disciples themselves are also 'kept', held protectively in the Father's love, sustained by the power of the Name (17:11) and defended, not from persecution or suffering, but from the destructive lies and seductions of the Evil One (17:15). There is a keeping involved in discipleship, a free obedience based on love and the conviction that Jesus' command is of worth; and there is a divine keeping, a treasuring of disciples, who are enclosed in the Father's love, and in the Son's cherishing of the Father's word.

It is important to bear in mind that the language and imagery of friendship in John 15 is metaphorical rather than literal. This means that it can stand alongside other imagery with which it is in some tension (at a literal level). Obedience is the obvious example, but there are others. Disciples in this Gospel are not just friends but even more fundamentally children of God, re-birthed with a new status—an original status once lost—through the work of the divine Spirit. We have had cause to refer to this imagery several times already. It is based christologically on Jesus' own status as Son in which disciples share. Johannine imagery of disciples as sons and daughters of God—sharing the filiation of Jesus—is not precisely inconsistent with that of friendship: both, after all, are expressions of love. Nevertheless, being a friend of the household is not the same as being a son or daughter. More difficult is Jesus' earlier use of the master-servant paradigm to describe the relationship between disciples and Jesus, though the language is usually that of service (*diakonia*) rather than slavery: 'Whoever serves me must follow me, and where I am, there will my servant be also.

Whoever serves me, the Father will honour' (*diakoneô, diakonos*, 12:26).[59] Taken together, the imagery—in all its seeming tensions and contradictions—expresses a relationship that cannot easily be defined or encapsulated in language: service, friendship, intimacy, shared knowledge, filiation, each offering a different dimension of what it means to be a disciple in this Gospel.

Conclusion

John's understanding of discipleship is built on a spirituality that is characterised by images of believing, learning, abiding, loving, following, and obeying. Each, in a different way, expresses the deep bond that exists between the Johannine Jesus and his disciples, and each captures aspects of what it means to belong within the community of friends. The images denote relationship, grounded in intimacy and self-giving love, but they also include divine authority and human dependence as the grounds for surety and trust. This latter is part of the covenant language and imagery of the Fourth Gospel, where each is committed to the other in a mutual yet not equal way—a way that re-shapes but does not dissolve the fundamental distinctions between God and humankind.

In a number of ways, the response of disciples is dependent on the example of the Johannine Jesus who (with some qualification) demonstrates these qualities in his life, ministry and death. Admittedly, the Gospel does not explicitly portray Jesus as 'learning'—ironically, his opponents describe him as a 'man of letters' yet without (formal) learning (*grammata oiden ... mê memathêkôs*, 7:15). Jesus' openness to the Father's words, and to the mission with which he is entrusted, provides a parallel, though there is no hint that the Johannine Jesus himself moves from a state of ignorance to knowledge. Still less can the imagery of 'following' be easily applied to Jesus. On the contrary, in each case, Jesus is the one who leads while the disciples follow. Yet Jesus is characterised by abiding and love, both of which are intrinsic to his relationship with the Father and his own disciples. He is submissive to the Father, the one who is 'greater than I' (14:28). The character of his mission, as 'the one sent' by the Father, determines this relationship. There is a wholeheartedness in his response to God, which is implicitly set before disciples as the path they too must tread.

In each case, discipleship in the Fourth Gospel emanates from the theologically prior relationship of the Son to the Father: the Son who is sent to fulfil the Father's will, whose gaze is eternally 'turned towards' the Father, who abides in the Father, and whose love for the Father characterises his identity and mission. The Spirit too belongs within the same circle of love and friendship. In turn Jesus calls disciples to enter the circle, opening the gateway to the Father's love and life. John's spirituality of discipleship is active in the sense that it bears fruit, creates love within a vibrant community, leads to mission in the world, follows the call of Jesus, and holds fast to Jesus' word. But its roots lie in contemplation: in the gaze of adoration, in restful abiding, in meditative love, and in the welcoming embrace of God, as reflected in the life of the community. As beloved disciples, as friends of Jesus, the reader of the Gospel is summoned to share the same vocation as the Johannine disciples: to enter the divine life which lies at the heart of creation.

End Notes

[1.] Craig R. Koester, *The Word of Life. A Theology of John's Gospel* (Grand Rapids: Eerdmans, 20008), speaks of four 'word pictures' that John uses to depict the life of discipleship: walking in the light, seed falling into the earth, washing one another's feet, and abiding in the vine (188-196).

[2.] Note the distinction between 'person' and 'individual' in Orthodox theology, the one implying community, the other self-containment; see Rowan Williams, *Silence and Honey Cakes: The Wisdom of the Desert* (Oxford: Lion Publishing, 2003), 52-4.

[3.] Explicitly 'church' language is found on three occasions in Matthew (16:18; 18:17 [twice]), and is frequent in Acts, the Pauline epistles, and Revelation 2-3.

[4.] On the theme of church in John's Gospel, see especially R. Alan Culpepper, 'The Quest for the Church in the Gospel of John' *Int* 63 (2009) 341-54.

[5.] On the link with the Feast of Dedication, which is concerned with the reconsecration of the Temple, and Jesus' dialogue with his increasingly hostile opponents (10:36), see F.J. Moloney, *The Gospel of John* (SP;

Collegeville: Liturgical Press, 1998), 316-7.

6. See Dorothy Lee, 'John', in B.R. Gaventa & D. Petersen (eds.), *The New Interpreter's One Volume Commentary on the Bible* (Nashville: Abingdon, 2010), 724-5.

7. John Ashton, *Understanding the Fourth Gospel* (2nd ed.; Oxford: Oxford University Press, 2007), argues that the concept of 'truth' is integral to John's central depiction of revelation, which he sees as being both universal and yet also esoteric (529-531).

8. See Johannes Beutler who argues that the purpose of the Gospel is not just to strengthen faith, but also to lead to confession of faith, as evident in the main characters of the Gospel ('Faith and Confession: The Purpose of John' in J. Painter, R.A. Culpepper & F.F. Segovia [eds.], *Word, Theology, and Community in John* [St Louis, MI: Chalice Press, 2002], 19-31).

9. See, e.g., the narrative of John 6 which depicts an initial movement towards faith, the hostile questioning of 'the Jews', and the final rejection of all but the Twelve; on the narrative structure see Dorothy Lee, *The Symbolic Narratives of the Fourth Gospel: The Interplay of Form and Meaning* (JSTNSS 95; Sheffield: Sheffield Academic Press, 1994), 126-160.

10. The verb occurs nearly a hundred times in the Gospel, spread throughout the Johannine narrative, usually found in such expressions as 'believe in' (e.g. 1:12; 3:36; 4:21; 6:35; 9:35; 11:25-26; 12:11;14:12; 17:20), 'believe that' (e.g. 6:69; 8:24; 11:27, 45; 17:8; 20:31), or simply 'believe' (e.g. 1:50; 3:12; 5:44; 9:38; 12:39; 14:29; 19:35; 21:31); cf. 20:27 for the adjective *pistos/apistos* ('believing/ unbelieving'). While the noun 'belief/faith' does not appear, the participial 'the one who/those who believe' acts as a noun (3:18; 6:47; 14:12; 17:20). See Raymond E. Brown, *The Gospel According to John* (2 vols.; AB29-29A; New York: Doubleday, 196), 1.512-514.

11. For a summary of 'believing' as it operates in the plot of the Gospel, see Derek Tovey, *Jesus: Story of God. John's Story of Jesus* (Adelaide: ATF Press, 2007), 103-137.

12. Tovey, *Jesus*, 104-107.

13. Sandra M. Schneiders, *Written that You May Believe: Encountering Jesus in the Fourth Gospel* (New York: Crossroad, 1999), 87.

14. As noted in a previous chapter, John Calvin expresses this Johannine duality of revelation: 'without knowledge of self there is no knowledge of God', and 'without knowledge of God there is no knowledge of self'; J.T. McNeill (ed.), *Calvin: Institutes of the Christian Religion* (Philadelphia: Westminster, 1960), I.1.1 & 2. See above, chapter 2.

15. Tovey, *Jesus*, 105.

16. The term is not to be interpreted in a nationalistic sense.

17. In John's Gospel, the essence of sin is unbelief, the rejection of Jesus which also signifies the rejection of life; see Dorothy Lee, *Flesh and Glory. Symbol, Gender and Theology in the Gospel of John* (New York: Crossroad, 2002), 166-196.

18. Schneiders, *Written*, 85.

19. On 'glory' in relation to honour in the ancient world, see Jerome H. Neyrey, *The Gospel of John* (NCBC; Cambridge: Cambridge University Press, 2007), 216-218.

20. The term can mean not only 'learner' but also 'adherent' in the sense of 'requiring one to adhere to a great teacher and his school'; Craig S. Keener, *The Gospel of John. A Commentary* (2 vols.; Peabody: Hendrickson, 2003), 1.468.

21. Keener, *John*, 1.685-686.

22. Catherine M. McCahill, 'Making God Known': Jesus, the Teacher of the Fourth Gospel and the Contemporary Christian Religious Educator (PhD Thesis, Melbourne College of Divinity, Dalton McCaughey Library, 2006).

23. On John's understanding of knowledge in relation to other views within his own environment (Qumran, Philo, Hellenistic, Gnostic), see Keener, *John*, 1.234-247.

24. The verbs associated with knowing (especially *ginôskô* and *oida,* used interchangeably) and with making known (*gnôrizô*) are frequent throughout the Gospel. Keener has a list of these verbs and their occurrences in the Johannine narrative (*John*, 1:244-245).

25. Rudolf Schnackenburg, *The Gospel According to St John* (3 vols; New York: Seabury & Crossroad, 1980 & 1982), 2.227-228.

26. Schnackenburg, *St John*, 2.228. For a theological summary of truth in John, see also pp. 236-237.

27. Brown, *John*, 1.273.

28. See Lee, *Flesh and Glory*, 88-99.

29. See F. Hauck, *menô, TDNT* 4.574-74, and Jürgen Heise, *Bleiben. Meinen in den Johanneischen Schriften* (Tübingen: J.C.B. Mohr [Paul Siebeck], 1967), pp. 22-28.

30. Xavier Léon-Dufour draws an important parallel with the story of Mary Magdalene's search for Jesus (20:11-18; *Lecture de l'Evangile selon Jean* (4 vols.; Paris: Editions du Seuil, 1988), 1:189.

31. In the biblical world, a vision is not primarily an internal, subjective experience, but something objective that not everyone can perceive due to their limitations. For the fourth evangelist, Jesus' baptism in the Holy Spirit is an external event to which he is the witness. It may also be that

John's Gospel simply assumes Jesus' baptism in water and chooses to focus only on the descent of the Spirit. What is significant, however, is that John does not relate the event directly—as do the Synoptics (Mk 1:9-11/pars.)—but through the preaching of John the Baptist. This narrative feature to intensifies the role of the Baptist as witness to Jesus' true identity: twice his testimony is alluded to in the Prologue (1:6-8, 15) and he dominates the first section of the narrative proper (1:19-37), witnessing to Jesus as the Lamb of God and Bearer of the Spirit, a witness that draws the first disciples from him to Jesus (see 3:28-30).

32. See C.K. Barrett, *The Gospel According to St John. An Introduction with Commentary and Notes on the Greek Text* (2nd ed.; London: SPCK, 1978), 243.

33. On the link between Wisdom and abiding, see Martin Scott, *Sophia and the Johannine Jesus* (JSNTSS 71: Sheffield: SJSOT Press, 1992), 157-159.

34. On the question of the sacramentality (or anti-sacramentality) of this section of the dialogue, see Keener, *John*, 1:689-691, who points out the focus of these verses is on Jesus' saving death.

35. The word is rare in Greek, and clearly linked to the verb *menô* which, as we have seen, is 'a theologically loaded term throughout the Gospel' (Keener, *John*, 2.935).

36. Koester, *Word of Life*, emphasises that discipleship always belongs, and functions, within community, understood in terms of family, friendship and worship (196-209).

37. Rekha M. Chennattu argues that the notion of covenant lies at the heart of John 13-17, with the image of the vine and the branches signifying 'the intimate and abiding covenant relationship between Jesus and his disciples' (*Johannine Discipleship as a Covenant Relationship* [Peabody: Hendrickson, 2006], 113 [89-139]).

38. Fernando F. Segovia, *The Farewell of the Word: The Johannine Call to Abide* (Minneapolis: Fortress, 1991), 123-135.

39. http://www.orthodoxphotos.com/Icons_and_Frescoes/Icons/Jesus_Christ/30.shtml

40. Turid Karlsen Seim admits that this scene inaugurates the *familia Dei*, but argues that the mother of Jesus has little significance beyond the material; the Johannine language, in her view, remains stubbornly patriarchal ('Descent and Divine Paternity in the Gospel of John: Does the Mother Matter?' *NTS* 51 [2005], 361-75).

41. Schneiders, *Written*, 49.

42. So Keener, *John*, 1.566-567.

43. Further on this, see Lee, *Flesh and Glory*, 99-104.

44. Sjef van Tilborg, *Imaginative Love in John* (Leiden: Brill, 1993), 149.

45. Further on the symbolics of this scene, see Lee, *Flesh and Glory*, 197-211.

46. Barrett, *St John*, 215.

47. On footwashing in the ancient world, see John Christopher Thomas, *Footwashing in John 13 and the Johannine Community* (JSNTSup 61; Sheffield: JSOT Press, 1991), 26-60.

48. The meaning, as Schnackenburg points out, is soteriological, pointing to the saving significance of Jesus' death: it is 'a symbolic action in which Jesus makes his offering of himself in death graphic and effective' (*St John*, 3.19); see also Withington, *John*, 237.

49. Brown argues that John has brought together two distinct and duplicate interpretations of the footwashing here (*John*, 2.559-562).

50. The Greek is literally: 'One of his disciples was reclining in the bosom of Jesus (*kolpos*), the one whom Jesus loved.' In the Prologue the same word is used of Jesus' relationship with the Father: 'God the only Son, who is in the bosom (*kolpos*) of the Father' (1:18).

51. It is not easy to know what the Johannine Jesus means by 'do you love me *more than these*' (21:15). Most likely the meaning is general and not a comparison between the other disciples' love for Jesus and Peter's: 'Do you love me more than you love these friends?'; so Ben Witherington, *John's Wisdom. A Commentary on the Fourth Gospel* (Cambridge: Lutterworth, 1995), 356, and Moloney, *John*, 559. As Ilaria Ramelli says, 'Peter should love Jesus more than anything else, so he should even die for him' ("Simon Son of John, Do You Love *Me*?" Some Reflections on John 21:15' *NovT* 50 [2008], 334). Another possibility is that it refers to Peter's fishing tackle, and thus his occupation (cf Mk 1:17/par.); so Charles H. Talbert, *Reading John. A Literary and Theological Commentary on the Fourth Gospel and the Johannine Epistles* (London: SPCK, 1992), 261, but this is unlikely, especially within a Johannine context.

52. In the Greek, the differences between the two verbs for 'love' (*agapaô* and *phileô*) have no significance beyond the stylistic. Elsewhere in the Gospel, John uses these two words and their cognates interchangeably. See Barrett, *St John*, 584, and Keener, *Gospel of John*, 1236. The word 'friend' is, in any case, *philos* and carries the full meaning of someone beloved, much more intense than casual acquaintanceship.

53. The main verb used is *akoloutheô* ('to follow') which can have a literal meaning (e.g. 11:31; 18:15), but generally the sense is theological and symbolic (1:37, 40, 43; 6:1; 8:12; 10:4, 5, 27; 12:26; 13:36-37; 21:19, 22). John can also occasionally use other expressions such as *opisô erchomai*

('come/go after', e.g. 12:19). Ironically, in the first place, it is Jesus who
'comes after/follows' John the Baptist (1:17, 27, 30).

54. Jerome H. Neyrey speaks of this passage in John as illustrating
'recruitment' rather than volunteering, with one disciple recruiting another,
a pattern that continues throughout the Gospel (*The Gospel of John* [NCBC;
Cambridge: Cambridge University Press, 2007], 56). See also Keener who
points out, with some qualification, that students normally sought out their
own teachers, rather than the other way round (*John*, 1.481).

55. Koester, *Word of Life*, 187.

56. From a literary point of view, this assumes the unity of John 21 with
the rest of the Gospel, as we saw in the Introduction, despite the points of
narrative unevenness (which are to be found, in any case, throughout the
Gospel); see Lee, 'John', 732-4. For a narrative reading that still regards
John 21 as additional to the Gospel, see Francis J. Moloney, 'John 21 and the
Johannine Story' in T. Thatcher & S.D. Moore (eds.), *Anatomies of Narrative
Criticism. The Past, Present, and Futures of the Fourth Gospel as Literature*
(Atlanta: SBL, 2008), 237-251.

57. Ernst Haenchen asks the rhetorical question, 'May one say that Peter, in
the judgment of the author, was honored by martyrdom—and precisely this
martyrdom?' (*John 2. A Commentary on the Gospel of John Chapters 7-21*
[ET: Hermeneia; Philadelphia: Fortress, 1984], 232).

58. See above, chapter 1.

59. Only one context uses the word 'slave' in relation to discipleship (13:16)
where the point of comparison is the real issue: 'the slave is not greater than
the master'. In one place, Jesus speaks of his servants being prepared to fight
if the nature of his kingship were otherwise (*hypêretai*, 'attendants', 18:36).

Chapter 6
Spirituality and the Senses

Discipleship in the Fourth Gospel is closely linked to imagination. To be a disciple for John depends on the ability to grasp imaginatively the core symbols of the Gospel, to comprehend them at a deep level and to weave one's life around them. In this view, imagination involves cognition as well as intuition, thought, and feeling, and signifies a new way of envisioning reality, a way that is based on 'the way, the truth, and the life' (14:6). To imagine this new life is already to embark upon it, already to commit oneself to its transforming power. Not unlike the notion of 'myth', imagination does not refer to what is unbelievable, escapist, and impossible, but rather to belief in the truth about God and about the world, according to John, a truth unveiled only to the eyes of faith. To believe in the Johannine Jesus means to believe imaginatively that his flesh is the bearer of divine glory, that to adhere to him bestows the restored status of a child of God, that the life of God's future can transform the present, and that life, both now and in the future, overcomes death—indeed, has already done so, in the experience of the Johannine Jesus and the characters of the Gospel. To participate in the spirituality of the Johannine text requires imagination, therefore, the imagination to experience what the Gospel offers.

Though in one sense profoundly spiritual and other-worldly ('from above'), Johannine spirituality is also fleshly and this-worldly ('from below'). The Gospel of John uses a number of images to express its understanding of what it means to believe in Jesus and to belong to the community of faith. These images are drawn from the material world and used to become symbols or vehicles of the divine world.[1] Discipleship cannot develop without such imagery, so foundational is it to the symbolic world of the fourth evangelist. Of particular pertinence are those images that focus on the senses, all of which are found in the Gospel in contexts that deal with believing existence.[2] These images are remarkably cohesive and relate to all five senses throughout the Johannine narrative—sight, hearing, taste, touch, smell—a narrative presence that is grounded in John's central theological motif, the incarnation. The Fourth Gospel is centrally focussed on the incarnation, the entry of God into the world in material form; as a consequence of this core symbol, the Gospel itself shares the same 'incarnate' quality confirmed in the Johannine Jesus whose tangible humanity radiates divine glory. The imagery focuses on those senses which respond to that incarnate, divine presence. Faith, in this Gospel, is determinative and it is also sensual.

In physiognomic terms, the five senses—the number and identification of which are generally attributed to Aristotle[3] —are the means by which human beings apprehend external reality. Each is associated with one organ or aspect of the body, and each corresponds to a particular segment of the brain.[4] Sight or vision, associated with the eyes and the physiological intake of light through the cornea and pupil, enables us to discern colour, movement, shape, distance, size. Hearing or audition involves the movement of sound through the ears to the ear-drum which sends messages to the brain, telling it of volume, type, intensity and balance. Taste or gustation occurs on the tongue with its manifold taste buds, detecting sweet and sour, salt and bitter, and conveying the appropriate messages to the brain. Touch, or somatic feeling, takes place on the skin of the body, in the middle layer which has nerve endings connected to the brain, discerning whether the touch is soft or hard, gentle or sharp, safe or dangerous, painful or painless, pleasant or unpleasant. And finally smell or olfaction employs air and breath through the nose and the nerves in the top of the nasal cavity to transmit messages of pleasant or unpleasant, threatening or soothing, as well as to summon memory.

Each of these senses may be lacking in any person and each, therefore, has its opposite. Each too works together with the others— for example, taste and smell combine to discern flavour. Generally the sense of sight, hearing and smell belong together as involving no necessary contact, unlike taste and touch which do; yet taken together, the five senses 'enable us to see the world in a unified way.'[5] The senses, in short, are intrinsic to what makes us human: the means of our apprehension and communication, and the basis of our experience.[6] Their capacity for metaphorical or spiritual signification is also important, as is evident in the way Aristotle sees them as forming part of the soul.

Sight

The first Johannine image of faith related to the senses is that of sight. The sense of sight has rightly been described as 'mankind's most noble and dependable sense';[7] in physiological terms, it 'trumps' all the other senses.[8] In the ancient world, likewise, the dominance of vision among the senses was widely recognised: 'the eyes are the most important marker of character and are frequently used in this way.'[9] It is not surprising that the most significant Johannine image based on the senses is that of sight, mostly found in the verbal form 'to see'. While there is a more mundane meaning, there is also a metaphorical meaning to this verb in the Gospel—or, rather, cluster of verbs.[10] The pronoun 'we' at 1:14 (*etheasametha*, 'we beheld') makes clear that we are speaking, from the start, of more than physical sight. In the Fourth Gospel, many see Jesus with physical eyes but only believers truly see him. In fact, to see Jesus in this Gospel is to see God, since sight of the Johannine Father is through, and only through, the palpable presence of the Son (12:45; 14:7-9; 17:24). The invisible God is made visible in the Johannine Jesus (1:18; 5:37; 6:46), making possible the beatific vision in the here-and-now. Furthermore, Jesus' divine ability to see into the human heart in the Gospel narrative (1:48-49; 2:23-25; 4:18), beyond all concealment and pretension, is because theologically he is the one who has first, and uniquely, seen the Father (5:19; 6:46; 8:38). In Johannine Christology, the unique sight of the divine leads to prophetic insight into the human.

While there is a general and more mundane meaning for 'see' in John's Gospel, there is also a very specific and nuanced meaning which only the context can display. Beyond its common occurrence, vision has a strongly metaphorical usage throughout the narrative of the Fourth Gospel, in relation particularly to faith and discipleship. The linkage reflects common usage in the ancient world where 'an audience would not only think of blindness on the literal level—lacking eyesight—but ... would also likely think in metaphorical terms, that is lacking spiritual vision.'[11] For John, those who come to faith see in Jesus that divine life (3:36; 6:40) and glory (11:40) belonging to God. They see not just the son of Mary and Joseph (6:41-42) but also, in the language of John 6, the Bread from heaven (6:35, 48, 51); they see, in other words, the glory in the flesh,[12] that deeper reality which, without dismissal or denial, lies beneath the surface.

The metaphorical use of sight is apparent in the arrival of the Greeks, a seemingly small incident that has a disproportionate effect on Jesus (12:20). Towards the end of the first half of the Gospel, the desire of the Greeks to 'see Jesus' is most likely metaphorical for discipleship[13]—given that there is no mention of their appeal being met and Jesus' answer points to the deeper significance of their request. With Philip's announcement that these Gentiles desire to 'see' Jesus, Jesus recognises this as the arrival of the 'hour', the sign for which he has been waiting (12:23). Their wish to 'see' is clearly more than literal: their desire is for faith, for belonging among the 'we' who behold the glory in the flesh. Their movement towards faith signals to Jesus that, in the unsuspecting words of the Pharisees, 'the world has gone after him' (12:19). His mission of self-revelation is complete with the ingathering of the Gentiles, perhaps incorporating those 'sheep that are not of this fold' to which Jesus refers earlier in the Gospel (10:16). Now is the time for Jesus' mission to reach its climax in his lifting up on the cross.

Vision imagery is also closely allied to the core symbolism of light and illumination (1:9; 8:12; 9:5-7, 37), with its corresponding theme of unbelief expressed as blindness and darkness. Sight and light are connected in the closest way, both biologically and metaphorically.[14] Aristotle, for example, notes that 'the object of sight is the visible', which he sees as linked to colour and thus, by implication, light.[15] In John's account, human beings come to possess such sight, not by nature or their own capacities (1:12-13), but through a miracle of the Spirit (3:3-8). It is equally possible to see the Johannine 'signs' without perceiving their Christological meaning, a response that leads to rejection (e.g. 2:23; 4:48; 6:19, 27, 36; 9:41). In this sense, the crucified Jesus is the icon of salvation and judgement for all who turn their gaze upon him, whether in faith or unbelief: 'they will look on the one they have pierced' (19:37; Zech 12:10).

The exclamatory 'behold' (*ide, idou*) is part of the same dynamic in the Fourth Gospel, demonstrating the iconic nature of the Johannine Jesus.[16] Based on what he has seen at the baptism (1:32-34),[17] John the Baptist proclaims, 'Behold, the Lamb of God' (1:29, 36). Similarly, the evangelist declares at Jesus' entry into Jerusalem, 'Behold, your king comes', 12:15; Zech 9:9), a kingship that is tauntingly acclaimed by Pilate in the context of the trial ('Behold the man', 'behold your king', 19:5, 14; cf. 19:4).[18] The believing community possesses a similarly iconic quality, as apparent in several Johannine characters: 'Behold truly an Israelite in whom there is no guile' (1:37); 'Behold your son … behold your mother'(19:26-27).[19] These declarations invite the reader to behold not just Jesus himself, but central characters in the drama—particularly the mother of Jesus and the beloved disciple—who themselves take on an iconic quality in the Johannine worldview.

The use of sight imagery is fundamental to the life of the community beyond Easter, as evidenced particularly in the second half of the Gospel. The beloved disciple's faith-filled seeing is the basis for its future life and witness (19:35). Mission and spirituality, in the Johannine sense, can be summarised in the injunction, 'Come and see' (1:39, 46; 4:29; 12:21; cf. also 11:34). In the Farewell Discourse, John plays on sight imagery with the impending absence of Jesus; the disciples see and do not see, they will no longer see yet they will see, the seeing will be taken from them but then restored for ever (16:16-22). This sight is also projected into the past: Abraham, Isaiah and especially Moses have foreseen Jesus (8:56-57; 12:40; cf. 5:46).

In John's spirituality, it is gazing on the incarnate Christ that, in some sense, defines discipleship. Two Johannine texts are pertinent here. First, as we have noted, the unseen God is now seen in the shape and form of the incarnate Son. To gaze on the flesh of the divinely human Word is itself saving, for John, and it is the chief response of the community of faith, born from God, who bear witness to the incarnation. Believers see the glory and recognise it for what it is: 'we saw his glory, the glory of the Father's only Son, full of grace and truth' (1:14). Contemplating the flesh and perceiving the emitted glory, as we have seen, is a sign of discipleship for John, intrinsic to the Gospel's spirituality.[20] It is not for nothing that the tradition has sometimes perceived this statement as a perfect superscription to the Synoptic transfiguration story, a story that does not appear in the Johannine text—or, if so, only obliquely. There on the mountain-top, before the three disciples, Peter, James and John, the Synoptic Jesus is transfigured to reveal the 'glory in the flesh', his body and clothing radiating with divine splendour, the sign both of his future destiny and his sublime identity (Mk 9:2-8/pars.). There too the gaze of the disciples—for all their misunderstanding—is ultimately transfiguring for them.[21]

The second relevant text is the crucifixion. The climax of the Johannine symbols which cluster around this narrative is the flow of blood and water from the side of the crucified Christ (19:31-37). At the end of this scene, John refers to the unnamed (beloved) disciple as the witness who attests to these events and their inner meaning (19:35)— a meaning that finds its roots in the Old Testament. Two biblical quotations sum up John's point here, one referring to the wholeness of the paschal lamb and the other to the piercing of the side: 'None of his bones shall be broken' ... 'They will look on the one whom they have pierced' (19:36b, 37; Exod 12:46, Zech 12:10). It is the second quotation that is of significance here. Although it is unclear to whom, in John's interpretation, 'they' refers, and whether the two references point to the one group, it is probable that the very vagueness of John's quoting leaves open the possibilities. Whether it is the enemies of the Johannine Jesus who will gaze on the bleeding figure on the cross or whether it is disciples who are to gaze with love and faith, is unclear, and perhaps deliberately so. The same disciples who behold the glory in the flesh at 1:14 are among those who gaze on this icon of the incarnation: the crucified figure whose death is paradoxically the source of sacramental love and life.

In the closing chapters of the Gospel, seeing refers specifically to the signs surrounding the resurrection, which function as images of new life. Metaphorically, the disciples are in darkness after the crucifixion, unable to believe that Jesus' death is anything but the end of everything. Significantly, Mary Magdalene approaches the tomb immediately before dawn and peers into the darkness of the vault; what convinces her of grave robbers is the yawning mouth of the tomb, the rolling away of the heavy stone (20:1-2). Gradually, as the light of day dawns, Mary comes to see the risen Lord both physically and spiritually. Her sight needs renewal, conversion (perhaps that is why John mentions twice that she 'turns', 20:14, 16).[22] She needs to 'see' the emptiness of the tomb for what it is: the presence of life, the triumph over death, the coherence of transcendence and immanence. Only in the calling of her name does she perceive that the one who stands before her is the Good Shepherd (20:16), risen from the dead and unexpectedly present to her—even if in not quite the way she assumes. The folded linen-cloths, the numinous presence of angels, the wounds, the catch of fish, the charcoal fire—all these images point symbolically to the presence and power of the Johannine Jesus in the community beyond Easter (Jn 20-21). Without sight, none of the disciples comes to Easter faith and none grasps the Easter implications of Johannine spirituality. Mary Magdalene's testimony encapsulates this: 'I have seen the Lord' (20:18), a sight and a proclamation that the other disciples too are given (20:20, 25).

There is one Johannine text that seems to have a rather different perspective on seeing. To Thomas, after his confession of faith, Jesus pronounces a beatitude on those who are not in the fortunate position of the disciples immediately following the resurrection: those who 'have not seen and yet have believed' (20:29).[23] These blessed ones are the future generations of believers who do not have the same immediate access to the crucified Lord as Thomas, Mary Magdalene and the other disciples. Indeed, there is an unusual play on 'seeing' throughout John 20. The beloved disciple 'sees' the head-cloth inside the tomb and apparently believes (20:8)—yet in the next verse the narrator explains that he and Peter did not believe the Scriptures (20:9). Next, Mary Magdalene sees but does not at first 'see' Jesus; she mistakes him for the gardener and must 'hear' before she believes. Then Thomas refuses to believe until he sees for himself. Finally Jesus commends those who have not seen yet have believed. Is John in this chapter undermining the spirituality of previous imagery of 'seeing' as symbolic of faith?

The symbolism of John 20, however, needs to be read within its narrative context. The 'seeing' of the disciples in this chapter refers specifically to seeing the immediate signs of the resurrection, whether the folded grave-clothes or the risen Christ himself. Without sight of these, none of the disciples—not even the beloved disciple—can come to Easter faith. Jesus' last words to Thomas are to be read with the giving of the Spirit in mind, a scene that is the centre of this section of the Gospel (20:19-23), around which the episodes with Mary Magdalene (20:1-18) and Thomas (20:24-29) turn. Through the presence of the Spirit-Paraclete, future believers are dependent on the material vision of the apostolic community for their spirituality, gaining complete access to the 'seeing' of faith[24] Sight, therefore, is still a significant, spiritual metaphor for the fourth evangelist, even if in some sense it is also a mediated experience, based on the eyewitness testimony of the first disciples.

The implications of the sight imagery for John's understanding of discipleship are extensive. This kind of spirituality, as we saw in the first chapter, is both sacramental and iconic. The reality of life in Jesus is conveyed through matter and sight, through the contemplative gaze of faith. To be a disciple, in John's account, is not primarily about activity but repose, not chiefly about initiative and effort but about the wordless gaze of faith that directs itself to the flesh of God incarnate, offering life ironically through death. Painting and icon, therefore, become close comrades of the Johannine evangelist on this point. To see, to behold, to gaze upon, are metaphors for the imaginative sight that comes from reading or listening to the Gospel for those separated by time and distance from the Johannine Jesus. Here is John's sacramental spirituality once more; the apprehension that the contemplative soaring of the spirit on the eagle-wings of Johannine theology does not lose its grounding in the earth, in matter. It concerns the transformation of matter to become the vehicle of God's grace and glory.

The capacity for faith, for sight, is a miracle of God's re-creating in this Gospel. Flesh of itself, as we have observed several times, does not have the necessary wherewithal to perceive the divine glory revealed in the Johannine Jesus. The miracle which opens blind eyes is the gift of the one who is the Light of the world. As Psalm 36:9 puts it: 'in your light we see light'. Jesus in this Gospel illuminates the eyes of faith to enable disciples to see themselves aright and to see the presence of God in flesh and blood. Vision is the gift of light, the gift of sight, drawing people out of the darkness of ignorance, or the darkness of sin (for they are not the same in John's Gospel) into the light of life. Throughout the Johannine narrative, sight becomes a core symbol and the most prominent of the Johannine senses in frequency and import.

Hearing

The second most important sense is that of hearing (used in the verbal form, *akouô*).[25] According to Aristotle, hearing is linked to sound and breath just as vision is to colour and light.[26] As with the image of sight, hearing in the Fourth Gospel has a mundane as well as a metaphorical meaning. Its occurrences are less frequent and less complex than that of sight. The physical act of hearing does not guarantee faith or understanding, any more than sight does. However, to hear truly means to recognise the Word in the words; to know that in the Johannine Jesus we listen to the voice of God. The Johannine Jesus definitively hears the Father's voice and utters it (8:26, 40), so that to hear his words is to hear the words of God (14:24). The narrator allows us, as it were, to eavesdrop on the conversation between Father and Son, so that we too 'hear' the words promising the Son's glorification as he faces the cross (12:28). On the one occasion God actually speaks, those standing around do not hear it aright, in contrast to Jesus himself (12:29). This aural capacity distinguishes Jesus from all others: only he hears the Father's voice and the Father, in turn, hears the voice of the Son— even before utterance is made (11:41). The Spirit shares in the same dynamic communication, voicing only that divine truth which has first been heard (16:13).

We have already explored something of the power of Jesus' speech in this Gospel.[27] The appropriate response to that word is right hearing and the Gospel naturally gives emphasis to this theme, presenting several stories in which characters show their faith by listening attentively and faithfully. In these cases, hearing becomes another image for authentic faith. The Fourth Gospel has nothing like the Synoptic saying, 'Let anyone with ears to hear listen' (e.g. Mk 4:9, 23), yet there is an implied contrast between the hearing that is internal and leads to faith—the 'ears of the heart'—and the hearing that is external and results in indifference or even rejection. To hear means, for John, to recognize the Word (*logos*) in the words (*logoi*). This is the basis of discipleship: to hear aright, to recognise and to follow. In this sense, to hear in the true sense is to gain eternal life, since hearing is the sign that final judgement has taken place (5:24). The same heightened sense of hearing is evident from the beginning, above all in the testimony of John the Baptist who witnesses to Jesus, by word and by water, a testimony so vital in this Gospel that it is the source of faith for believers: 'that all might believe through him' (1:7). The baptism of Jesus—if indeed it is depicted as a baptism[28]—is the moment at which John recognises Jesus' identity, not through logical deduction but through divine revelation (1:29-34). John not only sees; he hearkens to the divine voice announcing the sign by which he will recognise Jesus as the Lamb of God, the bearer of the Spirit, the Son of God. As the friend of the bridegroom, he hears with joy the bridegroom's voice, happy to give way before him (3:29). John the Baptist is the primary human witness to the voice of God that speaks (3:31), his joyful listening becoming the source of the Church's life and faith, opening the door for Israel to greet its Lord. The first two disciples hear the testimony of the Baptist and follow Jesus (1:37, 40), just as the Baptist himself has heard the voice of the bridegroom (3:29).[29]

In the Cana to Cana cycle (2:1-4:54), the mother of Jesus exhorts the servants at the wedding, in effect, to hear the commands of her Son (2:5). The Samaritan villagers come to faith on the basis of hearing, not just the woman's words, but more importantly those of Jesus himself: 'we have heard for ourselves and we know that this is indeed the Saviour of the world' (4:42). They hear for themselves and believe (4:42). Hearing is associated in this context with knowing, the kind of knowing that is cognitive and relational—the heart-felt recognition of Jesus' true and universal identity which gives rise to faith. In the next episode the royal official, most likely a Gentile, is content to hear only the healing word of Jesus for his son to believe, returning home to find his faith confirmed (4:50-53).

In the next cycle, the Feasts of Judaism (5:1-10:42), in the context of Dedication, the sheep hear and recognise the voice of the one who has consecrated himself to God. As the Good Shepherd, he names them one-by-one (10:3, 27), while his knowing of them is matched by their recognition of his voice and naming. Their true identity as the flock belonging to his fold is indicated by their capacity to hear his voice and respond in faith and trust. To be a believer is to be among those who hear, in the voice of Jesus, the Father's voice. The sheep hear the voice of the Good Shepherd naming them (10:3, 27), just as Mary Magdalene hears the voice of the Shepherd calling her name on Easter Sunday (20:16); she hears and recognises the beloved voice and finds the transfigured presence which has eluded her (20:16).

Disciples are 'friends' of Jesus (*philoi*) because they have become privileged hearers of the Father's voice (15:15). Most dramatically of all, Lazarus hears the Word of life summoning him to return to life through the impenetrable walls of death, in that grim silence where no echo is heard (5:25, 28; 11:43-44). When Jesus arrives at Bethany it is to find Lazarus four days buried, lying in the tomb, dead beyond the possibility of recall, his body decomposing and his soul long departed. Even in that most silent of all places, the tomb, where no sound of earth can reach, the dead man miraculously hears the voice which alone penetrates the stone walls of his mortality. He hears, he rises to life, he emerges from the tomb, as the imperious voice of the Son of God summons him to life, still wrapped in the garments of death and burial (11:43-44). Earlier in the Gospel, speaking of his authority to give life and judgement, even on the sabbath—an exemption that only God possesses—the Johannine Jesus proclaims: 'Very truly, I tell you, the hour is coming, and is now here, when the dead will hear the voice of the Son of God, and those who hear will live' (5:25). This proclamation is hereby fulfilled, and Lazarus reveals his identity as one of the sheep of the Good Shepherd, hearkening to his voice and responding to it in trust.[30]

Not only do believers hear the words of the Word, but God also hears the words of believers and is attentive to their needs. The man born blind points this out, under interrogation by the authorities, as he reaches the conclusion that, far from being a sinner, Jesus must be 'from God' since God does not listen to sinners (9:31); and God has clearly listened to Jesus in bestowing the gift of the man's sight. Later, in the Farewell Discourse, the disciples are assured that God will give them whatever they ask: God will hear them and grant their requests (16:23-24, 26-27). The hearing, in other words, is two-way in this Gospel: God hears those who hear God and who recognise in Jesus the true and authentic divine voice.

There are times in the Johannine narrative when such divine hearing is not always apparent. God's ears seem on occasions rather deaf. Sometimes the Johannine Jesus hears and responds yet does not act as if he has heard—perhaps aware of other factors that those around him have not grasped (7:1-13). At other times, he hears well enough but does not respond in the way that the readers—and the characters who have supplicated him—expect. When Jesus hears of Lazarus' illness, as we have seen in other discussions,[31] he declares it to be (literally) 'not unto death' and promptly stays where he is for two days (11:4-6). As it transpires, everyone's expectations in the narrative are overturned: the disciples' (11:11-14), Martha's (11:17-27, 39), Mary's (11:32), and the mourners' (11:35-37). Yet this distance in hearing is more imagined than real. Jesus does respond, though with a timing and a method not always comprehensible to human beings, even those of faith. Despite appearances to the contrary, the evangelist seems to be saying, God does hearken to the cry of faith and will, in God's own time, respond in a way that exceeds human expectations.

Hearing has also an implicitly trinitarian dimension that undergirds all the other aspects of this image. The Son is the one who speaks what he hears from the Father (5:30; 8:40, 47)—an active hearing that authenticates his testimony. He is the Father's Word, yet that function is dependent entirely on his capacity to hear. It is also mutual, since the Father hears the Son just as the Son hears the Father; indeed, the ears of both Father and Son are perpetually attuned to one another: 'Father, I thank you for having heard me,' Jesus prays at the tomb of Lazarus, 'I knew that you always hear me ...' (11:41-42a); to the disciples he says, 'I have made known to you everything I have heard from my Father' (15:15). The Spirit too declares only what has been given by Jesus and the Father, only what has been heard; the Spirit participates in that divine circle in which each is alert to the living voice of the other. Hearing, then, is a mark of the divine realm, but is also characteristic of the community of believers whose faithful hearing opens them to a share in the celestial realm.

Elsewhere, John speaks in synonymous language of keeping Jesus' words or commands (*têreô*).[32] This is another image for hearing but in the sense of hearkening to (12:47; 14:15, 23; 17:6), as demonstrated by the Johannine Jesus himself (8:55; 15:10). In this sense, faith can be described as 'hearing the voice or the words of Jesus ..., in the sense of "obeying'... an inward hearing ...'[33] It is possible to hear and not believe (12:47), to listen to the words but not keep them. Hearing is associated with truth: for the reader, to hear aright is to recognise the voice of Jesus as the definitive utterance of God and to find a new identity in belonging to the truth (18:37). To be a believer in this Gospel is to stand among those who hear, in the Johannine Jesus and the Paraclete, the Father's voice and keep it. Audition is fundamental to the life of faith in this Gospel.

Taste

Sight and hearing are the two main senses that serve, metaphorically, to depict what it means to have faith in this Gospel. The other senses are also represented in the Johannine text, including that of taste, although explicit language is infrequent and often implied. One of the psalms encourages the reader to 'taste and see that the Lord is good' (Ps 34:8). John does not quote this verse, but its spirit pervades the Gospel in respect to both taste and sight. Disciples in the Fourth Gospel are called to taste God's goodness, a goodness revealed in Jesus himself. John makes two explicit references to tasting (the verb is *geuomai*,

2:9; 8:52) but the imagery is implicit elsewhere.[34] The symbolism goes back to the first 'sign' at Cana, a wedding banquet (2:1-11), where the bewildered steward is the first to taste 'the water made wine' (2:9). The provenance of this imagery in the prophetic literature of the Old Testament suggests the messianic banquet of the end-time where the sumptuous feast flows with the best wines (Amos 9:13; Joel 3:18; Hos 2:21-22; Isa 25:6). There are also overtones of Wisdom as hostess who summons people to her banquet: 'Come, eat of my bread and drink of the wine I have mixed. Lay aside immaturity, and live, and walk in the way of insight' (Prov 9:5-6). Already the imagery of wine operates metaphorically to suggest God's provision in the future and God's way of wisdom in the present. The steward who 'tastes' the wine exclaims at its excellence and the unusual style of hospitality in serving good quality wine when the guests—though obviously not the steward himself—have lost something of their powers of discernment. What the steward tastes is, in effect, the 'goodness of the Lord', revealed in the incarnate Son whose divine glory is manifest in the 'sign' (2:11).

Elsewhere John uses imagery of food and drink as symbolic of the revelation. Jesus offers the Samaritan woman 'living water' (4:10-14) to quench her thirst for life, and promises an internal fountain of water as a lasting gift (4:14), the same stream that will flow, at the crucifixion, from the wounded side of Jesus himself (19:37). The Johannine Jesus hungers and thirsts, while also giving food and drink: he is tired and thirsty at the well (4:6-7); at Tabernacles he summons the thirsty to quench their thirst in him (7:37-39), employing images of both Wisdom and the Spirit. As the hostility and misunderstanding escalate at the feast of Tabernacles, Jesus' opponents accuse him scathingly of claiming, 'if anyone keeps my word, they will never ever taste death', despite the deaths of Abraham and the prophets ('if anyone keeps my word, they will never taste death', 8:52). Jesus' actual words are, 'they will never see death' (8:51), yet the two are parallel: sight and taste, vision and gustation, both express, in their own ways, access to the deathless life which the Johannine Jesus bestows.[35] After the raising of Lazarus, Jesus reclines at table with the Bethany family, sharing in the banquet (12:1-8), as Jesus does with the other disciples at the Last Supper (13:1ff.). To taste is a vivid metaphor for faith and for the abundant life that Jesus offers the believer, a metaphor based on the human need for sustenance. In the same way, the water that Jesus supplies gives life eternal. The alternative, in this Gospel, is spiritual and eternal death, just as human beings die physically without material food and drink.

The most powerful example of tasting imagery is in the dialogue following the feeding of the five thousand, where eating and drinking are not just optional but essential for the life of faith (6:1-71). The biblical context is that of the manna in the wilderness expressing God's providence for the people of Israel, as symbolic of the bread that Jesus gives, the bread from heaven. As the dialogue progresses and Jesus' interlocutors become more and more alienated, the revelation intensifies (6:41-65). The wider Passover setting (6:4) suggests also the paschal lamb, eaten at the Passover celebration in commemoration of God's deliverance (6:53-58).[36] Both the manna and the lamb are symbols not just of the new thing that Jesus brings, but more radically of the Johannine Jesus himself. He is the true bread from heaven whose imperishable (risen) flesh sustains eternal life, just as perishable food sustains physical life. In John's crucifixion story the theme of Passover runs beneath the narrative, explaining the ironical piety of Jesus' opponents and the dating of Jesus' death at the hour of slaughter of the paschal lambs. This confirms John the Baptist's testimony at the beginning of the Gospel (1:34). Jesus' side is not pierced, in order that his self-offering to the Father may be unbroken, undefiled, as is the offering of the paschal lamb (19:36-37). In both images, the bread and the lamb, the deeper truth is that these images symbolise Jesus himself. Paradoxically, the food which believers must taste to gain eternal life is Jesus, the Bread of heaven and Lamb of God. The material becomes symbolic of the eternal; the material is itself the medium for the eternal. The eating and drinking refer symbolically to feeding on Jesus by faith, tasting his life, his very self which overcomes death and bestows eternal life. Once again, the symbolism points to faith— and to a faith that is nourished by the ongoing, sacramental life of the believing community.

Note also Jesus' own readiness to taste that which belongs to the human condition. In opening the conversation with the woman of Samaria, he asks for a drink of water even though 'Jews do not share things in common with Samaritans' (4:9). That is, he is prepared to drink from the woman's water jar, rendering himself unclean. It is precisely this willingness to taste the Samaritan's water that enables her to recognise and taste his. Perhaps it is not stretching the metaphor too far to see in the incarnation God's readiness to 'taste' human experience, to enter the human condition and partake of human life so that human beings may taste God's divine life; here taste can be used as metaphorical, not just of faith, but of the incarnation. In John's Gospel, Jesus' hunger and thirst operate not only biologically but also metaphorically, especially in his passionate commitment to the Father's will (4:31-34), attested to in the Scriptures—a commitment that finally devours him ('zeal for your house will consume me', 2:17). In the Passion, Jesus confirms his intention (unlike Simon Peter) of drinking the Father's cup (18:11). At the crucifixion, this metaphorical thirst for the divine will is uttered and 'quenched' in Jesus' last words, closely connected in meaning as well as time: 'I thirst … it is finished' (19:27-28). The raging thirst heralding the imminence of death becomes metaphorical for the driving passion which takes the Johannine Jesus to the cross.

Touch

The sense of touch or somatic feeling is different from vision and hearing (and smell), as we have noted, because it implies contact and cannot be perceived from a distance, the same being true for taste: 'the medium of the tangible is flesh'.[37] This factor suggests a certain intimacy to the sense of touch, a closeness and directness that can imply anything from the deepest intimacy to the harshest tactile acts of repulsion and violence.[38] References to touch are less numerous in John than imagery of tasting, the verb occurring only once in the Gospel (*haptomai*, 20:17).[39] Yet there are several occasions where images of touch, in different language, take on symbolic value in the narrative of the Fourth Gospel. Christologically, John uses the striking metaphor of the Father giving all things into the Son's hands (3:35;

13:3), a metaphor that encapsulates the agency of the Johannine Jesus and the unique role he plays in bridging the gulf between Creator and creation. As a consequence, believers can never be taken from the Son's—and therefore the Father's—hands (10:28-29). The handing over of all things to the Son includes the community of faith, who are protected even in the midst of persecution because they are secure in the hands of the Good Shepherd, a hold that is stronger than death.

Touching is figurative for faith, either as the expression of believing or for the purposes of enabling belief. Mary of Bethany is the best exemplar of this first kind of touch. The sensuous description of her anointing of Jesus' feet with oil and wiping them dry with her unbound hair signifies, by this symbolic action, faith and gratitude to Jesus for the gift of her brother's life. More than that, it depicts the costliness of her faith matching the costliness of Jesus' action in rising Lazarus to life (11:45-57). Mary's unconventional touch, her loose hair in the context of the banquet, and the profligacy of the oil—as Judas' objection makes plain (12:5)—all serve to articulate faith in Jesus and love for him, a love that reciprocates his love for her. Touch is the means by which she expresses, in vivid and sensuous terms, belief in the one who has embraced flesh for the sake of flesh. Her action corresponds to the costliness of Jesus' dangerous and subversive act in raising her brother to life (11:45-57). Mary's unconventional touch of Jesus' feet articulates the reciprocity of love in this Gospel. It also foreshadows the footwashing where Jesus touches the feet of his disciples at the Last Supper, a ritual and symbolic expression of union in his death, indicating both intimacy and service (13:8).[40]

The imagery of touch can also be used in a hostile fashion, indicating the desire of the *kosmos* to overpower the light (1:5). In the section that circles around the 'feasts of the Jews', Jesus' opponents attempt to lay hands upon him (7:30, 44; 10:39) but are unable to do so without divine consent; there is a celestial timing to which they are unwittingly subject. On trial, Jesus is struck by the hands of both the high priest's servants and the Roman soldiers (18:22-23; 19:3). These blows are abusive and taunting, indicating the voluntary subjection of Jesus to 'the ruler of the world' (14:30; 16:11), a subjection that ironically spells the latter's ultimate end. The paradox is that the Johannine Jesus gives himself into the hands of the world in order that all things might be given over into his hands.

If we can speak of the incarnation in the Fourth Gospel as God's readiness to taste the human condition, we can speak in parallel terms of God's touch. The God of this Gospel makes contact with flesh and blood in a radical sense, joined intimately to humanity. That incarnate touch is apparent in the footwashing where Jesus touches the feet of his disciples at the Last Supper, his final symbolic act before his arrest and death (13:1-20). The footwashing is often interpreted as an act of lowly servitude, as we have observed already,[41] where Jesus plays the role of the slave, to the horror and dismay of the disciples, giving them an example of lowly service to the world. Yet the footwashing is primarily about the intimacy of union with the Johannine Jesus, sharing in his sacrificial death: 'unless I wash you, you have no share with me' (13:8). The real act of humble service is the cross, the extension of the incarnation, and the result of this act is the union of believers with Jesus. The ritual aspects have priority in the footwashing, because the one who embodies the temple of God's glory—the one whose own feet have been 'washed' by Mary of Bethany—prepares his disciples, ritually and symbolically, for his death: 'having loved his own who were in the world, he loved them to the end' (13:1b). What follows for the community is their comparable love for one another, embodied in the ritual act of footwashing, expressing the love and faith into which they are drawn and which they share with one another (13:12-15).

The fact that such humble and loving touch is life-giving is already apparent in the Gospel in the story of the man born blind. The important point here is the manner of the man's healing. Using his own spittle and mixing it with soil, the Johannine Jesus anoints the man's eyes with the paste, instructing him to wash in the Pool of Siloam, the Pool that the evangelist informs us means 'Sent' (9:6-7; 15). It has long been noted that the man's eyesight is not restored but created, since he is born blind; significantly, Jesus uses the dust of the ground, the material from which Adam was made (Gen 2:7). The spittle, holding like blood the essence of life, the dust, the physical touch, and the water of the

Pool, work together as primal elements to give the man a sight he has never possessed. This is the only healing story in John's Gospel where Jesus uses touch (unlike the Synoptics—cf. Mk 1:31; 5:29, 41). In the end the man is brought to faith, his life as well as his eyes illumined, because he is able to perceive the spiritual and theological implications of Jesus' healing touch.

Finally, the resurrection narratives make reference to touch, although the imagery is ambiguous, somewhat akin to that of sight. John 20 can be confusing for the reader at a number of levels. In this context, why is the believing Mary Magdalene told not to touch the risen Christ, while the unbelieving Thomas is invited to touch the wounds (20:17a, 27)? The wording in each case is different, however, and only on the first occasion is the verb 'touch' used. The full force of the present tense of the imperative (*mê mou haptou*, 20:17), as we saw in the previous chapter, suggests that Jesus is not so much forbidding Mary's touch as instructing her not to hold on. In that case, the quality of her touch would indicate a degree of misunderstanding on her part: that Jesus has returned for ever in this guise. The explanation that follows makes it clear that Jesus' 'ascending'—John's imagery for the entire event of cross, resurrection and ascension into heaven—is incomplete. He will indeed remain with her, but until his final coming that presence will be through the Spirit-Paraclete which he is about to bestow (20:19-23). Touch here becomes symbolic of a faith that is still developing, still partial, yet a faith that is set on the right path and will finally reach fruition.

Jesus' invitation to Thomas to touch is of a different quality. The language, if anything, is more direct and shocking: 'Thrust your finger here [literally] … 'Reach out your hand and thrust it in my side' (20:27). The narrative does not record whether Thomas does touch, and we may well assume he does not, at least in the mind of the narrator. Without hesitation, Thomas quickly exclaims, in a climatic confession of faith, 'My Lord and my God' (20:28). In the end, the hearing and seeing seem to be enough for him though, as Jesus points out, future disciples will not be so fortunate (20:29).[42] The imagery of touch is important, nonetheless, for it stresses the tangible reality of Jesus' risen presence and the ongoing presence of the wounds, testimony to the incarnation and the cross in this Gospel. Though the community of future believers will not literally see, hear or touch, they will possess the same quality of contact with Jesus in the sacramental life of the community. Johannine spirituality, even in the absence of the Risen One, remains fleshly and tangible: to touch, as to see, hear and taste, remain vivid metaphors for the life of faith, made visible in the sacraments and in the love that flows among believers.

Smell

The last sense, that of smell, would seem at first glance to be the least significant of the five senses in the Gospel of John. Perhaps because we are least aware of the sense of smell in general and its impact on us, we easily ignore its presence in the Johannine narrative. While the verb 'smell' occurs only once in the Gospel (*odzô*, 11:39, along with the noun, 'odour', *osmê*, 12:3), there are two distinct references to olfaction. These are interconnected in different narrative contexts where the evangelist evokes a similar vivid contrast between the stench of death and the fragrance of life. Smell functions metaphorically as a symbol for both life and death, and John uses it to underscore the tangibility, not only of human mortality, but also of eternal life. This perpetual fragrance draws believers figuratively to faith, as they are drawn on a material level to pleasant odours: flowers, fruits, spices, perfumes.

The first and most explicit references to smell occur in the story of the raising of Lazarus, which we have already examined for its imagery of touch. The narrative incorporates the anointing at Bethany (11:1-12:11),[43] mentioned first at the beginning of the story as if it has already taken place (11:2)—a narrative device to drawn the anointing into the Lazarus story, which is of direct relevance to the imagery of smell.[44] Despite her earlier declaration (11:27), Martha's faith wavers at the mouth of the tomb, the stench of death overwhelming her: 'Lord, already there is a stench because he has been dead for four days' (11:39). Martha smells only decomposition and decay, not understanding the reason Jesus boldly confronts it. Perhaps she assumes, like the mourners, that he wishes to pay his last respects to his deceased friend. In any case, she perceives only death and cannot comprehend what it means when the one who is 'resurrection and life' stands face-to-face with death. The deathly stench invades her nostrils with hopelessness and despair, at least for the present (though earlier she demonstrates belief in the resurrection of the dead, 11:24). But Jesus puts an end to death and its malodorous smell, calling Lazarus from the dead to the living, from decay to growth and life. He alone can eradicate the terrifying stink of the grave.

In the scene that follows the plot to kill Jesus, there is a further reference to smell that stands in contrast to the scenario at Lazarus' tomb (12:1-8). At the banquet given in honour of Jesus and in gratitude for the restoration of Lazarus to life, Mary anoints Jesus' feet with perfumed myrrh (12:1-8). We have already recognised the sensuality of this story in relation to touch; but it is equally important for its emphasis on smell. In contrast to the tomb, the home of the Bethany family is flooded with the scent of life, the odour of the myrrh: 'The house was filled with the fragrance of the perfume' (12:3).[45] The contrast is not accidental. Just as, at the open tomb, Martha recoils from the smell of death, now her home is drenched with the scent of perfume poured liberally over Jesus' feet. The smell, heavy and sensuous, wafts through the house like incense, enduring for days as such perfumes will. In place of the stench of death is the odour of life, a life exemplified in Lazarus himself but having its source in the Johannine Jesus who embodies in himself the odour of life, a life that transcends death. The fine scent has the last say, after all, not the rotting smell from which Martha shrinks.

Yet Mary's myrrh, and the faith that inspires it, is not simply about life in opposition to death. Jesus explicitly relates the myrrh to his own death and burial (12:7).[46] In this Gospel, Jesus is the resurrection and the life but he offers it by way of his death, surrendering his life to give life. Whether Mary perceives the full implications of her action is not clear in the text, although Jesus seems to imply her awareness of his impending death. But probably that awareness, at this stage, goes no further. John retains the Synoptic tradition of the myrrh-bearing women, but places it here in the few days before Jesus' death rather than after the crucifixion (Mark 16:1).[47] Nevertheless, for John, the odour of life is bought at a price, just like Mary's myrrh. All this is implied in the story of the anointing, though only later is its full meaning unveiled.

The second reference to smell is in the Passion and resurrection narratives. Although John does not refer to the stench of crucifixion, the author presupposes such knowledge, along with other details of Jesus' suffering. Death by crucifixion involves the evacuation of the body, and the stench of such a death is only one part of its horrors. In the burial narrative, by contrast, Jesus' body is embalmed in the powerful and invigorating aroma of the myrrh and aloes, prepared by Joseph of Arimathea and Nicodemus (19:38-42). We tend to note the sheer weight of the spices prepared by Joseph of Arimathea and Nicodemus for Jesus' burial (19:38-42). Yet the distinctive and powerful odour of the myrrh and aloes should not be forgotten as we imaginatively enter the scene. This body does not decay as does Lazarus'. On the contrary, its short sojourn in the tomb and the fragrant spices which embalm it ensure no ugly stench. Although Joseph and Nicodemus do not imagine that Jesus will rise from the dead (in company with the other disciples), the kingly burial they offer Jesus, both in the quantity and the rich scent of the spices, is the expression of their faith, limited though it may be. Indeed, the mode of burial points forward to the Easter garden (18:1, 26; 19:41), the fragrance of Spring and new-blossoming flowers and herbs.[48] In this place of aromatic odours, another disciple, Mary Magdalene, discovers new life in the unexpected presence of the 'gardener' (20:15). Here again the stench of death is overcome by the odour of life, a life whose perfume never fades. Thus, in two contexts, olfaction functions in the Fourth Gospel as symbolic for both life and death, where the evangelist underscores the tangible reality not only of human mortality but also, and more portentously, of life.

Conclusion

The five senses capture the embodied dimensions of the human existence that is aware of the diversity of experience as it bears upon our human lives. Through the senses we apprehend the world around

Illustration 6: Raphael, Crucifixion 1502-1503. Oil on panel.
National Gallery, London, UK

Raphael's Crucifixion above has a number of distinctly Johannine features. The two angels on either side, each with a chalice— one foot delicately perched on a wisp of cloud—underlines the sacramentality of this scene, the blood representing the eucharistic cup. The colours are bright, the sky a deep blue (the two suns at the top connoting the Synoptic eclipse), and the gold hue of Christ's body capturing something of the Johannine glory of the event. Most significant for us are the two kneeling figures at the foot of the cross: the mother of Jesus and the beloved disciple. Both gaze rapturously at the figure of the crucified Christ, reflecting the testimony of 19:35 and the gaze in faith on 'the one whom they have pierced'. The other two figures, both female, are presumably Mary Magdalene and another of the women at the foot of the cross (19:25).[49] The fact that their gaze is not on the Crucified One but on the two kneeling figures is suggestive, turning the viewer's attention to their reverent stance and inviting him or her to share the same devout gaze, the same mystic beholding beneath the cross.[50]

us, the people who are important to us, and the things which give meaning. Judith Wright expresses this awareness in her poem 'Five Senses':

> Now my five senses
> gather into a meaning
> all acts, all presences;
> and as a lily gathers
> the elements together,
> in me this dark and shining,
> that stillness and that moving,
> these shapes that spring from nothing,
> become a rhythm that dances,
> a pure design.
>
> While I'm in my five senses
> they send me spinning
> all sounds and silences,
> all shape and colour
> as thread for that weaver,
> whose web within me growing
> follows beyond my knowing
> some pattern sprung from nothing—
> a rhythm that dances
> and is not mine.[51]

The poem offers a vivid portrayal of the role of the senses in our apprehension and appreciation of reality: both as a totality and in its variegated dimensions. In the second stanza, it concludes with an understated but nonetheless spiritual consciousness of the senses as something given or bestowed, something that is not ours in origin but comes from beyond ourselves.

The fourth Gospel uses the five senses to signify the vividness of human existence and its metaphorical import for understanding spirituality. John employs the senses in the narrative as images pertaining to faith; they represent that material comprehension by which the reader makes connection to the divine source of life. To grasp this spiritual reality, the evangelist makes use of metaphor and symbol, making tangible the message of life that the Gospel enacts, since the transcendent God in the Johannine framework can only be perceived and apprehended through such imagery (3:12).[52] Here the five senses operate symbolically to point to a deeper reality.[53]

Such apprehension requires, first and foremost, a transformation in the reader's imagination. As James Alison points out, in John's Gospel the implied reader does not possess this ability naturally, because his or her reason, education and thus imagination 'are marked by death and its consequences.'[54] What is called for in this Gospel, he argues, is the new imagining of a God 'who does not know death' and who reveals to the religious authorities that 'the secret of [their] satanized god is death'.[55] It is the focus on imagination that is important here: the imagination that conceives of life within and beyond death and all forms of death-dealing, not just at the end of life but in its midst. Although this is not precisely the language of the fourth evangelist, it is synonymous with what the Fourth Gospel means when it speaks of eternal life as the consequence of believing in Jesus as the divinely-human Son: 'in order that, in believing, you may have life in his name' (20:31). The senses thus work on two levels, the material and the symbolic, through appeal to the imagination.[56] Though separated by time and distance from the characters of the Gospel, the reader gains access to the same symbolic imagining and therefore the same reality through the literal and material apprehension of the Johannine narrative.[57] The text—its plot, characters and imagery, including its focus on the five senses— becomes the symbolic medium which donates new life to the implied reader of the Gospel.[58]

John's attention to the five senses underlines the centrality of the incarnation as the basis of Johannine spirituality; to employ the opening words of the first Johannine epistle, 'that which was from the beginning, which we have heard, which we have seen with our own eyes, which we have beheld and our hands have handles ... that which we have seen and heard'. This pronouncement, whatever its precise meaning in the epistle, can serve to encapsulate the sensuous dynamic of the Gospel itself (1 Jn 1:1).[59] The words of God in the past—creative, dynamic, saving—now resolve themselves into the one Word, Jesus

Christ. This utterance, for the Fourth Gospel, becomes the centre, so that the reader looks back at the words of God in the past from the vantage-point of the Logos, to whom the senses of believers are now attuned.[60] That is why John describes the community as 'beholding' the glory of God in the flesh.[61] The God who is invisible, beyond human ken ('no-one has ever seen God', 1:18), is the same God in the Fourth Gospel whose glory is seen, heard, tasted, touched, and smelt, not just in epiphany and temple, Torah, holy Wisdom and prophets, but more completely in the Word made flesh.[62] Augustine says of the risen Christ in his resurrection appearances: 'Because he was seeking the inner sense of faith, he presented himself also to their outer senses.'[63] For the fourth evangelist, the incarnation, in and through the resurrection, evokes not only the self-revealing of the Johannine God but also the dynamism inherent in creation and the possibilities of new life in the unceasing (re-)creativity of God. The incarnation expresses the hope of flesh revived in a palpability that death cannot annihilate. In short, the five senses of vision, audition, gustation, feeling and olfaction are roused in the Gospel narrative, enabling the reader to grasp the incarnational texture of salvation through imagination. In this sense, Johannine spirituality is tied inextricably to Johannine Christology: matter to matter, spirit to spirit, the one giving rise to the other within the Fourth Gospel's sensuous and symbolic worldview.

The fourth evangelist uses the five senses to image faith in the spiritual lives of believers. Through the symbolism of sight, hearing, taste, touch and smell, the reader can enter imaginatively the world of the text and find new impetus for faith and a transfigured life, grounded in the identity of the Johannine Jesus and his self-revelation. John's incarnational theology stresses the manifestation of God through the body and images of the body. In this sense, the reader apprehends the meaning of the incarnation—divine glory unveiled in mortal flesh—and appreciates that spirituality as fleshly, carnal, grounded, communicating the other world through the medium of this world: through the senses and the imagination, through body as well as soul. This kind of spirituality sees the body, not as incidental but essential, the means of redemption: the salvation of flesh by flesh. John's spirituality is an embodied one, uniting body and soul, matter and spirit, established by the movement of God to embrace mortal flesh in the Johannine Jesus.

End Notes

1. For an outline of recent scholarship on imagery in the Gospel of John, see Ruben Zimmermann, 'Imagery in John. Opening up Paths into the Tangled Thicket of John's Figurative World,' in *Imagery in the Gospel of John. Terms, Forms, Themes, and Theology of Johannine Figurative Language*, ed. J. Frey, Van der Watt, J.G., Zimmermann, R., *WUNT 200* (Tübingen: Mohr Siebeck, 2006), 76-79.

2. A shorter version of this chapter, 'The Gospel of John and the Five Senses', is published in *JBL* 129 (2010), pp 115-127.

3. For an understanding of this subject in the ancient world, see Aristotle's extended discussion of the five senses: *De Anima* II.v-xii, in W.S. Hett, ed. *Aristotle—on the Soul,* Loeb Classical Library (London: Heinemann,1957), 94-139.

4. Augustine, in his exegesis of the 'five oxen' in Luke 14:19, interprets them in relation to the five senses, identifying each as pairs: two eyes, two ears, two nostrils, tongue and palate, outer and inner touch: Sermon III/4, E. Hill, ed. *The Works of Saint Augustine: A Translation for the 21st Century* (New York: New City Press,1992), 112.3-7.

5. Maya Pines, 'More Than the Sum of Its Parts', Part 4 in 'Seeing, Hearing and Smelling the World', Howard Hughes Medical Institute, http://www. hhmi.org/senses/a110.html.

6. It is well-known that people with sensory disabilities often intensify the remaining senses to compensate for the one or more missing. The remarkable story of Helen Keller, born blind and deaf, demonstrates the compensating use of touch that liberated her from a world of inner darkness and silence (*The Story of My Life* [New York: Modern Library, 2003]).

7. David Lindberg, *Theories of Vision from Al-Kindi to Kepler* (Chicago: Chicago University Press, 1976), 1.

8. See John J. Medina, *Brain Rules. Twelve Principles* (Seattle: Pear Press, 2008), 221-240.

9. Chad Hartsock, *Sight and Blindness in Luke-Acts: The Use of Physical Features in Characterization* (Leiden: Brill, 2008), 60. Mikeal C. Parsons speaks of a 'physiognomic consciousness' that pervaded the ancient world *Body and Character in Luke and Acts: The Subversion of Physiognomy in Early Christianity* [Grand Rapids: Baker Academic Press, 2006], 76-79), and describes 'the connection of the eye to moral character' in several ancient texts, including Cicero (77).

[10.] There is no single word for 'see/sight' in the Greek of John's Gospel. Several synonymous verbs are used (*horaô, theôreô, theaomai, blepô, emblepô*; also *anablepô*) with meanings that, in most cases, can only be distinguished in their specific linguistic context. Verbs associated with vision occur more than 130 times in the Fourth Gospel. The noun *eidos* also appears ('sight', 5:37).

[11.] Hartsock, *Sight and Blindness*, 53.

[12.] On the symbiotic relationship between 'flesh' and 'glory' in the Fourth Gospel, see Dorothy Lee, *Flesh and Glory: Symbol, Gender and Theology in the Gospel of John* (New York: Crossroad, 2002), 29-64.

[13.] So, for example, Raymond E. Brown, *The Gospel According to John*, 2 vols., Anchor Bible 29-29a (Garden City, New York: Doubleday, 1966), 1:466, Xavier Léon-Dufour, *Lecture de l'evangile selon Jean*, 3 vols., Parole De Dieu (Paris: Editions du Seuil, 1988, 1990, 1993), 2:459, and Francis J. Moloney, *The Gospel of John*, Sacra Pagina 4 (Collegeville, MN: The Liturgical Press, 1998), 359. On the other hand, C.K. Barrett, *The Gospel According to St John. An Introduction with Commentary and Notes on the Greek Text*, 2nd ed. (London: SPCK, 1978), 422, argues that 'to see' (*horaô*) here only means the request for an interview.

[14.] The close link may be explained by extramission theories of vision, common in the ancient world and Judaism, in which light emanates from the eye itself (as against intromission, where rays of light enter the eye along with visible objects, a theory also found in the ancient world). Further on debate in the ancient Greek world on vision, see H.D. Betz, 'Matthew vi.22f and Ancient Greek Theories of Vision' in *Text and Interpretation. Studies in the New Testament Presented to Matthew Black* (Cambridge: Cambridge University Press, 1979), 46-64, D.C. Allison, 'The Eye Is the Lamp of the Body (Matthew 6:22-23=Luke 11:34-36),' NTS 33 (1987): 62-66 and Parsons, *Body and Character*, 67-82.

[15.] *De Anima* II.vii.

[16.] The form occurs some twenty times in the Fourth Gospel. Unfortunately, it is obscured in the NRSV, which substitutes 'here is' (1:29; 1:47; 3:26; 7:26; 19:5, 14, 26-27) and on occasions uses 'look!' (1:36; 4:35; 12:15, 19; 19:4), 'see!' (5:14; 11:36; cf. 20:27) or 'yes' (16:29)—and sometimes fails to translate it at all (11:3; 16:32).

[17.] The sight imagery comes to a climax at the end of the chapter in Jesus' words to Nathanael and the other disciples, 'You will see greater things that these ... you will see the heavens opened ...' (*opse(i), opsesthe*, 1:50-51).

[18.] The taunts are most plausibly directed at the Jewish authorities ('the Jews') in the trial narrative, rather than at Jesus himself; see Warren Carter, *John and Empire: Initial Explorations* (New York/London: T & T Clark,

2008), 289-314, who rightly reads the character of Pilate—and the Roman imperial system which he represents—as violently opposed to the Johannine Jesus and everything for which he stands in the Gospel.

[19.] It is true that, in several occurrences of this verbal usage, there is no distinctly iconic quality in John, though some references (e.g. 5:14) may have potentially iconic overtones.

[20.] See above, chapter 5.

[21.] Dorothy Lee, *Transfiguration* (London/New York: Continuum, 2004).

[22.] Further on this motif, see Dorothy Lee, 'Turning from Death to Life, A Biblical Reflection on Mary Magdalene (John 20:1-18)' *Ecumenical Review* 50 (1998), 112-20.

[23.] Dorothy Lee, 'Partnership in Easter Faith: The Role of Mary Magdalene and Thomas in John 20,' *JSNT* 58 (1995): 37-49.

[24.] Richard Bauckham, *Jesus and the Eyewitnesses. The Gospels as Eyewitness Testimony* (Grand Rapids, Michigan/Cambridge, UK: Eerdmans, 2006), 403-6, argues that the language of 'sight' in the Fourth Gospel is the language also of the eyewitnesses, for whom there is both a literal and metaphorical perception; if so, it has important implications for what he sees as the ancient world's preference for eyewitness 'seeing' (114-54).

[25.] The verb, without direct synonyms, occurs in John over fifty times; W. Michaelis, '*horaô* et al.', *TDNT* V, 316.

[26.] Aristotle, *De Anima* II.viii.

[27.] See above, chapter 1.

[28.] Unlike the Synoptics, it is not clear in John's Gospel whether Jesus is actually baptized by John the Baptist. One possibility is that the fourth evangelist finds the story too embarrassing and difficult. But it is also possible that John assumes his readers know the story, just as he assumes knowledge of other details (e.g. characters such as the mother of Jesus); so Barrett, *St John*, 177-78.

[29.] On the evangelist's use of the bridegroom imagery, particularly in relation to John the Baptist, see Mary L. Coloe, 'Witness and Friend. Symbolism Associated with John the Baptist,' in Frey et al., *Imagery in the Gospel of John*, 319-22.

[30.] It is perhaps ironical that Simon Peter cuts off the ear of the high priest's slave, Malchus (18:10). Peter is one who has heard and yet, in another sense, has not heard Jesus' true identity. He is rebuked for his inability, unlike Jesus, to hear the divine voice and accept the Father's will (18:11).

[31.] See above, especially chapter 4.

[32.] The verb occurs, mostly in the Farewell Discourse, some twenty times with distinct christological overtones.

33. Rudolf Schnackenburg, *The Gospel According to St John*, 3 vols. (New York: Seabury (vols 1-2) Crossroad [vol 3], 1980 & 1982), 1:564 Excursus VII.

34. There are more than thirty references to taste, including eating and drinking, in the Fourth Gospel. Note that Aristotle, who argues that taste has no actual medium, observes that it requires liquid and is concerned with flavour; *De Anima* II.x.

35. On hunger and thirst as expressions of Johannine anthropology, see especially Craig Koester, 'What Does It Mean to Be Human? Imagery and the Human Condition in John's Gospel,' in Frey et al., *Imagery in the Gospel of John*, 409-14.

36. See Dorothy Lee, 'Paschal Imagery in the Gospel of John: A Narrative and Symbolic Reading,' *Pacifica* 24 (2011), 13-28.

37. Aristotle, *De Anima* II.xi.423.

38. Leucippus, the pre-Socratic atomist philosopher, is credited with the saying, 'all the senses are a variety of touch'; see Allison, 'Eye Is the Lamp,' 63.

39. There are also about thirty references to touch in relation to fingers, hands and feet.

40. See Lee, *Flesh and Glory*, 197-211.

41. See above, chapter 5.

42. Literally, 'thrust' (*ballō*); Thomas also speaks of needing to see 'with my hands' (20:25).

43. Further on the structure, see Dorothy Lee, *The Symbolic Narratives of the Fourth Gospel. The Interplay of Form and Meaning* (Sheffield: Sheffield Academic Press,, 1994), 191-97., and Lee, *Flesh and Glory,* 198-200.

44. Lee, *Symbolic Narratives*, 191-92.

45. On the contrast between the two odours, see *Symbolic Narratives*, 222, n. 2, and *Flesh and Glory*, 205-6. Also Gail R. O'Day, 'John,' in *The Women's Bible Commentary*, ed. C.A. Newsom & S.H. Ringe (London: SCM, 1998), 299.

46. Brendan Byrne, *Lazarus: A Contemporary Reading of John 11:1-46*, Zacchaeus Studies (Minnesota: Liturgical Press, 1991), 86-89; also Lee, *Symbolic Narratives*, 224-26.

47. A perspective John shares with the Gospel of Matthew, where the women on Easter morning come only to 'see the tomb' (Matt 28:1). A form of the Bethany story occurs in Mark, but it does not overtake the role of the mourning women after the crucifixion (Mk 12:3-9/par.).

[48.] On the Paradise overtones in John's garden imagery, see Nicolas Wyatt, "Supposing Him to Be the Gardener' (John 20,15). A Study of the Paradise Motif in John' *ZNTW* 81 (1990), 21-38.

[49.] The four women parallel the four Roman soldiers (19:23); so E. Hoskyns, *The Fourth Gospel*, 2 ed., 2 vols. (London: Faber & Faber, 1947), 630-31.

[50.] A number of other mediaeval and Renaissance paintings show angels flying around the cross, with chalices in their hands to catch the drops of blood from Jesus' hands and side, emphasizing the imagery of eucharistic drinking and portraying, if a trifle bluntly, mediaeval belief in the 'real presence'. See, for example, Giotto di Bondone's depictions of the cross with their flocks of small angels in the upper half, three of whom hover around Jesus' body with extended bowls (*Crucifixion,* 1304-06, Fresco, 200 x 185 cm, Cappella Scrovegni, Padua; *Crucifixion,* 1310s, Fresco, North Transept, Lower Church, San Francesco, Assisi; and *Crucifixion*, 1330s, Tempera on wood, 39 x 26 cm, Musées Municipaux, Strasbourg).

[51.] *A Human Pattern. Selected Poems* (Sydney: Angus & Robertson, 1990), p. 105.

[52.] Rainer Hirsch-Luipold, 'Klartext in Bildern. *alêthinos* ktl., *paroimia - parrêsia, sêmeion* als Signalwörter für eine Bildhafte Darstellungsform im Johannes-Evangelium,' in Frey et al., *Imagery in the Gospel of John*, 66.

[53.] One of the most powerful evocations of the five senses is found in the late fifteenth century series of six tapestries, *La Dame à la licorne*, located now in the Musée de Cluny in Paris, though originating in Flanders. Each tapestry represents one of the senses; the final in the series depicts the Lady removing her jewels and placing them in a casket, with the inscription, *A mon seul désir*. Interpretation cannot be certain, but at least the tapestries point to the lavishness of sensual existence and the final and ultimate moment of renunciation. See A. Erlande-Brandenburg, *La dame a la licorne* (Paris: Editions de la Réunion des Musées Nationaux, 1978).

[54.] James Alison, *Living in the End Times. The Last Things Re-Imagined* (London: SPCK, 1966), 77.

[55.] Alison, *Living in the End Times*, 64.

[56.] Lee, *Flesh and Glory*, 119-28.

[57.] Despite John's spiritual and moral dualism in the contrasting pairs of the Gospel—light/darkness, sight/blindness, truth/falsehood, life/death—the movement from one to the other in the narrative occurs gradually and in distinct stages. Indeed, the movement can work in both directions at the same time, as the story of the man born blind makes plain; in John 6, by contrast, the movement is finally negative. Further on the stages of faith, see Lee, *Symbolic Narratives*.

[58.] This includes its tangibility in papyrus or parchment, as well as its aurality in public performance.

[59.] Note that 1 John in these opening verses places particular emphasis on 'seeing'.

[60.] The Fourth Gospel also points beyond itself to the community to which it is addressed. In this sense, there is a parallel literal and symbolic sensory experience to which the Gospel attests. For John, the community itself takes on a life to which the senses can connect: there is a seeing and hearing, a tasting and touching, a fragrance, all of which, understood aright, give Johannine believers access to life. Significantly, it is the presence of the Spirit-Paraclete which breathes life into the symbols of the community, just as the Johannine Spirit is the one who gives life to believers and brings to life the words and deeds of Jesus' ministry.

[61.] On the parallels with the Synoptic transfiguration story, which contains both seeing and hearing but with priority (arguably) for the former, see Lee, *Transfiguration*, 100-111.

[62.] Marianne Meye Thompson has demonstrated the strong lines of continuity between the Johannine God and the God of the Old Testament, now revealed in Jesus: '"Everyone Picture Tells a Story": Imagery for God in the Gospel of John', in Frey et al., *Imagery in the Gospel of John*, 259-277.

[63.] Augustine, *Sermon* 112.7.

Part I: The Johannine Epistles and Book of Revelation

Chapter 7
Spirituality in the Johannine Epistles

The three epistles of John, placed towards the end of the New Testament, display important aspects of Johannine spirituality. Their genre is different from that of the Gospel, being letters addressed to a community or individual. The pattern of epistles in the New Testament is that they begin by naming and/or describing the author (often in the third person), followed by the audience to whom the letter is addressed, then a greeting. The ending includes further greetings, both to the community in general and sometimes to individuals specifically named. In the New Testament, these formal aspects of the epistle are christianised, reflecting not just the Christian ambience of the letter but also the spiritual authority of the implied author (e.g. Rom 1:1-7; 16:21-27; Gal 1:1-5; 6:18). The same is true of the second and third Johannine epistles, which begin and end with appropriate (albeit brief) greetings. As noted in the Introduction, it is unclear whether or not 'elect Lady' at 2 John 1 corresponds to 'Gaius' in 3 John 1, as another figure in the Johannine community:[1] perhaps a woman and her family,[2] or the female head of a house-church where the 'children' refer to the members of the church. In either case, it is strange that the author concludes with a greeting from 'the children of your elect sister' (2 Jn 13).[3] Most popular is the view that the language represents figuratively the church, in line with biblical imagery of Israel-church as woman or bride.[4] Only 2 John 1 and 3 John 1 describe the author as 'the elder' (*ho presbytêros*).

By contrast, 1 John, the longest and fullest of the three, lacks a proper epistolary beginning and ending, and has no direct reference to the author. It is possible that the beginning and ending have been lost, or that 1 John is a tract rather than an epistle. Yet epistolary language occurs throughout, along with first person pronouns and references to writing (1 Jn 1:4; 2:1, 7, 12-14, 21, 26; 5:13), making it hard to believe it is not some kind of direct communication, however unusual or incomplete. Perhaps the best possibility is that it is 'an admonition in written form' addressed to a number of house churches in and around Ephesus.[5] Moreover, the author gives the impression of being an old man. The attribution of 'elder', in addition to ecclesial status,[6] seems to fit the identity of the author of 1 John as much as it does the other two.[7]

Illustration 7: Giotto di Bondone, St John the Evangelist, 1320-25. Tempera on wood, 81 x 55 cm Musée Jacquemart-André, Châalis[8]

Giotto portrays St John above as an old man, bearded and balding, with pen and parchment in hand, his thoughtful, dark gaze turned to the right, as if pondering his next words, while the ink dries on the nib of his pen. The portrait, in fact, gives the impression of depth of reflection, maturity, wisdom: all the attributes of an older man who has been a friend and pastor to his people.

One of the remarkable features of the Johannine epistles is that their tone and mood are affectionate throughout. This is not to say there is no warning, no solemn caution or caveat. But what does emerge is the fondness in which the elder holds his correspondents, a fondness that is mingled with a sense of authority. The implied author sees himself as responsible for the spiritual lives of this community, his role being one of guidance, direction, admonition, consolation and encouragement. He expresses the hope of meeting with them again in the near future (2 Jn 12; 3 Jn 13), aware of how poor a substitute 'pen and ink' are for seeing them face-to-face. The elder addresses his correspondents as 'children' (*paidia, tekna*), or in the diminutive form, 'little children' (*teknia*)—often preceded by the pronoun 'my'—which underlines the long-standing warmth and authority of his relationship with them (2:1, 12, 18, 28; 3:1, 7, 10, 18; 4:4; 5:2, 22); he also calls them 'beloved' (*agapêtoi*, 1 Jn 2:7; 3:2, 21; 4:1, 7, 11; 2 Jn 1-2, 5, 11). He writes as the spiritual father of a much-loved flock, a teacher and spiritual advisor whose reputation is already established among them, but who uses caritative language to considerable rhetorical effect.

The epistles deal with a number of themes in which teaching, spirituality and ethics are stitched together, implying that each is connected to the other. The same claim could be made for other epistles, such as those of Paul, and in a sense it is true; but the Pauline letters usually reserve ethical exhortation ('parenesis' is the technical term) till the end, as if drawing out the implications of what has been proclaimed in earlier sections. In the Johannine epistles, no such classification is found. Spiritual encouragement, moral exhortation, pastoral care, and theological instruction go hand-in-hand, one folding into another, and all of it directed to the lived experience of believers: 'If there is a single theme in 1 John, it is that claims to religious experience or status have no validity if they remain independent of life as it is lived.'[9] Alongside the pastoral and spiritual dimensions, there is also a polemical note woven into the other elements, aimed at those whom the elder considers his opponents.[10]

This merging of themes and approaches makes it difficult to outline the structure of 1 John. At times the subject matter seems to leap intuitively from one thing to another. In another sense, we find a characteristic Johannine pattern of circular argument, repeating and enlarging earlier material in a way that has its own interior logic. The same is true for the themes and imagery of all three epistles: they have their own circular movement—a feature associated with the discourse material in the Fourth Gospel.[11] A simple structure divides 1 John into five broad sections:

Prologue	1 Jn 1:1-4
Walking in the Light	1 Jn 1:5-2:27
Love as the Mark of Those Born of God	1 Jn 2:28-3:24
Commands to Test the Spirits, Love and Believe	1 Jn 4:1-5:12
Concluding Encouragement	1 Jn 5:13-21

In this structure 1:5 acts as a bridge between the prologue and the first main section, and 2:28 begins a new section (though this is not universally agreed upon).[12] The second and third epistles, so much shorter, can each be divided into three:

Opening Formula (2 Jn 1-3; 3 Jn 1-2)

Body of Epistle: Reminder of Core Teaching (1 Jn 4-11);

      Hospitality (3 Jn 2-12)

Conclusion (2 Jn 12-13; 3 Jn 13-15).[13]

Teaching: Jesus' Identity

The teaching which emerges from the Johannine epistles concerns the nature and identity of Jesus. That this is not just cerebral knowledge, unconnected to spirituality, is made clear in uncompromising statements such as, 'Anyone who ... does not abide (*menô*) in the doctrine (*didachê*) of Christ does not have God' (2 Jn 9a). The converse is equally true, since to grasp the teaching is to grasp something of God: 'the one who abides in the doctrine, this one has the Father and the Son' (2 Jn 9b). Teaching, in this text, lies at the basis of spirituality, since abiding—as in the Fourth Gospel—is inherently relational and possesses cognitive content. Indeed, for the elder, to reject the core truth about Jesus Christ is to ally oneself with deception and antichrist (1 Jn 2:22; 4:3; 2 Jn 7)—as in the case of those who have recently, it would seem, seceded from the Johannine community.

What is the nature of the christological teaching on which John places such emphasis? There are three aspects, all connected to what the elder regards as rejection of Christ. In the first place, the core issue appears to be that some have denied the incarnation, the belief 'that Jesus Christ has come in the flesh' (1 Jn 4:2; see 2 Jn 7). Linked to this would seem to be the problem of those who do not perceive Jesus as Messiah/Christ or Son (1 Jn 2:22-23; 4:15; 5:1, 10; 2 Jn 9).[14] As a consequence, for the elder, they have thereby rejected Jesus as Saviour and Paraclete/Advocate who saves believers from sin by his sacrificial death (I Jn 1:7; 2:1; 4:14). In the epistles, this denial has implications for the life of the Christian community. True believers, on the contrary, are those who believe in, and confess, Jesus as Son of God and Saviour, whose lives are shaped by the conviction that he is the revelation of God: that the Father and the Son are one, attested to by the Spirit (1 Jn 5:6).[15]

It is difficult to discern the opponents' theology, since we only have one side of the conversation; nor can we be sure that all the opponents believe the same thing. Some, at least, appear to have held docetic views: the belief that Jesus' humanity was not real but only a matter of appearance.[16] This issue would account for the emphasis on 'flesh' in the epistles, including the opening verses of 1 John, with their emphatic proclamation of a tangible and palpable reality, based on firsthand, eyewitness knowledge: 'that which we have heard, which we have seen with our eyes, which we have beheld and our hands have touched … that which we have seen and heard' (1 Jn 1, 3).[17] Yet it does not explain why the dissidents should deny Jesus as Messiah, Son, Saviour or Advocate, since these titles could all be understood in docetic or non-docetic ways. It may be that the elder assumes that to deny the flesh of Jesus is to deny his entire identity (in which case there might be an element of misunderstanding on his part). More likely, the denial extends to Jesus' role as Saviour, especially if (some of) the dissidents reject the notion that they are capable of sin. Whatever the opponents have believed and done, they are to be cut off from social intercourse because their presence is regarded as contaminating (2 Jn 10-11).[18] In all this uncertainty what is clear is that, regardless of the opponents' actual position, John the elder asserts his own christological perspective that sees Jesus as the incarnate Son from whom alone forgiveness and salvation come. For this author, such a Christology lies at the core of Christian theology and spirituality. Right practice is based on right teaching, the one issuing in the other:

> right behaviour flows from right relationship; the two are inseparable ... not only ... faith and practice ought to go hand in hand, but also ... one's relationship with God (or the devil) is itself a transforming relationship. Practice is both a requirement beside faith and a fruit of faith.[19]

What 1 John stresses here is that believing experience cannot be divorced from teaching: the affective and the cognitive belong together. In Johannine spirituality, true teaching is needful for Christian life. In effect, this perspective bypasses a form of dualism in which thinking and experience are disengaged from each other, neither having anything to say to the other. The Johannine epistles show no sympathy for this neatly divided world; for them, spirituality is grounded in the identity of Jesus and therefore his capacity, as the divine Son, to save believers from sin, falsehood, hatred, and death.

Sin and Forgiveness

As we have observed, the Christology of the Johannine epistles is critical for comprehending its spirituality; the identity of Jesus provides their orientation. Jesus is presented as Paraclete and Saviour, both titles pertaining to sin and the cult. Unlike the Gospel and the Book of Revelation, the elder does not use the title 'Lamb of God' in the epistles, although there is a similar perspective on Jesus' death as a sacrifice for sin. In the first epistle the elder describes Jesus' death as an 'atoning sacrifice' for sin (*hilasmos*, 1 Jn 2:2; 4:10),[20] drawing on cultic imagery associated with the temple and its rites of forgiveness. 'Paraclete' is used of the Holy Spirit in the Fourth Gospel, but in the first reference in the Gospel, Jesus speaks of giving '*another* Paraclete', implying that he is the first (Jn 14:16). Here in 1 John, the meaning seems more limited than the Gospel usage, restricted to the forensic imagery of Jesus engaging in advocacy on behalf of those guilty of sin. He can play the role of advocate, in this text, because his atoning death has dealt with sin once and for all. At this point, 1 John shares with the Fourth Gospel the same universal understanding of the saving efficacy of Jesus' death (1 Jn 2:2b; Jn 1:29).

1 John's references to sin can be confusing. Unlike the Fourth Gospel, the stress is not so much on 'sin' as rejection of Jesus, but 'sins' as culpable acts within the community. The fourth evangelist does sometimes move between 'sin' in the singular and 'sins' in the plural (e.g. Jn 8:21, 84), but for the most part the emphasis is on a singular attitude underlying specific actions. The elder, too, has a general sense of 'sin' in the singular, but this he defines as 'lawlessness' (*anomia*, 1 Jn 3:4), a life lived beyond the umbrella of the law.[21] For the most part, the epistles are concerned with 'sins' as acts that harm the common life of believers. But this is where the confusion lies. Are sins part of the ongoing life of believers, as the first reference suggests (1 Jn 1:8-10), or is the committing of an act of sin a sign of one's alienation from God and thus comradeship with the devil, as later on the elder seems to suggest? Over against those who 'say they have no sin', being self-deluded and far from truth (1 Jn 1:8, 10), are those incapable of sin by virtue of their new birth: 'everyone born of God does not commit sin, because God's seed abides in them, and they cannot sin, because they are born of God' (1 Jn 3:9).[22]

Taking all the references to 'sin' and 'sins' into account in 1 John (the other two epistles do not mention it), it would seem that the elder is making a distinction between sinful acts and a sinful orientation of life.[23] The ultimate aim is that believers *not* sin, that their lives become replete with the love and life of God, hallowed and truthful (1 Jn 1:2a); but in the meantime the reality is that they do fail, and the elder sees this as inevitable. His message is one of consolation for those troubled by awareness of their own failures and inadequacies. There is remedy at hand for believers in the sending of the sinless Son of God (1 Jn 3:5). Even for them, despite their high calling, there is a compassionate God who stoops down to them when they fall and raises them to their feet. On the other hand, those whose lives are oriented towards sin—manifesting itself in lack of love, untruthfulness and self-delusion—do not belong within the household of faith. Protestations notwithstanding, their life-style suggests a different orientation, a hatred and deceitfulness that, in the elder's view, is characteristic of the devil and not of God (1 Jn 3:8). Rudolf Bultmann sees the seeming contradiction as resolved in the tension between 'gift' and 'demand'. Believers in 1 John are given the possibility of not sinning, a gift that 'remains for the believer a possibility not to be lost, so that he can always call upon that gift, even though in fact he sins.' The gift has priority but 'always includes a demand'.[24]

In his comments on forgiveness in the church of 1 John, David Rensberger suggests that 'confession' in the New Testament context was most likely not a private and internal affair, even in the context of worship, but both 'public and specific'.[25] He argues that 1 John's language in 1:8-10 of 'saying', 'confessing' and 'denying' suggests such a context, where sins are openly acknowledged within the believing community based on faith in the forgiving love of God.[26] If Rensberger is right, it confirms that I John presents a communal understanding of sin and fellowship, rather than an individualistic one.

There is a further problem on the issue of sin. Towards the end of the first epistle, a distinction is made between sin that is 'towards death' and sin that is 'not towards death' (*pros thanaton*, 1 Jn 5:16-17). This distinction is not a variation on the difference between sin as an individual act and sin as an orientation of life. Clearly the idea of non-mortal and mortal sin envisages a specific act committed by a brother or sister within the community: the one which can be forgiven, with intercession, and the other which cannot. It is not at all clear of what the deathly sin consists. Despite later mediaeval tradition, which distinguished between venial and mortal sins—those which required absolution before death and those which did not— it may be that what the elder has in mind is a warning against idolatry, as apparent in the final verse of the epistle, which seems otherwise inexplicable (1 Jn 5:21). Alternatively, what John may have in mind is the one who turns back to sin—meaning those who have left the community and no longer walk with Johannine believers.[27] Whatever the author means is beyond our knowledge but, like the unforgiveable sin in the Synoptic Gospels (Mk 3:28-29), does not take away from the reality of forgiveness in 1 John. It does not affect the Johannine insight that believers can and do go on sinning and that, in each case, the Advocate stands beside them to uphold, defend, and forgive.

What are the implications of the elder's writings on sin for understanding the spirituality of the Johannine epistles? Once again, in the first place, we find a perspective that refuses to separate thought from feeling, belief from action. Believers are regarded as whole persons, not fragmented beings where one part has no connection with another. The orientation of believing existence is turned firmly away from sin—from hatred and deceit—and towards the goodness of God. There is a challenge to believers to live out their identity and calling, and to resist the temptation to turn back to what they have left behind. Secondly, there is assurance of forgiveness along the way, an assurance that their faults and failures are forgiven and their hearts cleansed. This perspective, in the view of the elder, gives hope, joy and confidence, even in failure, because what believers depend upon is not their own efforts but the gift of God continually renewing and restoring.

The epistles emphasise these points by means of the imagery of light, another close link with the Fourth Gospel.[28] If God is characterised by the radiance of light and the absence of darkness (1 Jn 1:5), then the spiritual life of believers should reflect the same luminosity, the same horror of 'night'. In John's eschatology, the old age of darkness is already passing away; the dawn is at hand. Therefore it makes sense that believers should walk in the light of day and not seek to turn back to darkness (1 Jn 1:7).[29] Such a journey undertaken in daylight guarantees the companionship of other believers, as well as the purifying and cleansing love of Christ. The elder articulates the hope of transformation in ultimate terms, closely allied to light;

children of God are promised that the *sight* of Jesus will finally and eternally transfigure them: 'we know that when he is manifest we will be like him, because we will see him as he truly is' (1 Jn 3:2). To walk in the light and in the truth (3 Jn 3-4), to perceive the Son who has come in flesh, in these texts, opens a new future beyond sin, failure and death.

Life and Love

The theme of life is found mainly in the first epistle, sometimes explicitly designated as 'eternal life' and at other times 'life' by itself, although implying the same qualitative experience. As with the Fourth Gospel, this life essentially is a description of God: God *has* life, in the same way that the Son also *has* life (1 Jn 1:1-2; 5:12, 20). It is a fundamental characteristic of the nature of God. Therefore, this life is both a gift and a promise bestowed on believers in and through the Son (1 Jn 2:25; 5:11); in this derivative sense, they too can be said to *have* life (1 Jn 5:13). This life is a feature of present existence, and not just delayed in an ever-receding future—although 1 John stresses the future dimension somewhat more than the Gospel. The elder writes of the community having already 'crossed over from death to life' (1 Jn 3:14), a knowledge that is confirmed and vindicated in love of others. Life is found in fellowship with the Father, in and through the Son, and also in fellowship with other believers within the community (*koinônia*, 1:3, 6). As with the Gospel (e.g. Jn 17:3), life has its origins in God, is given as gift and promise in the incarnation of the Son,[30] and becomes a key feature of believing existence: a circle of life into which the community is drawn.[31]

In the epistles, life is closely allied to love, since love lies at the basis of authentic ('eternal') life. The elder has much to say on the subject of love, especially throughout the first epistle. It begins in the heavenly realm, in the relationship between God and Jesus which is characterised by love. Love also characterises the nature of God: God is love, as well as life (1 Jn 4:8b). This divine love, shared between Father and Son, is graciously given to believers as a gift, furnishing them with a new status and a new identity as God's beloved children (1

Jn 3:1). Love is primarily a divine quality, as it is in the Gospel of John; not something believers manufacture but something they are freely given. Locating love in this way is essential in John's spirituality. His is a spirituality of love (and life), but the love comes from outside, originates elsewhere, and is bestowed in mercy and grace. Johannine spirituality is first and foremost a spirituality of receptivity and gift.

Love has its challenge as well as givenness, its activity as well as receptivity, its command as well as grace. The epistles have a good deal to say about keeping the commandments (singular or plural), and these seem to come down to love (1 Jn 2:3-5; 4:21; 2 Jn 5-6). They are described as both old and new, new in their manifestation in Christ, and old in their grounding in the Old Testament (1 Jn 2:7-8); new and old because they are part of the core of Christian teaching. The main image is that of 'keeping' (têreô), in the sense—as we saw with the Gospel—of safeguarding and protecting what is of value. Other synonymous expressions are 'doing' God's commands (usually translated 'obeying', poieô, 1 Jn 5:) and 'walking according to' God's commands (peripateô kata, 2 Jn 6). The latter especially communicates the sense of a life lived in love, where love is part of everyday life, as regular and frequent as walking. The epistles speak of this obedience-in-love as the sign of believers' 'abiding' in God and in God's love (1 Jn 3:24), the sign of God's Spirit within them. The failure to love is a terrifying abiding in death (1 Jn 3:14b).[32]

The logic of love in the Johannine epistles is characteristically circular. Believers love because they are first loved; they love in response to being loved (1 Jn 4:10a, 19); they love the God who demonstrates prevenient love for them in the sending and crucifixion of the Son (1 Jn 3:16; 4:9, 10b). As a consequence of this demonstrated love, they also love one another—all who live within the same covenant of divine love. They do so because God commands them to love (1 Jn 3:23) and also because, according to this text, 'to love the parent is to love the child' who is the parent's offspring and image (1 Jn 5:1). Furthermore, given Jesus' departure, there is no divine object for believers' love except in the faces of others. To love others is to demonstrate the authenticity of love for God, a love evident in practical acts of kindness (1 Jn 3:16b-

17; 4:7). Love of one another, then, is the sign of the new life believers have entered, the evidence that they abide in God who is love. In fact, to hate a brother or sister is to deny one's identity as a child of God and to make a mockery of God's love—according to 1 John, is an act tantamount to murder (1 Jn 3:15; 4: 20).

The opposite of love is not only hatred but also fear: 'In this, love is perfected with us, so that we may have confidence on the day of judgement … Fear does not exist in love, but perfect love casts out fear, for fear has punishment in mind, and the one who fears is not perfected in love' (1 Jn 4:17-18). There is again a circularity to these verses: perfected love—perfect love—perfected in love. The author has in mind the fear of final judgement, the anxiety of being finally and ultimately rejected. The verb used, 'to perfect' (*teleioô*), has a sense of goal or end, so that it suggests 'the conditions under which God's love reaches its goal.'[33] Being perfected in love means resting securely in the knowledge of divine love; elsewhere in the first epistle, it also means displaying that (divine) love to others, to brothers and sisters within the believing community. This is not simply a matter of duty. To be perfected in love means living a life surrounded by love; becoming so filled with love, towards God and others, that there is no room for fear, anxiety, or dread. Spirituality in the epistles involves a growing away from fear and a growth towards love, a love that has its source and origin in God.

The Spirit and the Spirits

Nothing has been said so far of the role of the Spirit in the Johannine epistles, despite the importance of this theme in understanding New Testament spirituality. There are several explicit references to the Spirit in 1 John. Two of these speak of the Spirit as given to believers by God (1 Jn 3:24; 4:13). In both cases, the gift of the Spirit is the donation of God to believers, part of God's gracious self-manifestation and self-giving, and is associated with abiding and knowledge. The reason we know that God abides in us, says 1 John, is because of the gift of the Spirit within us, which testifies to God's loving and life-giving presence. This kind of knowledge has a cognitive basis but is also experiential; there is a mysterious knowledge that the Spirit grants, for this author, as the expression of divine immanence, which bestows assurance and consolation.[34]

The kind of 'mysticism' implied in the writings of John the elder is not dependent solely on subjective experience. The Spirit who inhabits the human spirit is the expression of divine truth in 1 John: 'and the Spirit is the one who bears witness, because the Spirit is the truth' (1 Jn 5:6). The Spirit's role within the life and hearts of believers is to confirm the truth of God—the truth of God's love, the truth of the gift and the demand. It is the opposite of lies and deceit, including self-deceit. Even in its interiority, therefore, there is an objectivity to the Spirit in 1 John which unites with the believer's own experience: exterior and interior, objective and subjective melded together in the reconciling testimony of the Spirit.

In a notoriously difficult passage, the elder speaks of the Spirit as the first among three witnesses to truth, the three being in complete agreement: 'there are three who bear witness, the Spirit and the water and blood, and the three are one' (1 Jn 5:7b-8).[35] In the Old Testament, for a case to succeed in the courts requires the evidence of 'two or three witnesses' (Deut 17:6; 19:15). Here too the elder, as part of what he understands to be the objectivity of truth, speaks not only of the Spirit's witness but of two further witnesses, both of them palpable and fleshly. The most likely reference of 'water and blood' is to the baptism and death of Jesus, as attested to by the witness of the beloved disciple at the foot of the cross in the Fourth Gospel (Jn 19:31-37),[36] with its sacramental overtones. These witnesses bring us back to the beginning of 1 John with the tangibly of the 'word of life' as revealed in Jesus Christ, perfect in his self-evident humanity. The Spirit's witness is not in competition with Christ, but rather confirms the witness of Jesus' own saving life and death: 'the reason for the significance of the water and the blood is that they both are vehicles of the Spirit.'[37]

As 'the Spirit of truth' (see Jn 14:17; 15:26; 16:13), the Spirit also plays a role in the discrimination of truth from error and truth from lies, especially where the distinction is difficult and ambiguous. Over against the Holy Spirit in 1 John stands 'the spirit of antichrist' (1 Jn

4:3) which, as we have seen, teaches false doctrine about Jesus, and is the source of all deceit and untruthfulness. The elder is convinced that believers need to learn and practise the discernment of spirits: 'do not believe every spirit, but *test* the spirits if they are of God' (*dokimazô*, 1 Jn 4:1a). This testing or discerning is to be based on the identity of Jesus Christ, and that of the believing community. The warning is particularly aimed at the 'false prophets' (1 Jn 4:1b), those who claim to possess religious truth and spiritual insight but whose teaching and spiritual guidance is, in the eyes of the elder, dangerous and destructive. Discerning the voice of prophecy is an important aspect of Johannine spirituality in the epistles.

Conclusion

Johannine spirituality extends beyond the Gospel to the epistles. Though they do not possess the same literary and theological qualities—the scope or depth—they have a distinctive spirituality of their own. As epistles, they are responding to a more immediate context, where division and discord have been a painful part of the community's recent life. There is warning and even a fierceness in parts of the epistles that is characteristic also of the Fourth Gospel: they are frankly inhospitable to those with whom the author is at enmity. At the same time, there is warmth and love for the implied readers, and a concern to guide them on a spiritual path that will not delude or deceive them. Regardless of the specific contours of those denoted as 'antichrist', we can still gain an appreciation of the spirituality of the epistles. The perspective on love and knowledge, on hatred and fear, and on the discernment of spirits, is characteristic of the spirituality found in the epistles. They are not identical to the Gospel, but they have their own value and their own way of articulating their viewpoint. The spirituality of the epistles is perhaps a little more mundane, and less lofty than the Gospel, but its contours are similar and, like the Gospel, its bearings well tuned to the daily struggles of believing existence.

End Notes

[1] For a list of five options for this phrase, see Raymond E. Brown, *The Epistles of John* [AB 30; New York: Doubleday, 1982], 651-655.

[2.] See, e.g., the Introduction to 2 John in *The ESV Classic Reference Edition* (Wheaton, IL: Good News Publishers, 2001), 1231.

[3.] See Judith Lieu, *The Theology of the Johannine Epistles* (Cambridge: Cambridge University Press, 1991), 3.

[4.] So Robert W. Yarbrough, *1-3 John* (BECNT; Grand Rapids: Baker Academic, 2008), 333-334.

[5.] Martin Hengel, *The Johannine Question* (ET London: SPCK, 1985), 47.

[6.] On 'elder' as a church title for pastoral leadership in the New Testament, see Yarbrough, *1-3 John*, 329-330.

[7.] See John Painter, *1, 2, and 3 John* (SP18; Collegeville: Liturgical Press, 2002), 18-19.

[8.] See http://www.lib-art.com/artgallery/10930-st-john-the-evangelist-giotto-di-bondone.html.

[9.] Lieu, Johannine Epistles, 106.

[10.] Painter makes this point, arguing that, while the schism is over, the community is living in its painful aftermath (*1, 2, and 3 John*, 16-17). Not all commentaries support the view that schism is a major factor in the Johannine epistles, a warning perhaps not to overstate this point.

[11.] Lieu makes a strong case for reading the first epistle in its own right, and not as an appendage to the Gospel, despite the 'family likeness' between Gospel and epistles (*Johannine Epistles*, 98-107).

[12.] So Georg Strecker, *The Johannine Letters. A Commentary on 1, 2, and 3 John* (Minneapolis: Fortress, 1996), 79. Rensberger interprets 2:28-3:10 as a unit (*Epistles of John*, 43-52); similarly, I. Howard Marshall connects 2:28-3:3, under the theme of 'the hope of God's children' (*Epistles of John*, 164-175), with 3:4-10 as 'the sinlessness of God's children', 3 (175-188). C.H. Dodd places 2:28-4:12 under the rubric, 'life in the family of God' (*The Johannine Epistles* [London: Hodder & Stoughton, 1946], 65-113).

[13.] These structures for the epistles are based, with some modification, on Pheme Perkins, 'The Johannine Epistles' in R.E. Brown, J. A. Fitzmyer, & R.E. Murphy (eds.), *The New Jerome Biblical Commentary* (London: Geoffrey Chapman, 1990), 988-995. See also the concentric structure proposed by John Christopher Thomas, 'The Literary Structure of 1 John' *NovT* 40 (1998), 369-81.

[14.] The title 'Son' occurs twenty-two times throughout 1 John (1:3, 7: 2:22, 23 [twice], 24; 3:8, 23; 4:9, 10, 14, 15; 5:5, 9, 10 [twice?], 11, 12 [twice], 13, 20 [twice]; cf. 2 Jn 3, 9), usually in relation to the Father, which is the primary title for God.

[15.] On the Christology of 1 John, see especially Lieu, *Johannine Epistles,*

71-79.

[16.] Further on the docetism of 1 John, see especially Georg Strecker, 'The False Teachers in 1 John (Docetism)', Excursus, in *The Johannine Letters* (ET: Hermeneia; Minneapolis: Fortress, 1996), 69-76.

[17.] It is not entirely clear whether the prologue of 1 John is referring to Jesus as the incarnate Word or to the message and proclamation of the gospel, given that the relative pronoun in verses 1 and 3 is neuter rather than masculine (*ho*, 'that which'). For the latter view, see Painter, *1, 2, and 3 John*, 119-120, and David Rensberger, *The Epistles of John* (Louisville: Westminster John Knox, 2001), 15-16. In contrast, Yarbrough argues that 'Jesus Christ is the slightly veiled subject of this section' (*1-3 John*, 31); see also Brown who takes the neuter as covering '*comprehensively ... the person, the words, and the works*' (*Epistles of John*, 154). On the parallels between the Gospel and 1 John in their prologues, see Rudolf Schnackenburg, *The Johannine Epistles. Translation and Commentary* (ET: New York: Crossroad, 1992), p. 50.

[18.] There is a parallel case in 1 Corinthians 5 of a member of the community who is engaged in sexual immorality; Paul's instructions are similar: 'Cast out the evil person from among you' (1 Cor 5:13b; Deut 17:7). The attitude seems harsh to us today but is based on a communitarian rather than individualistic notion of identity, where evil in the individual is seen to corrupt the community (and even the land; see, e.g., Num 35:33; Ps 106:38; Jer 3:1-2, 9).

[19.] William Loader, *The Johannine Epistles* (London: Epworth, 1992), 33. Talbert entitles 1 John 4:7-5:12 as 'perfect love and proper belief' (*Reading John*, 37).

[20.] The word is not easy to render into English. Sometimes it is translated as 'expiation' or 'sacrifice to expiate sins' (e.g. RSV, NJB), with the implication that Jesus' death radically redresses sin through his self-offering; others prefer 'propitiation' (e.g. KJV, ESV, NAS, ASV), implying that the Son assuages divine wrath on the cross. The NRSV and NIV's 'atoning sacrifice' is preferable, as it leaves the question of meaning somewhat ambiguous, while confirming that Jesus' death is sacrificial (which seems to be about as far as the elder goes). See the helpful discussion in Brown, *Epistles of John*, 217-222.

[21.] *Anomia* is a thoroughly Jewish definition of sin, referring to breach of the Mosaic Law; in the context of 1 John it may mean breaking the Johannine commandments (Painter, *1, 2, and 3 John*, 222). On the other hand, Brown interprets *anomia* as 'iniquity' in an apocalyptic sense rather than as a breaking of the Mosaic Law (*Epistles of John*, 398-400); Schnackenburg prefers to translate it as 'evil' (*Johannine Epistles*, 170-172). For Colin

Kruse, *anomia* is rebellion rather than breach of the law ('Sin and Perfection in 1 John' *AusBR* 51 [2003], 60-70).

22. Some commentators prefer 'begotten' to 'born' (2:29) because of the predominant use of Father language; e.g. Brown, *Johannine Epistles*, 384-391, and Painter, *1, 2, and 3 John*, 213. On 'born' see Schnackenburg, *Johannine Epistles*, 162-169, and Bultmann, *Johannine Epistles*, 45-46. Both ideas are present, although 'born' is the more complete term.

23. The present tense of the verb *poieô* ('I do', 1 Jn 3:9) needs to be given its full force, suggesting an ongoing commitment to sinful acts, a commitment that implies an underlying state of alienation from God and other believers, nullifying their status as 'children of God'; Talbert, *Reading John*, 30.

24. *Johannine Epistles*, 53.

25. *Epistles of John*, 21.

26. 'In the polite and often impersonal atmosphere of many modern churches, we are seldom inclined to acknowledge anything specific about our lives, least of all our sins. Perhaps real "fellowship with one another" implies something radically different, a level of intimacy that would let us abandon what amounts to a claim—in public—that "we have not sinned", and open ourselves to our brothers and sisters as we do to God' (Rensberger, *Epistles of John*, 22).

27. Brown outlines the various theories (*Epistles of John*, 612-619), his own preference being that John is distinguishing between sins committed by believers (non-mortal) as against sins committed by unbelievers (mortal), the latter referring most likely, in his view, to the secessionists.

28. Thompson, *1-3 John*, describes light as 'the thesis of the epistle' (40).

29. Schnackenburg points out that the dualism of this language—light and dark—is not metaphysical: darkness is not a realm in its own right, as heaven is; rather, in asserting that God is light, 1 John wishes to lay stress on 'the unblemished holiness of the deity ..., the fullness of his divine being.' To walk in the light is primarily moral, concerned with holiness of life, rather than a form of pagan mysticism characteristic of the ancient world in which the focus is on the individual's subjective experience of union with the deity (*Johannine Epistles*, 74).

30. See Bultmann, *Johannine Epistles*, 8-9, who rightly interprets 'and the life was made manifest' (1:2a) as the equivalent of 'the Word became flesh' (Jn 1:14).

31. On the centrality of family imagery in 1 John, see Gail R. O'Day, '1, 2,3 and 3 John' in Newsom, C.A. & S.H. Ringe (eds.), *The Women's Bible Commentary* (London: SPCK, 1998), 374-5.

32. Thompson warns of the danger of watering down the demands of the

gospel: of preaching 'only what God generously gives to us and not what God also expects of us (*1-3 John*, 81).

33. Painter, *1, 2, and 3 John*, 281.

34. Schnackenburg's illuminating discussion of the Spirit in 1 John concludes that 'the doctrine of the Spirit in 1 John is to a great extent in agreement with GJohn' (*Johannine Epistles,* 195 [191-195])

35. There is a famous textual addition within these verses, found in the KJV, which reads: '*For there are three that bear record in heaven, the Father, the Word, and the Holy Ghost: and these three are one*. And there are three that bear witness *on earth*, the spirit, and the water, and the blood …' The italicised words are not present in the best and earliest editions of the epistle. For a brief summary of the history of the 'Johannine Comma' see D. Moody Smith, *First, Second, and Third John* (Interpretation; Louisville: John Knox, 1991), 121-122 see also Grantley McDonald, *Raising the Ghost of Arius. Erasmus, the Johannine Comma and Religious Difference in Early Modern Europe* (unpub. PhD dissertation; University of Leuven).

36. So Robert J. Schreiter, *In Water and In Blood. A Spirituality of Solidarity and Hope* (New York: Crossroad, 1988), 104-105.

37. Schreiter, *In Water*, 105.

Chapter 8
Spirituality in the Book of Revelation

The Book of Revelation (or The Apocalypse) is one of the most neglected books in the New Testament, at least in mainstream religious circles. There is a certain irony to this, given that this book has had more effect on Christian doctrine, art and literature than almost any other.[1] Moreover, spirituality is not something commonly associated with Revelation in the popular imagination. Its strongly apocalyptic flavour, its bewildering visions and the seemingly dominant motif of divine judgement, seem a long way from the concerns of the spiritual life or mystical theology. But this is far from the case, whatever initial appearances might suggest. The judgement motifs are really the prelude to its true emphasis, which is salvation and hope. The ensuing discussion of the Book of Revelation follows its dramatic structure, focussing on the spirituality that emerges from letter and vision, myth and symbol, liturgy, hymn and narrative.[2]

Revelation is the most overtly symbolic book in the New Testament. As one writer has aptly put in, the book 'presents itself as a cascade of imagery, with vivid and often grotesque scenarios tumbling from the page one after another.'[3] While symbolism is present in the Letters to the Seven Churches (2:1-3:22), it is most profuse in the apocalyptic visions which constitute most of the rest of the book. Whether sited in the heavenly sanctuary or on the earth below, the visions are replete with imagery, metaphor, symbol and myth, a number of which are not explained by the author.[4] In some ways these literary tropes may seem profligate and even absurd—like that of the Lamb, slaughtered and risen, a picture of vulnerability and innocence, who is nonetheless a warrior and a bridegroom, married to a city—but they have their own internal logic, and are carefully organised within the structure of Revelation. Ben Witherington rightly comments that there is 'not a syllogistic logic to Revelation, but there is a narrative logic'.[5] The mythic logic of Revelation includes also the recapitulation of major symbols and themes. It would be a mistake to conclude from this visual and aural panoply, engaging the senses, that the plethora of literary forms is thrown together, without rhyme or reason. In many respects the symbols have something of the character of dreams—the same bizarre quality when viewed in the cold light of day, the same slippage in time between past, present and future, the same vividness and credibility within their own framework, the same capacity for analysis.[6] The literary profusion of Revelation belongs together, fits together, within the exquisite tapestry of the whole work.[7] It portrays 'an impressive sacral architecture'.[8]

In addition to its complex symbolism—or perhaps because of it—Revelation has been interpreted in widely disparate ways.[9] Traditionally, it has been read within a straightforward, historical frame, as a blueprint of the last days. In some groups, generally of marginal status, it has been read in a millenarian fashion, taking seriously the 'one thousand year reign' of Christ and the saints on earth before the final victory and resurrection of the dead (20:2-7).[10] A more contemporary interpretation shows greater awareness of the nature of apocalyptic in the ancient world. This latter approach does not necessarily contradict political and economic readings. These interpret Revelation in relation to its situation in the Roman empire, where it is seen to function as a form of resistance to the imperial cult within Asia Minor.[11] Feminist readings have focussed on female imagery and characters, asking the question of whether the male-centred language of Revelation is conventional or whether it assumes a male readership and marginalises women.[12] There are interpretations that link the imagery of Revelation to astrology and the zodiac in the ancient world in a Judaeo-Christian context.[13] This diversity of interpretation makes the reader's task challenging and difficult.

The images and symbols of Revelation have their primary source in the Old Testament, and most explicitly the second part of the Book of Daniel, where Daniel receives a series of apocalyptic night dreams and visions (Dan 7:1-12:13). In its use of other biblical books, Revelation reads the Old Testament through the same apocalyptic lens. The wider influence of Jewish apocalyptic is apparent, as well as imagery and myth from the Ancient Near East. Another important source is the mythology of the Greco-Roman world. Sometimes these myths come together, as with the dragon monster narrative, which has versions in the Old Testament, the Greek world and the Ancient Near East.[14] Although the primary orientation of Revelation is biblical and Jewish, there are signs of selective borrowing from the environment of Asia Minor and Hellenism.

In this complexity, it can be difficult for the contemporary reader to know how to read the Book of Revelation. Jean-Pierre Prévost has suggested five keys for reading Revelation. First of all, he suggests, the reader should focus on what Revelation has to say of Christ, who is central to the message of the book.[15] Secondly, the prophecy of Revelation should be interpreted from the horizon of the author's (and communities') present experience of Roman imperialism and the imperial cult, avoiding the danger of turning Revelation into a blueprint for the future and John the Seer into a 'futurologist'.[16] Thirdly, the reader needs to find the key to the symbolism, beginning with those symbols which John himself explains within the text (e.g. 1:20; 11:28; 17:9), and moving to those less apparent, including numerical symbols.[17] Fourthly, the reader needs to become familiar with other apocalyptic writings of the period, both Jewish and Christian, which will aid in grasping the significance of less obvious tropes.[18] The last key to understanding Revelation is to read the book from an 'evangelical' perspective, where 'John gives us a message of hope with an unprecedented power.'[19] These five interpretative keys are in line with most contemporary readings of Revelation, and help uncover the positive spirituality of the book, even amid scenarios of destruction and death.[20] As with the Gospel of John, Revelation's spirituality is closely tied to its symbolism.

Time and the Number Seven

Perhaps the most conspicuous symbols of Revelation is its numerology. Even a cursory glance at the Book of Revelation reveals the frequency and import of the number seven. There are seven churches to whom seven letters are written (1:4, 11, 20; 2:1), represented by seven golden lampstands and presided over by seven stars who are seven angels (1:4, 11-12, 16-20; 2:1). There are seven spirits of God (3:1; 4:5; 5:6), and seven torches of fire (4:5). There follow three series of 'sevens' in the ensuing chapters: seven seals of a scroll released one-by-one (5:1-8:5), seven trumpets blown by seven angels (8:6-11:19), and seven plagues instigated by seven angels with seven bowls of wrath (15:1-18:24). Various characters have emblems of the number seven on their person: the Lamb has seven horns and seven eyes (5:6); the fiery red dragon has seven heads with seven diadems crowning them (12:3); the beast from the sea has seven heads (13:1), as does the beast on which the whore of Babylon sits, associated with seven mountains and seven kings (17:3, 7-11). There are also seven beatitudes (1:3; 14:13; 16:15; 19:9; 20:6; 22:7, 14). The number seven possibly arises from the actual number of cities within the one region in Asia Minor, but it carries a symbolic function, as numbers often do in the ancient world. Here seven signifies completion or perfection: the wholeness of the faith community, for example, or the terrifying might of evil. The effect of this numerical symbolism is to give Revelation a universal appeal beyond the elements that make up its context—a specific time in a known geographical location in the Roman empire.[21] This kind of spirituality is highly symbolic.

Not only is the number seven puzzling, so too is the time-frame in which Revelation is set. Traditionally, the Book has been read as a blue-print of the end of time, as we have noted, a description of the events which will herald the Second Coming of Christ. Millenarian groups down through the ages, from the Montanists in the early Church onwards, have interpreted it—and continue to interpret it—in these terms. Yet Revelation is not so easily categorised. Its focus on God's future reign has a sense of present anticipation, as contemporary readings of Revelation tend to argue. As much as it envisages the future kingdom of God, Revelation addresses the present aspect of the seven churches, and the political and economic situation in Asia Minor. It speaks to a community struggling to maintain identity over against the synagogue, on the one hand, and the Roman empire, on the other. The latter is powerfully present, behind the scenes for much of Revelation, but becoming explicit in the designation of the Whore as the city of seven hills, with its imperial ideology, idolatry, and mercantile supremacy and wealth (17:1-18:24). The language and imagery of Revelation represent an alternative ideology, a religious viewpoint that is directly at loggerheads with the empire's dictatorial creed and pursuit of material in which the author 'seeks to startle complacent Christians

Illustration 8: Hieronymous Bosch, St John the Evangelist on Patmos, 1504-5
Oil on oak panel, 63 x 43,3 cm. Staatliche Museen, Berlin[22]

In the image above, Bosch depicts John the Seer gazing for inspiration into heaven at the Heavenly Woman in the top left-hand corner, his quill poised in his right hand. His face is open and receptive, focussed intently on what will be disclosed. Just above him an angel on the island's mound directs him heavenwards. On his left lurks a small but malevolent demon. The falcon on the bottom left most likely indicates the eagle, symbol of John the evangelist. The tree to the right, with its long, thin trunk and its foliage reaching almost to heaven, suggests the tree of life.

into seeing the contradictions between the claims of the empire and the claims of God.'[23] Its spirituality is counter-cultural, with distinctly political implications.

If Revelation is as much about the present as the future, it is also anchored in the past. The past manifests itself in the dependence on the Old Testament and the identity of Israel as God's covenant people. Its perspective is prophetic, both in its critique of idolatry and in its condemnation of social injustice. The more immediate past which gives meaning to the community of the seven churches is that of Jesus himself. John the Seer stresses Jesus' sacrificial death on the cross and his triumphant victory over death, encapsulated in the title 'Lamb', which is frequent in Revelation.[24] Three times the Lamb is described as 'slain' (5:6, 12; 13:8), and twice is his 'blood' alluded to (7:14; 12:11), emphasising the centrality of the crucifixion in John's apocalyptic spirituality. God's dwelling among mortals is associated with the descent of the heavenly Jerusalem, with its suggestion also of the incarnation (21:3). In this way, the spirituality of Revelation moves between past, present and future; or, to put it another way, the Christ event and thus the life of the believing community acts as the precursor for God's future reign. This orientation makes sense of the author's understanding of Jesus as the 'Alpha and Omega', the beginning and end, the first and last letter of God's alphabet, the medium by which God speaks (22:13)—an appellation that belongs in the first place to God (1:8: 21:6).[25] The spirituality of Revelation meets the reader out of the future, but it is also grounded in the past. Another way of putting this is to say that the present is the point of intersection between the two.

This kind of spirituality seems to provide a strange parallel to what we might speak of today as the unconscious, with its capacity to slide in dreams between past, present and future. The symbolism of John the Seer's spirituality has an interiority to it, a structure that connects to the exterior world but also has roots in the internal realm, the depths of the mind and heart. To call this perspective 'psychological' would be anachronistic. But, paradoxically, Revelation speaks the language both of politics and economics and also of the soul. That is perhaps why its spirituality has been so appealing in art, music and liturgy in the Western tradition, as well as to modern commentators concerned to highlight the political context and content of Revelation's visions.

The Spirit

Before examining the series of seven woes in Revelation, we need to turn to John the Seer's understanding of the Spirit, which lies at the basis of his spirituality. This is not an easy topic to grasp, since it is not always clear whether 'spirit' (*pneuma*) refers to the divine Spirit or a more general sense of spirit (e.g. 'the spirit of prophecy', 19:10). Moreover, Revelation oscillates between references to 'the Spirit' (1:10; 2:7, 11, 17, 29; 3:6, 13, 22; 4:2; 14:13; 17:13; 21:10; 22:17) and 'the seven spirits' of God (1:4; 3:1; 4:5; 5:6). There is also mention of evil spirits (16:13-14; 18:2). While it is possible that the 'seven spirits' refer to angelic beings, the seven archangels, it is quite possible that they refer to the one divine Spirit—especially since 'seven' conveys a sense of unity and completeness not necessarily tied to numerical value.[26] Although the Spirit is not portrayed explicitly as the object of worship, unlike God and the Lamb, the Spirit nonetheless 'plays an essential role in the divine activity of establishing God's kingdom in the world.'[27]

Essentially, the Spirit is responsible for the visions of John the Seer. Metaphorically speaking, the Spirit is the means of transport, the one who takes the Seer to each visionary place. John speaks of being 'in the Spirit' or 'in the spirit' (*en tô[i] pneumati*) four times in the text (1:10; 4:2; 17:3; 21:10), which on the first occasion is designated 'the Lord's day' (*en tê[i] kyriakê[i[hêmera[i]*); presumably the other visions occur on the same day. In other words, the Seer experiences the visions on the day in which the Christian community gathers to celebrate the resurrection. This liturgical context reflects a close bond between Jesus and the Spirit, who grants the Seer access to the divine sanctuary through heavenly ascent.

More than the means of access and transport enabling John's visionary experiences, the Spirit also speaks on two occasions in Revelation, both utterances of great significance. The first is a beatitude pronounced on the dead, spoken first by an unidentified heavenly voice, then reiterated by the Spirit: 'Blessed are the dead who die now in the Lord … Yes, says the Spirit, that they may have rest from their toils, for their deeds follow after them' (14:13). In confirming and extending the beatitude, the Spirit shows a close connection with God and the Lamb. Here the assurance is directed at the saints and martyrs, who will find sabbath rest from their struggles, their righteous lives attesting to them in the heavenly realm.

The second utterance illustrates one of the key roles played by the Spirit in Revelation in the last vision where, alongside the Bride, the Spirit summons those outside to enter the holy city of Jerusalem: 'The Spirit and the Bride say, Come.' (22:17). In this depiction, the Spirit has an ongoing function for the community, offering welcome and hospitality to those outside, designated 'dogs and sorcerers and adulterers and murderers and idolaters' (22:15). Here the Spirit embodies what John the Seer regards as the church's ongoing mission to stand at the entrance of the city. Just as the Spirit gives John access to the divine sanctuary and the visions he sees there, so also the Spirit gives access to the new Jerusalem for those who dwell outside— unclean, pagan, irreligious, sinful as they are. This gift of admission is the primary function of the Spirit in Revelation, a gift handed over to the church, but a gift for which the Spirit is primarily responsible. In this sense, the Spirit acts rather like Hermes: the god in the ancient Greek pantheon who is associated with the crossing of boundaries, with travellers, and with leading departed souls to the realm of Hades, to which he has ingress and egress. Like Hermes, the Spirit in Revelation possesses the capacity to cross unnavigable seas, to move between realms, and to lead people to their ultimate destination.

The role of the Spirit reveals much of the spirituality of Revelation. The Spirit draws the community to prayer and worship, and acts as their companion on the spiritual path, leading them to the vision of God. The Spirit is the gate-keeper, in Revelation, the one who holds open the gates and welcomes people to their true home. In this sense, the Spirit acts as a ladder between the earthly and the heavenly realms, the one who leads the saints heavenwards on their travels. The Spirit is also associated with God and the Lamb, drawing the community into a divine vision of joy, triumph, and consolation. Through the Spirit, Christians in Revelation can cross the threshold from earth to heaven, from the material to the spiritual, vaulting barriers that would otherwise keep them stagnant and earth-bound. This capacity of the divine Spirit is the consequence of the dwelling of God descending to earth: the ascent of believers is predicated theologically on God's descent.

To the Seven Churches (2:1-3:22)

Revelation's spirituality has a strongly demanding and moral tone in the letters to the churches (2:1-3:22). Each of the seven churches is given its own mini-letter, with its own encouragement or warning.[28] The address to each of the seven churches follows a similar pattern:

1. 'To the angel of the church in ..., write'

2. 'Thus says ...' [title for Jesus]

3. 'I know' [the good works and/or misdeeds of the church]

4. 'The one who conquers...' or 'To the one who conquers...' [plus reward]

5. 'Let the one who has an ear listen to what the Spirit is saying to the churches'.[29]

The spirituality of these letters draws an uncompromising line between what is acceptable and what is not, what is good and what is evil, what is idolatrous and what is faithful. It rewards patience and endurance in poverty and persecution (2:2-3, 9, 19; 3:10),[30] zeal and enthusiasm in faith (2: 4), openness to repentance (2:5, 16, 22; 3:3, 19), and faithful confession (2:10, 13, 25). It condemns laxness and lack of rigour in religious practice (2:4; 3:1-2, 15-16), compromise with the world (2:15), idolatry (2:20-23), and spiritual complacency (3:17-18). Those who conquer—who remain faithful and endure to the end—are promised the rewards of eternal life, while those who grow lax or careless are warned sternly of retribution. These chapters of Revelation consist technically of 'parenesis', the kind of spiritual and moral encouragement generally found towards the end of the Pauline epistles.[31]

This spirituality seems at first glance both uncompromising and harsh, with its stern demands and intolerance of any form of negligence.[32] But two comments need to be made about the spirituality of Revelation in these chapters. In the first place, it belongs within a context of hardship and persecution where what is called for, according to the Seer, is a whole-hearted commitment to the gospel; where anything less, for him, represents self-indulgence and failure. Secondly, it is addressed not primarily to individuals but to churches. The starkest threat is that 'I will come to you and remove your lampstand from its place' (2:5). True, it is an austere spirituality, yet it calls for a kind of asceticism which, in the Seer's view, promotes true life. In all the threats, there is promise, encouragement and reassurance for those communities who have struggled patiently and held to the faith, despite the temptation to conform.[33] It challenges secure lifestyle, complacent access to luxury, and material comfort, calling for something more vigorous, radical and counter-cultural in a context of suffering:[34] something that challenges the established world order and its values, calling for more than a lukewarm response.[35] This is a spirituality of resistance, with political as well as ethical implications, which does not tolerate what it perceives as indifference or apathy, challenging readers to live boldly and courageously, without concession of any kind. It is a spirituality that is not universally present in the New Testament, where sometimes there seems more room for compromise and moderation. Revelation's spirituality is intense, fervent, zealous—perhaps, to some, extreme.

The Scroll and the Trumpets

Revelation's spirituality emerges also in the apocalyptic visions that follow the letters to the churches. The series of seven woes (Rev 6-11, 16-18) is preceded by a vision of the heavenly sanctuary (4:1-5:14).[36] This is the first of several glimpses into that divine place where the heavenly hosts continually worship 'God the almighty, and the Lamb', day and night. Once again, the Spirit plays a dominant role in this divine disclosure; the Seer is taken up into heaven by the Spirit and given an insight into the life of heaven. The imagery of these chapters is rich in symbolism: jewels, climatic manifestations associated with the sky and the sea, fire, animal-like creatures, angelic beings, representatives of Israel and the church, all join together to depict the radiance of divine presence, and worship as the authentic response to that presence. Yet this is not a vision of the heavenly sanctuary for its own sake. It has a distinctive purpose. The issue is the need for the seven-sealed scroll to be opened and the absence of anyone 'worthy' to do so (*axios*, 5:2-3). Strangely enough, this lack makes the Seer weep because, without any prior knowledge of its contents, he is convinced that the scroll must be opened to avoid tragic consequences (5:4). As it transpires, only one is worthy and that one is the Lamb, whose worth is established not only by his proximity to the throne (where God is manifest yet unseen, 2:2-3), but also by the triumph of his death and resurrection (5:6, 12-14).[37]

What these visionary chapters reveal in the heavenly sanctuary is that the fundamental spirituality of Revelation revolves around worship. The worship of the living God is not incidental but essential to its spiritual vision.[38] According to Steven J. Friesen, worship in Revelation 'acknowledges beings who have authority ... is enfolded in the meaning of sacrifice; it entails submission and obedience; it enjoins acclamations, blessings, praise, and thanks.'[39] Sacred ritual is not a delicacy to be enjoyed by aesthetes in the Book of Revelation, but intrinsic to the meaning of authentic spirituality and ethics. True worship indicates where the heart lies; it becomes the foundation for radical action, behaviour and lifestyle. The observe is also true: the essence of sin in Revelation is idolatry, worship of the imperial powers which promote welfare for the few at the cost of the many, which seek material gain and are ready to bow the knee to whatever will guarantee prosperity and comfort. To worship the one, true God is the meaning of Christian life and spirituality for John the Seer. Worship stands at the beginning and end of the spiritual life, nurturing it along the way, and centring it in God. Not for nothing do these chapters commence the series of visions that follow: they set out the centre-ground, they locate the living heart of the message of this author.

What emerges from the opening of the seven seals is more terrifying than otherwise—a series of four horses, white, red, black, and pale, who execute judgement on the earth (6:1-8). These are followed by a glimpse of the martyrs in heaven who await with longing the completion of God's wrath (6:9-11), and by a series of apocalyptic signs—earthquake, eclipse, and the vanishing of the earth (6:12-17). The signs are reminiscent of material in the Synoptic Gospels: the apocalyptic discourse (Mk 13/pars.), and the crucifixion, with its unnerving signs of earthquake and darkness (Mk 15:33-38/pars). In Revelation these signs are accompanied by the gathering of the elect, the song of conquest which they sing in the heavenly sanctuary (8:10-12), and the proclamation of a world from which all pain and suffering, all hunger and need, have been banished, a world centred on God (8:15-17).

With the opening of the seventh seal, the response is unexpected. Amid the drama and action of the heavenly realm, in song, praise, proclamation, judgement, and battle, what now descends is a half-hour of silence in the sanctuary, even the celestial voices of adoration falling silent (8:1). The unnerving silence serves as the prelude to the next series of visions, the blowing of the seven trumpets, but it also injects a note of awe into the drama. It recalls older traditions of silence in heaven before the creation of the world (2 Esdr 7:30; Wis Sol 18:14-15; 2 Bar 3:7).[40] Connecting this scene with the glimpses into the divine sanctuary, the alternation of music and silence is rich in meaning and association. It depicts a spirituality of beauty, tranquillity, and mystical awe: both a musical and a silent response to the mighty acts of God, even divine judgement—although a judgement that has salvation as its end result: '[w]hat still remains is the coming of a new creation.'[41]

There is a passage in *The Screwtape Letters* where, in writing to his demon-nephew, Screwtape comments disparagingly on heaven as a place of music and silence, as against the 'diabolical din' which he and his like have carefully cultivated in Hell:

> Music and silence—how I detest them both!
> How thankful we should be that ever since our

> Father entered Hell ... no square inch of infernal
> space and no moment of infernal times has been
> surrendered to either of those abominable forces,
> but all has been occupied by Noise — Noise, the
> grand dynamism, the audible expression of all
> that is exultant, ruthless, and virile — Noise
> which alone defends us from silly qualms,
> despairing scruples, and impossible desires.
> We will make the whole universe a noise in the
> end. We have already made great strides in this
> direction as regards the Earth. The melodies and
> silences of Heaven will be shouted down in the
> end.[42]

With grim humour, C.S. Lewis reveals paradoxically the exquisite atmosphere in the heavenly sphere, as depicted in Revelation—the music of praise, the silence of awe before the dawning of the new creation, the capacity for wonder and contemplation reflected in celestial silence as well as music. This silence—and this music—is intrinsic to Revelation's spirituality.

The seven trumpets proclaim once again the voice of judgement, the woes of the end time, issuing in mass-scale destruction and violence: the earth and sea, rivers and mountains, the inhabitants of the earth (8:6-11:19). At the same time, the final trumpet proclaims the victory of God's kingdom and the hope of release for the dead and those who have suffered (11:17-18).[43] This is an important pattern, essential for understanding the spirituality of Revelation: the movement from judgement to salvation. It is not a spirituality with which modern readers may be particularly comfortable. Yet judgement is not dreaded by the community of John the Seer but, on the contrary, longed for and welcomed. It represents vindication after injustice, the triumph of good over evil, the final victory of God.

Later in the Book of Revelation, the sword which issues from the White Rider, a sword of vengeance and judgement, comes from his mouth (19:15); his name is 'The-Word-of-God' (19:13), indicating that the language of physical violence in Revelation is metaphorical.[44] The same metaphorical usage occurs in Isaiah where the 'shoot from the stem of Jesse' will make judgement to vindicate the righteous poor, and will 'strike the earth with the rod of his mouth' and kill the wicked 'with the breath of his lips' (Isa 11:4). So also the Epistle to the Hebrews speaks in parallel terms of the 'living and active' word of God as 'sharper than a two-edged sword, piercing through to the division of soul and spirit, joints and marrow, discerning the desires and thoughts of the heart' (Heb 4:12). The language of weapon and warfare in Revelation is figurative for the power of God's discerning word, a word that brings salvation through God's repudiation of sin, suffering and death.[45] This is not a spirituality which advocates violence, but rather expresses in fierce imagery what it sees as the prior necessity of judgement before salvation can be ushered in. The violence is symbolic rather than actual.

The Heavenly Woman and the Dragon

Revelation's spirituality, with its extremity and vividness of language and metaphor, takes an unexpected turn in the following chapters. Before the next series of 'sevens', the seven plagues leading to final judgement and salvation, a remarkable vision intervenes that seems, at first, unconnected to what has come before: the vision of the heavenly woman and the dragon (12:1-17).[46] With its aftermath in the rising of the two beasts, one from the sea and one from the land (13:1-14:20), John the Seer locates in mythological terms the present tribulation of the community.[47] He sets out in symbolic form the enemies against which God and the church are set, an enmity that is embraced by the assurance of victory. This vision paves the way for the plagues which ensue, these being the consequence of allegiance to the devil and his minions. At the same time, it follows the opening of the temple and the glimpse into the ark of the covenant, both symbols of God's faithful and unswerving fidelity to Israel (11:19).

Behind the narrative of the pregnant heavenly woman, confronted by the fiery-red dragon, is a mythological framework that is located in more places than one. From a political point of view, there are parallels with the goddess Roma, personification of the city of Rome, and the emperor, her son—imagery that originated in the period of Augustus

(27 BC – 14 AD), when the first altars were raised at Pergamum and Nicomedia. Religiously, the myth is present in the Old Testament (e.g. Isa 27:1, 51:9-14; Jer 51:34-37; Ezek 32:1-6), with overtones of the Garden of Eden and the serpent's role in bringing about the Fall.[48] The Greco-Roman world also has mother-son myths which followed a pattern of threat, escape, rescue, and vindication. Under these widespread influences, Revelation presents its own version of the powerful woman giving birth to her son under attack from the dragon-serpent, whom the son will finally defeat. These parallels enable the ancient reader to identify with the myth and understand it in terms of Christian spirituality.

The story as narrated in Revelation 12 is particularly striking and dramatic. Divided into three sections, the story begins and ends with the heavenly woman and her tribulations (12:1-6, 13-17). In the midst is set the heavenly battle between the archangel Michael and the dragon (12:7-12; see 1 Enoch 6-13), in which the latter is overcome and hurled from heaven to earth, whence he makes trouble for the woman and 'the rest of her offspring' (12:17). Note the vivid contrast between the two in the opening scene. The red dragon is concerned only to destroy, his vast power directed towards vandalism and desecration (12:3-4), the 'parody of God the Creator'.[49] In contrast, the woman, who holds considerable authority in her association with the heavenly powers (sun, moon and stars, 12:1), is in the act of giving birth; her power is fecund and life-giving, pointing to salvation (12:2).[50]

What spirituality emerges from this striking myth? The defeat of the dragon—identified as the devil (12:9)—spells victory in heaven for the saints and martyrs, and at the same time violence and suffering for the earth onto which he is cast (12:12). On the one hand, Revelation's spirituality presents a theology of hope, with victory already attained in the celestial realm and soon to be consummated on earth. On the other hand, it serves to account for the existence of evil and suffering, assuring the reader that these are temporary and that their end already indicated. The sorrows of earth are provisional: the devil has little time in which to wreak havoc before he too will be overthrown and the earth cleansed of its pollution (12:12). In the meantime, the saints on earth, the children of the woman who represents Israel and the church,[51] are in the grip of suffering and persecution.[52] They are not without sustenance or protection. On the contrary: the newborn child is swept up into heaven (12:5) and the woman, now in flight in the wilderness (Exod 19:4; Deut 32:11), is protected by God and by the earth itself which comes to her aid (12:6, 14-16; Exod 15:12; Num 16:32-34).[53] This is a spirituality which takes seriously suffering, sorrow and violence, yet foresees their doom and offers protection in the midst of trial and tribulation. It offers the resources to endure, to remain hopeful, to rest in the promise of rescue and deliverance.

Believing existence is thus depicted as a battle-ground, not so much between God and Satan, as between the devil and the woman's children (supported by heavenly and earthly powers), which parallels the heavenly battle between Michael and the dragon. Only in this context does the spirituality of Revelation have meaning. It is significant that the devil and his two servants—the beast from the sea and the beast from the land (13:1-18)[54]—form an unholy alliance, a 'trinity' of violent and vengeful power. In a parody of the divine being, the first beast is even wounded on one of its heads (13:3, 12).[55] Nonetheless, for all the hurt and destruction they cause, all the idolatry and blasphemy they promote, all the followers they tragically gain, their power remains unreal. It counterfeits goodness, for it can create nothing of itself; it can only destroy. There is something sobering in this apocalyptic vision of evil as the parody of good, of evil as actively malevolent towards goodness. The spirituality of Revelation takes evil seriously, warning the community of its capacity to enthral, to captivate, to feign a being and attractiveness that are delusional and false. John's spirituality is martial in tone, but it looks to the defeat of evil and the emptying of the wrathful, divine cup for the sake of the new creation.

The Seven Plagues

A concomitant feature of Revelation's spirituality is its focus on liberation and redemption. The last series of 'sevens' within its apocalyptic cycles is the revelation of the seven plagues (Rev 15:1-

18:24). There are strong overtones in this section of the ten plagues brought on the Egyptians by Moses at the time of the exodus (Exod 7:14-12:32), plagues which led to the liberation of the Israelite slaves.[56] It is significant that the series begins with another glance into the heavenly sanctuary where a song of victory is sung, the song of Moses, 'the servant of God and of the Lamb' (15:3). Just as the ten plagues in Egypt express the wrath of God against the stubbornness of Pharaoh in refusing to let God's people go, so the seven plagues complete the judgement of God against the imperial might of Rome and all that it embodies (15:1). The ending of judgement means the fulfilment of liberation.

The following chapters disclose the working out of divine judgement on the earth. Each of the bowls is poured out by an angel onto the earth, the sea, the rivers and springs, the sun, the throne of the beast, the Euphrates river, and the air, bringing hail (17:1-21). But the main result of the plagues is judgement on the great Whore, the city of 'Babylon', a representation of Rome. A Roman coin of the first century AD strengthens this identification. This 'Dea Roma' coin depicts on one side the head of the Emperor Vespasian (69-79 AD); on the observe side is the goddess Roman reclining on a mound of seven hills, a sword dangling from one hand, signifying the military might of Rome.[57] In Revelation, the woman is a personification of the city and its economic life, as the author explains,[58] presiding over its conquests of lands and peoples, and its traffic in human lives.[59] The sexual immorality described is metaphorical of its idolatry (17:1-6).[60]

The depiction of the city, which stands as the mirror opposite of the New Jerusalem, leads to the description of its downfall in the following chapter, which is set out as an Old Testament lament (*qinah*). It outlines the tragedy as well as triumph of the empire's overthrow (18:2-3, 9-20), with a summons to leave the imperial city, and the rich and idolatrous life-style it yields, and to confirm the divine judgement against it (18:4-7). The rich and abundant life of princes, merchants, and seafarers is lamented in fine detail in this chapter, the poem bemoaning the loss of jewels and spices, cloth and furniture, and the ending of its cultural life, its musicians and craftsmen, its celebrations. But behind the lament is a fierce joy—the joy of those who have suffered at the empire's hands, the joy of those now vindicated (18:20).

The spirituality of the seven plagues is not an easy one to contemplate. It unsettles, as does so much of Revelation, widespread notions of universal love and toleration. We do not like to ponder the picture of a deity treading 'the winepress of the fury of his anger'. The spirituality of Revelation is directed against those who live in economic ease, and the idolatry of wealth that is seen to accompany it, as well as those who engage in other forms of idolatry, both literal and figurative. The imagery of 'Babylon' describes such commercial success and idolatry in vivid terms. The city is depicted as repugnant in its affluence and indifference, its corruption, idolatry, and uncleanness. Beale argues that these chapters depict the extravagance and wealth arising from the trade and commerce of empire of any kind—although set in the context of the Roman empire in the first century AD— along with the idolatries and oppression that often accompanying such empire-building: '[a]ny institution or facet of culture that is characterized by pride … economic overabundance, persecution, and idolatry is part of Babylon'.[61] This comment captures the sense of John the Seer's spirituality, its fierce attempt to rouse the reader, through vivid imagery, from spiritual sloth and collusion.

At the same time, the spirituality Revelation summons the reader faith to that all such violence and devastation is overcome in Christ's death and resurrection. The language of wrath and judgement is integral to Revelation's spirituality: God's wrath, poured out on the earth, represents the repudiation of those forces which damage life and creation. In the terms of Revelation, this is cause of consolation and hope for those who suffer; a spirituality that is ready to look suffering in the face and see within it, writ large, the life-giving triumph of God. As Koester aptly expresses it, the visions of judgement are not 'simple predictions, but … warnings that are designed to move readers to repentance and endurance'. In terms of the structure of Revelation, 'the book's repeated spirals may move downward into visions of threat, but they return each time to scenes of glory in the presence of God.'[62] What seems a harsh and life-denying spirituality has, at its heart, the conviction of triumph and joy. Its purpose is to challenge and fortify those who are tempted to take an easier path, in the Seer's understanding, and to strengthen and console those who have chosen the difficult path, the path of suffering and resistance.

Final Vision: Jerusalem

A vibrant note of joy permeates the final chapters of Revelation and the spirituality depicted there (19:1-22:17). Beginning with the worship and hymnody of the heavenly courts—its sung cry of triumph ('Alleluia!' 19:1, 3, 4, 6)—the victory supper follows the final battle. This battle defeats both Satan and death ('Hades'), throwing them into 'the lake of fire' (20:7-15), which is where everything associated with death belongs.[63] But the victorious feast is also a wedding banquet (19:7-8). The imagery of the Lamb has been consistently paradoxical in Revelation, as we have noted, the picture of innocence, vulnerability and sacrifice linked also to sovereignty and wrath (5:12-13; 6:16), the Lamb being both shepherd and warrior as well as sacrificial victim (7:17; 17:14). Here the imagery is further enlarged: the same Lamb, sacrifice and victor, is the bridegroom at the final banquet, and his Bride is the holy city of Jerusalem, her white raiment signifying the radiance and light of righteousness (19:8).

The spirituality of these chapters is one of beauty, restoration, and harmony on a cosmic scale. Revelation takes pains in its description of the heavenly city, given as a gift to human beings in the restoration of all things. Its features are symbolic and allegorical, representing Israel and the church, the ancient and the new people of God, in the perfection of its dimensions and the beauty of its streets and edifices (21:9-21). At the centre is the (literally) illuminating presence of God and the Lamb, to whom full access is now given, and the nations bring their own treasures within its walls (21:22-27). But the new Jerusalem is as much a garden as a city. The river flowing through its centre is surrounded on either side by an avenue of trees,[64] whose leaves have healing properties: the union of nature and civilisation (22:1-5), the vision of Eden restored and magnified.[65]

This last is the most beautiful of Revelation's visions, the most uncomplicated and simple—always providing that its imagery is interpreted with the allegorical meaning in mind (otherwise it can appear slightly absurd). The imagery of jewels and stones, gold and silver, light without darkness, rivers and healing leaves, is rich and evocative, portraying the true wealth of which the saints are heirs, as against the false, deceptive, and oppressive wealth of Babylon. City for city, the two stand alongside: the one an image of prosperity, riches and idolatry at vast cost and with enormous suffering; the other an image of prosperity, riches and worship freely bestowed and spelling the end to suffering. Not only is there no idolatry, but there is no temple in this city, no place of sacrifice, forgiveness and atonement, since 'the whole city is At-one-ment', "God with us", its *temple* is God and the Lamb.'[66]

It is significant for this spirituality that the gates of the city seem never to close. Always the spiritual and bridal voice echo the invitation to the uncleanness which surrounds it (22:17), inviting the thirsty to come and drink of the waters of life—a spirituality that remains available for all who desire it. In this picture of the city with its beauty and hospitality, Paradise is regained: in a garden, in cosmic harmony, in sociality and community, the doors always open for those who seek entry.[67] The new community extends to all living things and all creation, an ecological spirituality of creation and re-creation living joyfully within the dynamic grace of God.[68] In this sense, for all its focus on judgement, the spirituality of John the Seer is one of delight, pleasure, reconciliation, joy and welcome.

Revelation's spirituality is also strongly apocalyptic in these chapters. The last section focuses on the future coming of the Lord, with its hope and joy, where the visions of beauty and reconciliation will be fulfilled: 'Behold I am coming soon!' (22:7, 12, 20). The language moves from vision seen to written book (22:10, 18-20), enabling the spirituality of hope to concluding with an epistolary ending (22:21) that parallels the epistolary opening near the beginning of Revelation (1:4-5a) and the letters to the seven churches.[69] For this author, the written words are inspired prophecy, claiming almost a 'canonical' status, with warnings of the danger of adding to, or subtracting from, its contents (22:18-19).[70] Revelation's spirituality is enshrined not simply in ecstatic experience and mystical vision, but in the literary shaping and constructing of a text, giving form and objectivity to what might seem otherwise elusive and subjective. Access to this spirituality is ensured for future generations.

Conclusion

The spirituality of the Book of Revelation is an unusual and complex one. Here we find a spirituality that endeavours to take evil seriously, that confronts the horrors of suffering, yet also inflicts its own in images of wrath and judgement. At the same time, for John the Seer, God alone has the capacity to reconcile all things, to 'wipe away every tear' (Rev 7:17; 21:4), to forgive and atone for all things, and to bring about victory over suffering, sin and death. God's love and sovereignty have the last word in the spirituality of Revelation, despite the harshness of its language and imagery, and the violence of the symbolism which often accompanies it.

By the end of Revelation, the primary title for God has been, in mythological and literary terms, vindicated: 'the Almighty' (*Pantocrator*, 1:8; 4:8; 11:17; 15:3; 16:7, 14; 19:6, 15; 21:22). As Eugene Boring points out, John the Seer seeks to justify the title for God in relation to human history which is not abandoned, despite the radical presence of evil.[71] God's 'omnipotence', he suggests, is significantly qualified and redefined by the death of Jesus, so that the cross becomes 'the definitive expression of the power and love of God'.[72] This redefinition of 'mighty', in light of the cross, happens 'without reducing its extent.'[73] In this spirituality, God does not abandon the world of divine creating, nor is history left to itself in evil, idolatry and violence. God definitively enters the stage, bringing hope as well as warning, so that by the end the implied reader is invited to join the victory cry, 'Alleluia! For the Lord God, the Almighty reigns!' (19:6).

This theological perspective on Revelation's spirituality is important, but with some qualification. The translation 'omnipotent one' for *Pantocrator* can give a misleading impression if it suggests divine dominance and arbitrary power or if it seems to bypass the cross, as we have seen, and the image of the slaughtered Lamb. The latter signifies not that which is 'all-powerful' but innocent suffering and self-sacrifice. It is true that the final chapters of Revelation celebrate God's definitive victory over evil and suffering, but the means by which this is achieved—with the cross at its centre—cannot be ignored, as Boring rightly notes. The 'might' of God is the might of suffering and death, freely-chosen. In this sense, divine sovereignty is confirmed in the paradoxical way in which God chooses to intervene in the world, according to Revelation, to bring to an end its suffering and its sin. In this sense, *Pantocrator* is perhaps better understood as 'all-ruling' or 'all-holding'. The spirituality of Revelation depicts a God who gathers all things and unites all things in the one gracious, liberating reign.

The obvious objection to this reading of divine sovereignty through the cross is the vehement language of judgement in Revelation, and the fiery nature of God's wrath. But once again we need to note the metaphorical nature of the language. Nowhere is there a call to arms against those who oppress the communities of the seven churches; nowhere is retaliation advocated, even if it were possible. In the spirituality of Revelation, salvation includes judgement, includes the expression of divine wrath against all that is unholy, deceitful, unjust; the rejection of what is evil and destructive.[74]

Another way to put this question is to ask how universal John the Seer's understanding of salvation is. Some parts of Revelation seem to imply this perspective, whereas others suggest the opposite. W.J. Harrington argues that 'positive eschaton' is a more adequate term than 'universal salvation', given the undoubted tension in Revelation between God's will and human freedom.[75] Yet the gates of the city remain open, and the call persists to those outside. If there is no 'negative eschaton', as Harrington suggests, and God's sovereignty is ultimately asserted, what becomes of human choice? For Harrington, the choice remains, but the consequences are real for those who knowingly choose evil over good: 'There is no future for such a one, because evil has no future'.[76] This reading makes a good deal of sense, holding together various tensions within the spirituality of Revelation:

divine sovereignty, the defeat of evil, the justice and goodness of God, human freedom. Yet the question remains: When, if ever, do the gates close?

One final comment on Revelation and its composition. While the Book of Revelation is largely an apocalypse, its epistolary beginning and end make clear that, whatever may or may not have happened on that Lord's Day on the island of Patmos, what we now have is something very different. The visions of Revelation are not poured forth spontaneously. On the contrary, despite their mystical origins, their written form is carefully arranged and crafted within the structure of Revelation, giving the impression of considerable reflection and literary prowess. The question of genre is a keen one for the Book of Revelation because of its mixed nature, as we have observed; but what it does provide is visionary experiences that have been meditated upon and crafted to address themselves to specific readers, the community of the seven churches. Perhaps the warnings at the end belong to this period of thoughtfulness and discernment, the author convinced that his letter has magisterial status and authority.

This too is a dimension of Revelation's spirituality. Spiritual experience, in this writing, does not have authoritative status without reflection and discernment. The movement from vision to pen, from ecstatic experience to rational composition, requires a level of perspicacity and critique on the part of the author. In such a spirituality, there is no raw experience that can be appealed to without its location in the liturgy, rituals and traditions of the communities from which it arises. A Johannine spirituality leaves room for consideration and discrimination, testing itself against prophetic witness and apostolic tradition. Such witness is concerned, for this writer, with the spirituality of believers, the living out of their lives in active and courageous resistance to the powers-that-be, in the hope of the transformation of all things, and the daily hallowing of their lives in truth and love.

End Notes

[1.] Christopher Rowland, 'Forward' in S. Moyise (ed.), *Studies in the Book of Revelation* (Edinburgh & New York: T & T Clark, 2001), xvii.

2. On the plot of Revelation see David L. Barr, 'The Story John Told. Reading Revelation for its Plot' in D.L. Barr (ed.), *Reading the Book of Revelation: A Resource for Students* (Atlanta: SBL, 2003), 11-23; also J.L. Resseguie, *Revelation Unleashed. A Narrative Critical Approach to John's Apocalypse* (BIS; Leiden: Brill, 1998), 160-192.

3. Ian Paul, 'The Book of Revelation: Image, Symbol and Metaphor' in Moyise (ed.), *Studies*, 131.

4. Further on symbolism in Revelation, see, e.g., Paul, 'Image, Symbol and Metaphor', 131-147, G.K. Beale, *The Book of Revelation. A Commentary on the Greek Text* (NIGTC; Grand Rapids: Eerdmans, 1999), 50-69, and Dan Lioy, *The Book of Revelation in Christological Focus* (Studies in Biblical Literature 58; New York: Peter Lang, 2003), 102-108. On artistic interpretations of the visions of Revelation, see Christopher Rowland, 'Imagining the Apocalypse' *NTS* 51 (2005), 303-27.

5. *Revelation* (NCBC; Cambridge: Cambridge University Press, 2003), 83. On the use of rational argument in the Letters to the Seven Churches, see David A. deSilva, *Seeing Things John's Way. The Rhetoric of the Book of Revelation* (Louisville: Westminster John Knox, 2009), 229-255.

6. Lynn R. Huber points out that the metaphorical language of Revelation is not adornment to be rifled through in order to attain meaning but rather 'allows humans to use their experience and understanding of the concrete to understand and express the abstract' (*Like a Bride Adorned. Reading Metaphor in John's Apocalypse* [Emory Studies in Early Christianity; New York & London: T & T Clark, 2008, 180). In this study of nuptial imagery in Revelation, Huber sees metaphor as the mapping of one concept ('the source domain') onto another ('the target domain'), showing that aspects of the target domain are emphasised while others are deliberately downplayed (179-184).

7. The image of a tapestry is used in Ian Boxall, *Revelation: Vision and Insight* (London: SPCK, 2002), 48-82, based on the discovery of the 'Angers Apocalypse' in 1843, an immense, mediaeval tapestry with seven sections and fourteen scenes from the Book of Revelation (48). It was produced by Nicholas Bataille and Robert Poinçon between 1375 and 1382. http;//sourcebook.fsc.edu/history/tapestry29.jpg.

8. Udo Schnelle, 'Revelation: Seeing and Understanding' in *Theology of the New Testament* (ET: Grand Rapids: Baker Academic, 2009), 751.

9. Beale, *Revelation*, gives a brief outline of the major interpretative approaches that are still current (44-49).

10. For a survey of interpretations since 1600, see Kenneth G.C. Newport, *Apocalypse and Millennium. Studies in Biblical Eisegesis* (Cambridge: Cambridge University Press, 2000); on mediaeval understandings, see R.K.

Emmerson and M. BcGinn, The *Apocalypse in the Middle Ages* (Ithaca and London: Cornell University Press, 1992); for a history of millenarianism from the early Church onwards, see Arthur W. Wainwright, *Mysterious Apocalypse. Interpreting the Book of Revelation* (Abingdon: Nashville, 1993), 19-103.

[11.] E.g. Elisabeth Schüssler Fiorenza, *Revelation: Vision of a Just World* (Edinburgh: T & T Clark, 1993); also the summary discussion in deSilva, *Seeing Things John's Way*, 27-63; also Wes Howard-Brook and Anthony Gwyther, *Unveiling Empire. Reading Revelation Then and Now* (Maryknoll: Orbid Books, 2000), 87-119, and J. Nelson Kraybill, *Imperial Cult and Commerce in John's Apocalypse* (JSNTSS 132; Sheffield: Sheffield Academic Press, 1996). See especially the series of four articles in *Revelation as a Critique of Empire, Int* 63 (1, 2009), 5-54.

[12.] See, e.g., Tina Pippin, *Death and Desire. The Rhetoric of Gender in the Apocalypse of John* (Westminster: John Knox, 1992), who takes the latter view.

[13.] Bruce J. Malina, *On the Genre and Message of Revelation. Star Visions and Sky Journeys* (Peabody: Hendrickson, 1995); also Jacques M. Chevalier, *A Postmodern Revelation. Signs of Astrology and the Apocalypse* (Toronto: University of Toronto Press, 1997), esp. 175-358.

[14.] See especially Adela Yarbro Collins, *The Combat Myth in the Book of Revelation* (Montana: Scholars Press, 1976), which draws on the Greek myth of Apollo slaying the Python, the earth-dragon, and establishing his prophetic sanctuary in the same place, Delphi. See below on the Heavenly Woman.

[15.] *How to Read the Apocalypse* (ET; New York: Crossroad, 1993), 1-11. On the centrality of John's Christology in the narrative and structure of Revelation, see Lioy, *Revelation*, esp. 161-172.

[16.] Prévost, *Revelation*, 23 (13-23).

[17.] Prévost, *Revelation*, 25-41. For a brief guide to the numbers, see, John Sweet, *Revelation* (2nd ed.; London: SCM, 1990), 14-15.

[18.] Prévost, *Revelation*, 43-57.

[19.] Prévost, *Revelation*, 66 (59-66).

[20.] For a history of interpretation that includes liturgy, art and music ('reception history'), see Judith Kovacs and Christopher Rowland, *Revelation. The Apocalypse of Jesus Christ* (Blackwell Bible Commentaries; Oxford: Blackwell, 2004), esp. 13-38.

[21.] In discussing the significance of 'seven', Austin Farrer concludes that Revelation is built around a series of six sevens, constituting 'a working week of God's judgement' that corresponds to the six days of creation in Genesis (*A Rebirth of Images. The Making of St John's Apocalypse* [Westminster: Dacre Press, 1949], 59 [36-90]).

22. http://www.wga.hu/index1.html.

23. Craig R. Koester, 'Revelation's Visionary Challenge to Ordinary Empire' *Int* 63 (2009), 18.

24. 'Lamb' in reference to Jesus occurs some twenty-eight times in Revelation (5:6, 8, 12-13; 6:1, 16; 7:9-10, 14. 17; 8:1; 12:11; 13:8; 14:1, 4, 10; 15:3; 17:14; 19:7, 9; 21:9, 14, 22; 22: 1,3). The second beast from the earth is described as being 'like a lamb', but this is part of its plagiarism (13:11). On the Lamb in Revelation, see Loren L. Johns, *The Lamb Christology of the Apocalypse of John* (WUNT 167; Tübingen: Mohr Siebeck, 2003), esp 150-205.

25. The use of such phrases as 'alpha and omega', 'beginning and end', and 'first and last', is called 'merism': a form of synecdoche in which the contrasting pairs include everything that lies in between; see Beale, *Book of Revelation*, 199, 1055.

26. So Richard Bauckham, *The Theology of the Book of Revelation* (NT Theology; Cambridge: Cambridge University Press, 1993), 109.

27. Bauckham, *Theology*, 110-115.

28. Further on the social and historical setting of the letters, see Colin J. Hemer, *The Letters to the Seven Churches of Asia in Their Local Setting* (JSNTSS 11; Sheffield: JSOT Press, 1986), which outlines, in some detail, the history and setting of each of the seven cities, showing the author's personal knowledge of topography and context.

29. Craig R. Koester, *Revelation and the End of All Things* (Grand Rapids: Eerdmans, 2001), 54-57.

30. It is not entirely clear how much persecution the communities of the seven letters were actually experiencing, given that so few concrete examples are given in Revelation. Perhaps it is more the fear and the possibility rather than the actuality.

31. Peter Adam makes this point: the parenesis is unusual in that it occurs near the beginning of Revelation, in the letters (*Hearing God's Words. Exploring Biblical Spirituality* [Downers Grove: InterVarsity Press, 2004], 115).

32. Further on this point, see Warren Carter, 'Accommodating 'Jezebel' and Withdrawing John: Negotiating Empire in Revelation Then and Now' *Int* 63 (2009), 32-47.

33. A good example is the commendation to Pergamum, with its resistance against the evil empire, even while dwelling 'where the throne of Satan is' (2:12-13); see Adele Yarbro Collins, 'Satan's Throne: Revelations from

Revelation' *BAR* 32 (2006), 26-39.

34. The only churches that receive a positive appraisal are Smyrna and Philadelphia, both associated with suffering; see the comments in Ben Witherington, *Revelation* (NCBC; Cambridge: Cambridge University Press, 2003), 108-111.

35. Note the comment of Allen Dwight Callahan: 'We live in a world at the beginning of the twenty-first century that John condemned at the end of the first.' ('Babylon Boycott: The Book of Revelation' *Int* 63 [2009], 54).

36. See Eugene M. Boring, *Revelation* (Louisville: John Knox, 1989), 120-121, for a helpful diagram of the 'sevenfold pattern of woes' in these chapters.

37. On Jesus as the object of worship within a monotheistic framework, see Richard Bauckham, *The Climax of Prophecy. Studies in the Book of Revelation* (Edinburgh: T & T Clark, 1993), 118-149.

38. See Maryanne Meye Thompson, 'Worship in the Book of Revelation' *Ex Auditu* 8 (1992), 45-54; also Bauckham, *Theology*, 23-53; also John T. Carroll, 'Revelation 4:1-11' *Int* 63 (2009), 56-58.

39. *Imperial Cults and the Apocalypse of John. Reading Revelation in the Ruins* (Oxford: Oxford University Press, 2001), 197, and Richard Bauckham, 'Creation's Praise of God in the Book of Revelation' *BTB* 38 (2008), 55-63.

40. Brian K. Blount, *Revelation. A Commentary* (Louisville: Westminster John Knox, 2009), 157-158.

41. Jürgen Roloff, *The Revelation of John. A Continental Commentary* (ET; Minneapolis: Fortress, 1993), 101.

42. C.S Lewis, *The Screwtape Letters* (London: Geoffrey Bles, 1942), 113-114.

43. Elisabeth Schüssler Fiorenza argues that the hymn of 11:15-19 is the literary and theological centre of Revelation, expressing its central theme (*The Book of Revelation: Justice and Judgment* [2nd ed.; Minneapolis: Fortress Press, 1998], 56).

44. Schnelle, 'Revelation', 770-1.

45. On the metaphorical and non-literal nature of the language of violence in Revelation, see W.J. Harrington, *Revelation* (SP 16; Collegeville: Liturgical Press, 1993), 229-230. See also Rebecca Skaggs & Thomas Doyle, 'Violence in the Apocalypse of John' *CBR* 5 (2007), 220-34.

46. Further on the narrative, see Dorothy Lee, 'The Heavenly Woman and the Dragon: Re-readings of Revelation 12' in F.D. Glass & L. McCredden (eds.), *Feminist Poetics of the Sacred. Creative Suspicions* (Oxford: Oxford

University Press, 2001), 198-220.

47. On the background of the imagery for the woman and the dragon, see Chevalier, *Postmodern Revelation*, 329-335.

48. Paul S. Minear, 'Far as the Curse is Found: The Point of Revelation 12:15-16' *NovT* 33 (1991), 71-77, Sweet, *Revelation*, 194-196.

49. Talbert, *The Apocalypse*, 49.

50. She is depicted as 'a cosmic queen who has power over the rhythm of night and day and over human destiny' (Adela Yarbro Collins, 'Feminine Symbolism in the Book of Revelation', *Biblical Interpretation* 1 [1993], 21). The woman's power is associated with both day and night (Gen 1:14-18; Ps 136:7-9); in Greek mythological terms, she is associated with the realms of Apollo (the sun, civilization, culture) and Artemis (the moon, the hunt, the feminine).

51. There are overtones of the Virgin Mary, as well as Eve, the mother of all living (Gen 3:15), and Zion, mother of Israel (Isa 26:16-27; 54:1; 66:7-11).

52. An alternative interpretation sees the woman as representing the individual believer in his or her struggle to give birth to the Christ, a reading based on the experience of mysticism: 'the "eternal birth" ... of the Son in the soul' (J. Ben-Daniel, 'Towards the Mystical Interpretation of Revelation 12' *Revue Biblique* 114 [2007], 606 [594-616]).

53. 'The earth is not just the stage ... but an actor in the drama; so Boring, *Revelation*, 153; see Roloff, *Revelation*, 151.

54. The number of the beast, 666 (13:18), is one of the most perplexing puzzles in the Book of Revelation and has received considerable attention. See Beale, *Revelation*, 718-728, who argues that the number has figurative meaning and cannot be located in any specific person or ruler. In the light of 'seven' signifying completion, the repetition of sixes suggests eternal incompletion; yet evil too can be represented by the number seven (e.g. 12:1, 13:1, 17:4). Robert H. Mounce concludes: 'the history of interpretation demonstrates that no consensus has been reached on whom or what John had in mind' (*The Book of Revelation* [NICNT; 2nd ed.; Grand Rapids: Eerdmans, 1998), 261.

55. The heads and horns, along with the crowns, on the two beasts portray intelligence, as well as power and authority.

56. On the parallelism with the plagues, see Beale, *Revelation*, 808-812.

57. David E. Aune, *Revelation 17-22* (WBC 42C; Nashville: Thomas Nelson, 1998), 920-922. Other features of the coin include a wolf suckling Romulus and Remus, and the figure of Neptune, the Roman sea god (emphasising Rome's might on the waters); the letters S and C stand for 'Senatus consultum' ('a resolution of the Senate').

58. The vision of Rev 17 consists of the vision itself (the Great Whore, 17:1-6) and its allegorical interpretation provided by the angel (17:7-18), the explanation making it unique within the book—although such interpretation is a feature of apocalyptic literature in general; see Aune, *Revelation* 17-22, 915, 919.

59. On the slave trade in the Roman empire (Rev 18:13), see Craig R. Koester, 'Roman Slave Trade and the critique of Babylon in Revelation 18' *CBQ* 70 (2008), 766-86.

60. See Beale, *Revelation*, 854-856.

61. Beale, *Revelation*, 856.

62. *Revelation*, 204-205.

63. On the 1,000 year reign and its background (Rev 20:1-8), see esp. Beale, *Revelation*, 1017-1021, which he interprets as figurative rather than literal; for other different kinds of millenarianist interpretations of Revelation, see pp. 972-974.

64. So Aune, *Revelation* 17-22, 1177-1178, who argues for many trees here, in accord with Ezek 47:7. Against this, cf. David Mathewson, *A New Heaven and a New Earth: The Meaning and Function of the Old Testament in Revelation 21.1-22.5* (JSNTS 238; Sheffield: Sheffield Academic Press, 2009), 189-190, who argues that there is only one tree, the Tree of Life (Gen 3:22, 24).

65. Sweet suggests that, while not explicit, the tree of the cross, 'healing the hurt caused by the tree of Eden', may be part of the metaphorical field here (*Revelation*, 311).

66. Sweet, *Revelation*, 308.

67. The main biblical texts that lie behind this vision of Paradise are Gen 2-3, Ezek 47, Zech 14 and Isa 60; further on this, see Mathewson, *New Heaven*, 186-215. Parts of the Song of Songs are also relevant here, with the garden imagery and the picture of union in love between the lovers (Song of Songs 2:10-13; 4:12-16; 5:1; 6:2-3; 7:11-13; 8:13).

68. Bauckham, 'Creation's Praise', 62-3. See also Richard Woods, 'Seven Bowls of Wrath: The Ecological Relevance of Revelation' *BTB* 38 (2008), 64-75, and Mark Bredin, 'God the Carer: The Book of Revelation' *BTB* 38 (2008), 76-86.

69. Aune, *Revelation* 17-22, 1205-1206, sets out a number of parallels between 1:1-3 and 22:6-10, 18.

70. It is likely that Rev 22 reflects a liturgical structure – see Aune, *Revelation* 17-22, 1206-1208, for various proposals, though he himself is sceptical.

71. Eugene M. Boring, 'The Theology of Revelation: "The Lord Our God the Almighty Reigns"' *Int* 40 (1986), 257-269.

72. Boring, 'Theology', 265. See John M. Court, *Revelation* (NT Guides; Sheffield: JSOT Press, 1994), 1171-118.

73. Boring, 'Theology', 261.

74. 'The path to the kingdom goes through, not around, the woes of history' (Boring, *Revelation*, 134).

75. *The Apocalypse of John: A Commentary* (London: Geoffrey Chapman, 1969), 229-235.

76. Harrington, *Apocalypse*, 234.

Conclusion

Our study of these texts has indicated that spirituality is an intrinsic aspect of their content, and not simply a personal and subjective response to their meaning. Spirituality has substance and is not confined to the experience of the reader. This understanding of spirituality assumes a close relationship to theology, the theology which emerges from the biblical writings. The difference in genre across gospel, epistle and apocalyptic vision makes both for theological differences and for varying perspectives in spirituality, quite apart from differences of authorship and community setting. Despite these divergences, there are a number of points that can be drawn out from the three, illustrating the spirituality they share. This spirituality shares much in common, although it is articulated in different ways and has different emphases.

Christology lies at the centre of Johannine spirituality, in each of its manifestations. In the Fourth Gospel and epistles, this conviction is tied in the closest way to the incarnation, the advent of God in mortal flesh; likewise, in the Book of Revelation, Jesus represents God's tabernacle among mortals (Jn 1:14; 1 Jn 1:1-2; Rev 21:3). The spirituality of this depiction includes an earthly quality in the presentation of Jesus; no matter how lofty a portrait is drawn of him—the divine Word and Son, the Alpha and Omega—his humanity is palpable in each text. This perspective serves as the basis for an embodied spirituality that reflects the belief that the world is the domain of God's creating. The role of the senses is apparent in all three texts; each has its own emphasis on sight, hearing, taste, touch and smell, which speaks first to the incarnation and secondly to the reader's imaginative entry into the world of the text. Each text, in its own way, depicts a vivid drama of salvation that engages the reader sensually and spiritually. The incarnation is paralleled by the confirmation of matter in these and other ways throughout our texts.

As the Creator of the universe, God is also its Redeemer, the one who does not let the world go, but steps onto the stage as a player in the drama, as *the* Player in the drama, the one through whom creation and history find their ultimate meaning and final victory. The spirituality of our three texts confirms the world as God's creation and, more significantly, affirms its destiny in the redemptive, re-creative divine will. The salvation of the world, in this sense, happens in and through Christ, the Word made flesh, the Son who has come in human form, the dwelling of God among mortals.

In all three texts, the cross holds a vital place. In John's Gospel it is the moment of glorification and exaltation, the lifting up of the Son to the Father, the ladder between heaven and earth. In the epistles, the self-sacrifice of Jesus on the cross is the means of forgiveness, the divine provider of advocacy and atonement for sinful humanity, in order that they might become children of God, those born of divine love. In Revelation, beside the throne stands the slaughtered Lamb (Rev 5:10), the one whose shed blood is ironically the source of cleansing and healing for the nations. In all three texts, the cross represents the incongruous and incomparable triumph of God over all that is evil and sinful. The triumphant utterance of the Johannine Jesus on the cross, 'It is finished!' (Jn 19:30), is echoed in the hymns of Revelation and the final victory cry (Rev 19:6). The world and human history—the earth itself—is the battle-ground on which God takes issue with 'the ruler of this world', challenging his presumptuous regime and overcoming him with the sword of the Word, liberating believers from the yoke of slavery and oppression, the violence of idolaters. The Johannine epistles speak of the evil one as conquered, the world (in the negative sense) overcome, and the spirit of antichrist cast out (1 Jn 2:13; 4:3-4; 5:4-5); the works of the devil are destroyed in the advent of the Son of God. The cross also redefines the way in which power is apprehended. While the victory is God's, and the evil usurper cast down, this victory is achieved ultimately not through military might or force but through vulnerability and self-sacrifice. As we have seen, this point seems hard to assert in view of the violence of Revelation's language, but once we understand it as metaphorical, the resultant effect is very different. The blood of Jesus has extraordinary significance in these texts—atoning, washing, cleansing, giving life. In this spirituality, Jesus the triumphant warrior is also, indeed primarily, the vulnerable and self-sacrificing Lamb.

Each of the three texts has God as its centre and the core of its spirituality. Salvation is the will and purpose of God, who is the origin of all things in creation and redemption. In the Fourth Gospel and epistles, the primary title for God is 'Father', a title that relates first and foremost to the identity of Jesus as Son. God is the Father of Jesus. Only in a secondary and derivative sense does God become the Father of believers, and only because they are incorporated into the filiation of Jesus. In Revelation, God is Pantocrator, the almighty and all-ruling one who holds creation in being and reveals divine sovereignty, a sovereignty disclosed in self-giving and sacrifice. God retains transcendence in all the texts, and within these metaphorical fields. In the Gospel of John, God cannot be seen or known (Jn 1:18; 6:46). In 1 John, the invisible God is manifest in the human face of the brother or sister in the community (1 Jn 4:12). In the Book of Revelation, the one who sits on the throne, in dazzling lustre and beauty, is never actually described, though everything else in the heavenly sanctuary is (Rev 4:2-3). God's immanence is articulated in Jesus, in the communion of the saints, in rainbow and jewel, in thunder and lightning, but the face of God is beyond mortal sight, just as the knowledge of God is beyond mortal ken. Even in revelation at its most overt, divine mystery remains; if anything, the Christ event intensifies the sense of mystery at what is paradoxically revealed.

The Spirit is of particular significance in the spirituality of each of our texts, inspiring, encouraging, enabling, challenging, supporting. John the Seer is granted his visions through the agency of the Spirit, who gives him access to the celestial sanctuary (Rev 1:10; 4:2). John's Gospel has a particular focus on the Spirit as Paraclete, ensuring the abiding of Christ within the community of faith (Jn 14:16). The epistles likewise give space to the Spirit as the gift of God to the children of God, bearing witness alongside the 'water and the blood', manifestations of Christ's sacrificial love (1 Jn 3:24b; 5:6, 8). In this sense, the Spirit is linked both to God and to Jesus, as well as closely allied to the believing community. The Spirit makes the connections—

within the life of God, between God and the community of faith, and within and among believers.

In rather different ways, each text acknowledges not only the hope of salvation but also the warning of judgement as intrinsic to its spirituality. The dialogue between Jesus and his opponents in the Gospel, his role as Light of the world and Son of Man, encompass the theme of judgement. In John's Gospel, Jesus both judges and does not judge (Jn 8:15-16): the response of people to the shining of the Light is judgement enough, evidenced in welcome or repudiation (Jn 3:18-21). The cross itself is, among other things, the articulation of divine judgement on the world, a judgement that overturns the world's presumption in putting Jesus on trial and that critically exposes its darkness. In the epistles, the beliefs and conduct of the secessionists, described as deceivers, antichrist, and sinful, expose them to the judgement of the writer, a judgement that displays itself as authoritative and definitive. Their false teaching leads them out of communion and thus out of fellowship with the Johannine community (2 Jn 10): they have been cut off—or, perhaps more likely, have cut themselves off. In either case, the response of the elder, with the authority he claims, represents divine judgement. The Book of Revelation is replete with symbols of judgement, particularly in the seven woes, and climaxing in the judgement on the Whore and the binding and destruction of Satan in the lake of fire. Yet these scenarios of judgement, however difficult we find them, reveal a spirituality that stands over against what is seen as evil, oppressive, unclean, violent and idolatrous.

The community of faith has a vital role to play in the spirituality of all three texts. Neither the Fourth Gospel and epistles, nor the Book of Revelation, have an individualistic or isolationist spirituality. Their concern is not with individuals but with persons in community. To make this point is not to deny the concern for personal spirituality within these writings. But personhood is understood communally; each believer belongs to God, first and foremost, as part of a community, a community that stretches between heaven and earth (Rev 6:10). This sociality is most apparent in Revelation and the Letters to the Seven Churches (Rev 2:1-3:22), but it is present also in 1 John's kinship language, especially the stress on familial love as the sign of belonging to God (1 Jn 3:14-17; 4:7; 3 Jn 5-8). In the Fourth Gospel it is most apparent in the parabolic allegory of the sheep and the fold, the vine and the branches, and the dragnet on the shores of Lake Galilee (Jn 10:1-18; 15:1-8; 21:1-14), all of which are organic symbols for the believing community. It is apparent in the gifting of the mother of Jesus and the beloved disciple to one another at the foot of the cross (Jn 19:26-27).

Worship plays an important part in the life of the community and is intrinsic to the spirituality of the Johannine writings. The Gospel of John, although the language is not frequent, implies a commitment to worship of the Father 'in spirit and truth', in the 'Spirit of truth' (Jn 4:23-24). This understanding of worship addressed to the Father is located in the identity of Jesus, and especially his self-offering on the cross, which signifies his worshipful exaltation to the Father's side, the ultimate prayer of his human life. The Johannine Jesus is the true worshipper, the object of worship, and also the locus of worship in and through the Spirit. In Revelation, worship and liturgy are practically ceaseless in the celestial realm—but for that ominous half-hour of silence (Rev 8:1)—and God and the Lamb are the objects of worship (Rev 4:1-5:14). Worship lies at the heart of Revelation's spirituality, standing in opposition to the idolatry characteristic of the Roman empire, to which John the Seer is adamantly opposed. In the epistles, worship is less explicit, yet the stress on confession of faith (1 Jn 4:2, 15)—particularly in relation to the identity of Jesus—suggests a liturgical context where the believing community gathers to affirm its faith in God and love for one another (1 Jn 3:1; 2 Jn 5). Believers share a common identity as children of God and a common, future destiny in becoming 'like Christ' (1 Jn 3:2), which is intrinsic to the spirituality of the epistles.

The Johannine writings display, each in its own way, the conviction of suffering as inevitable in the life of believers: suffering is part and parcel of spirituality. In the Fourth Gospel, the struggle is seen in those who move towards faith, who are drawn to Jesus but do not always understood; who are attracted to his message yet daunted sometimes by its implications. It is present in the hostility of the world and the inevitability of persecution. It is present in the painful unfinality of all things, despite the richness of what is made present. In the Johannine epistles, the community struggles to hold itself in union, to grasp its centre, to find itself anew in the loss of those who have left, those who have seceded from the gathered company. In Revelation there is the threat of persecution throughout, and the struggle to hold uncompromisingly to the faith, without surrender or concession to the powers that threaten the community: not just with violence but with indifference and compromise. In each case, suffering and struggle are part of the spiritual journey, yet also assured of their end, and of the advent of joy and union in the re-creative purpose of God.

To sum up: Johannine spirituality in all three texts is grounded in the life of God, the dynamic presence of the Spirit, the gracious love of the Father, and the incarnate presence of Jesus, crucified and risen. The story of God's dealings with the people of God is the framework which makes sense of believers' lives. In the incarnation, Jesus identifies with the human story and with the story of creation. In turn, believers are invited to encase their small stories within that larger tale. Such an outlook is both community oriented and personal. It is spirited and embodied, celestial and terrestrial, with the capacity to ascend from earth to heaven and heaven to earth. Nor need such a spirituality be restricted to the human domain: the extent of redemption is the extent of creation itself. Divine judgement is the observe side of salvation, not alien to its spirituality but framed by it. It looks expectantly, beyond judgement and negation, to divine affirmation—God's future as the source of life and hope, a future that already permeates the present, as the dawn begins to lighten the night sky. Such a spirituality awaits the future: the divine promise to wipe away all tears in the final overthrow of sin and death; yet it lives now within that anticipated reality, transforming the present. The spirituality of the Fourth Gospel, the Johannine epistles, and the Book of Revelation, is rich and variegated. It is pervaded by the conviction that is found on the spiritual path for believers and for the community of faith: the hallowing of their lives before God in truth and love.

Bibliography

Adam, Peter. *Hearing God's Words. Exploring Biblical Spirituality*. Downers Grove: InterVarsity Press, 2004

Alison, James. *Living in the End Times. The Last Things Re-Imagined* London: SPCK, 1966.

Allison, D.C. 'The Eye Is the Lamp of the Body (Matthew 6:22-23=Luke 11:34-36)' *NTS* 33 (1987): 62-66.

Alter, Robert & Kermode, Frank. *The Literary Guide to the Bible*. London: Fontana, 1987.

Anderson, Paul N. 'The Having-Sent-Me Father: Aspects of Agency, Encounter, and Irony in the Johannine Father-Son Relationship'. *Semeia* 85 (1999): 33-57.

———. *The Fourth Gospel and the Quest for Jesus: Modern Foundations Reconsidered* (Edinburgh: T & T Clark, 2007).

———. 'John and Mark—the Bi-Optic Gospels'. In Robert Fortna & Tom Thatcher (eds.), *Jesus in Johannine Tradition*. Philadelphia: Westminster, 2001: 175-88.

Anderson, Paul N., Just, Felix, & Tom Thatcher (eds.). *John, Jesus, and History, Volume 2: Aspects of Historicity in the Fourth Gospel*. Atlanta: SBL, 2009.

Ashton, John. *Understanding the Fourth Gospel*. 2nd edition. Oxford: Oxford University Press, 2007.

Augustine. *Confessions* (2 vols.; ET: W. Watts, LCL; Cambridge, MS: Harvard University Press, 1912.

———. *Sermones* in J.-P. Migne (ed.), Patrologia Graeca. 166 vols., 1857-66 87.1

Aune, David E. *Revelation*. 3 vols; WBC52; Dallas: Word Books, 1997.

Barr, David R. 'John's Ironic Empire'. *Int* 63 (2009): 20-30.

Barr (ed.), David R. *Reading the Book of Revelation: A Resource for Students*. Atlanta: SBL, 2003.

Barrett, C.K. *The Gospel According to St John. An Introduction with Commentary and Notes on the Greek Text*. 2nd ed. London: SPCK, 1978.

———. *Essays on John*. London: SPCK, 1982.

———. *The Prologue of St John's Gospel*. London: Athlone Press, 1971.

Barton, Stephen C. *The Spirituality of the Gospels.* London: SPCK, 1992.

Bauckham, Richard.   *The Climax of Prophecy. Studies in the Book of Revelation.* Edinburgh: T & T Clark, 1993.

―――. 'Historiographical Characteristics of the Gospel of John', *NTS* 53 (2007): 17-36.

―――. *Jesus and the Eyewitnesses. The Gospels as Eyewitness Testimony.* Grand Rapids, Michigan/Cambridge, UK: Eerdmans, 2006.

―――. *The Theology of the Book of Revelation.* NT Theology; Cambridge: Cambridge University Press, 1993.

Bauckham, Richard (ed.), *The Gospels for All Christians: Re-thinking the Gospel Audiences.* Grand Rapids: Eerdmans, 1998.

Bauckham, Richard. 'Creation's Praise of God in the Book of Revelation'. *BTB* (2008): 55-63.

Bauckham, Richard & Mosser, C. (eds.). *The Gospel of John and Christian Theology.* Grand Rapids: Eerdmans, 2008.

Beale, G.K. *The Book of Revelation. A Commentary on the Greek Text.* NIGTC; Grand Rapids: Eerdmans, 1999.

Beasley-Murray, George R. *John.* WBC; Waco: Waco Books, 1987.

Bell, Arthur A. 'The Date of John's Apocalypse: The Evidence of Some Roman Historians Reconsidered'. *NTS* 25 (1978): 93-102.

Ben-Daniel, J. 'Towards the Mystical Interpretation of Revelation 12'. *Revue Biblique* 114 (2007): 594-616.

Betz, H.D. "Matthew vi.22f and Ancient Greek Theories of Vision". In *Text and Interpretation. Studies in the New Testament Presented to Matthew Black.* Cambridge: Cambridge University Press, 1979: 46-64.

de Bhaldraithe, Eoin, 'The Johannine Prologue Structure and Origins'. *AusBR* 58 (2010): 57-71.

Bierenger, R. '"Greater than our Hearts" (1 John 3:20): the spirit in the Gospel of John' *Bible Today* 45 (2007) 305-9.

Blount, Brian K. *Revelation. A Commentary.* Louisville: Westminster John Knox, 2009.

Boring, Eugene M. *Revelation.* Louisville: John Knox, 1989.

―――. 'The Theology of Revelation: "The Lord Our God the Almighty Reigns"'. *Int* 40 (1986): 257-69.

Boxall, Ian. *Revelation: Vision and Insight.* London: SPCK, 2002.

Bredin, Mark. 'God the Carer: The Book of Revelation'. *BTB* 38 (2008): 76-86.

Brodie, T.L. *The Gospel According to John: A Literary and Theological Commentary*. Oxford: Oxford University Press, 1993.

Brouwer, W. *The Literary Development of John 13-17. A Chiastic Reading*. Atlanta: SBL, 2000.

Brown, Raymond E. *The Community of the Beloved Disciple. The Life, Loves, and Hates of an individual Church in New Testament Times*. New York: Paulist, 1979.

―――. *The Death of the Messiah. From Gethsemane to the Grave. A Commentary on the Passion Narratives in the Four Gospels*. 2 vols. London: Geoffrey Chapman, 1994.

―――. *The Epistles of John. A New Translation with Introduction and Commentary*. New York: Doubleday, 1982.

―――. *The Gospel According to John*. 2 vols, Anchor Bible 29. Garden City, New York: Doubleday, 1966.

Brown, R.E. et al (eds.). *The New Jerome Biblical Commentary*. New Jersey: Prentice-Hall, 1990.

Bultmann, Rudolf. *The Gospel of John: A Commentary*. ET: Oxford: Blackwell, 1971.

―――. *The Johannine Epistles*. Hermeneia; Minneapolis: Fortress, 1973.

Burge, Gary M. *The Anointed Community. The Holy Spirit in the Johannine Tradition*. Grand Rapids: Eerdmans, 1987.

Byrne, Brendan. *Lazarus: A Contemporary Reading of John 11:1-46*, Zacchaeus Studies. Minnesota: Liturgical Press, 1991.

Callahan, Allen Dwight. 'Babylon Boycott: The Book of Revelation' *Int* 63 (2009), 48-54.

Calvin, John. *The Gospel According to St John, Part 1, 1-10*. Calvin's NT Commentaries; ET: Grand Rapids: Eerdmans, 1961.

Carroll, John T. 'Revelation 4:1-11. *Interpretation* 63 (2009): 56-58.

Carter, Warren. 'Accommodating 'Jezebel' and Withdrawing John: Negotiating Empire in Revelation Then and Now'. *Int* 63 (2009): 32-47.

―――. *John and Empire: Initial Explorations*. New York/London: T & T Clark, 2008.

Casey, Michael. *Towards God. The Western Tradition of Contemplation*. Melbourne: Dove, 1989, 1995.

Charlesworth, James H. *The Beloved Disciple: Whose Witness Validates the Gospel of John?* Valley Forge: Trinity Press International, 1995

Chevalier, Jacques M. *A Postmodern Revelation. Signs of Astrology and the Apocalypse*. Toronto: University of Toronto Press, 1997.

Chettanu, Rekha M. *Johannine Discipleship as a Covenant Relationship*. Peabody: Hendrickson, 2006.

Coloe, Mary L. *God Dwells with Us: Temple Symbolism in the Fourth Gospel*. Collegeville: Liturgical Press, 2001.

———. *Dwelling in the Household of God. Johannine Ecclesiology and Spirituality*. Collegeville: Liturgical Press, 2007.

———. 'Witness and Friend. Symbolism Associated with John the Baptist'. In *Imagery in the Gospel of John. Terms, Forms, Themes, and Theology of Johannine Figurative Language*, edited by J. Frey, van der Watt, J.G., Zimmermann, R., 319-32. Tübingen: Mohr Siebeck, 2006.

Collins, Adela Yarbro. *The Combat Myth in the Book of Revelation*. Montana: Scholars Press, 1976.

———. 'Feminine Symbolism in the Book of Revelation', *Biblical Interpretation* 1 (1993): 20-33.

———. 'Satan's Throne: Revelations from Revelation', *BAR* 32 (2006): 26-39.

Conway, C.M. *Men and Women in the Fourth Gospel. Gender and Johannine Characterization*. Atlanta: SBL, 1999.

Countryman, L. William. *The Mystical Way in the Fourth Gospel. Crossing Over Into God*. Valley Forge PA: Trinity Press International, 1994.

Court, John M. *Revelation*. NT Guides; Sheffield: JSOT Press, 1994.

Crump, David. 'Who Gets What? God or Disciples, Human Spirit or Holy Spirit in John 19:30', *NovT* 51 (2009): 78-89.

Culpepper, R. Alan. *Anatomy of the Fourth Gospel: A Study in Literary Design*. Philadelphia: Fortress, 1983.

———. *The Gospel and Letters of John*. Nashville: Abingdon, 1998.

Culpepper, R. Alan. 'The Quest for the Church in the Gospel of John'. *Interpretation* 63 (2009): 341-54.

Cunningham Lawrence S. & Keith J. Egan, *Christian Spirituality. Themes from the Tradition*. New York: Paulist, 1996/

Davies, O. & Turner, D. (eds.), *Silence and the Word. Negative Theology and Incarnation*. Cambridge: Cambridge University Press, 2002.

Dodd, C.H. *The Interpretation of the Fourth Gospel*. Cambridge, Cambridge University Press, 1953.

———. *More New Testament Studies*. Manchester: Manchester University Press, 1968.

————. *The Johannine Epistles*. London: Hodder & Stoughton, 1946.

Dunn, James D.G. *Christology in the Making. A New Testament Inquiry into the Origins of the Doctrine of the Incarnation*. 2nd ed.; London: SCM, 1989.

Eliot, T.S. *The Complete Poems and Plays*. London: Faber & Faber, 1969

Elmer, Ian J. 'I, Tertius: Secretary or Co-author of Romans, *AusBR* 56 (2008): 45-60.

Ellis, Peter F. 'The Authenticity of John 21'. *St Vladimir's Theological Quarterly* 36 (1992): 12-25.

Elowsky, Joel C., ed. *John 1-10*. Edited by Thomas C. Oden, Ancient Christian Commentary on Scripture: New Testament IVA. Downers Grove, Il: InterVarsity Press, 2006.

————. *John 11-21*. Edited by R.C. Oden, Ancient Christian Commentary on Scripture: New Testament IVB. Downers Grove, Il: InterVarsity Press, 2007.

Emmerson, R.K. & BcGinn, M. *The Apocalypse in the Middle Ages*. Ithaca & London: Cornell University Press, 1992.

Erlande-Brandenburg, A. *La Dame À La Licorne* Paris: Editions de la Réunion des Musées Nationaux, 1978.

Evans, Craig A. *Word and Glory: On the Exegetical and Theological Background of John's Prologue*. Sheffield: JSOT Academic Press, 1993.

Farrer, Austin. *A Rebirth of Images. The Making of St John's Apocalypse*. Westminster: Dacre Press, 1949.

Fiddes, Paul. "The Quest for a Place Which Is 'Not-a-Place': The Hiddness of God and the Presence of God." In *Silence and the Word: Negative Theology and Incarnation*, edited by Oliver Davies and Denys Turner, 35-60. Cambridge: Cambridge University Press, 2002.

France, R.T. *The Gospel of Mark: A Commentary on the Greek Text*, The New International Greek Testament Commentary. Grand Rapids: Eerdmans, 2002.

Franzman, Majella & Klinger, M. 'The Call Stories of John 1 and John 21'. *St Vladimir's Theological Quarterly* 36 (1992): 7-25.

Friesen, Steven J. *Imperial Cults and the Apocalypse of John. Reading Revelation in the Ruins*. Oxford: Oxford University Press, 2001.

Gardner, Helen, ed. *The Metaphysical Poets*. 2 ed. Middlesex: Penguin, 1966.

Gordley, Matthew. 'The Johannine Prologue and Jewish Didactic Hymn Traditions: A New Case for Reading the Prologue as a Hymn' *JBL* 128 (2009): 781-802.

Grayston, Kenneth. *The Johannine Epistles*. Grand Rapids: Eerdmans, 1984

Gregory the Great. *Moralia in Iob*. http://www9.georgetown.edu/faculty/jod/ texts/moralia1.html.

Haenchen, Ernst. *A Commentary on the Gospel of John*. ET: Philadelphia, 1984.

Hägerland, Tobias. 'John's Gospel: A Two-Level Drama?', *JSNT* 25 (2003): 309-22.

Harrington, W.J. *The Apocalypse of John: A Commentary*. London: Geoffrey Chapman, 1969.

————. *Revelation*. SP 16; Collegeville: Liturgical Press, 1993.

Hartsock, Chad. *Sight and Blindness in Luke-Acts: The Use of Physical Features in Characterization*. Leiden: Brill, 2008.

Hauck, F. '*menô*'. In *Theological Dictionary of the New Testament*, 4:574-576.

Heise, J. *Bleiben. Meinen in den Johanneischen Schriften*. Tübingen: J.C.B. Mohr (Paul Siebeck), 1967.

Hemer, Colin J. *The Letters to the Seven Churches of Asia in Their Local Setting*. JSNTSS 11; Sheffield: JSOT Press, 1986.

Hengel, Martin. *The Johannine Question*. ET: London: SPCK, 1985.

Hett, W.S., ed. *Aristotle—on the Soul*, Loeb Classical Library. London: Heinemann, 1957.

Hill, C.S. *The Johannnine Corpus in the Early Church*. Oxford: Oxford University Press, 2004.

Hill, E., ed. *The Works of Saint Augustine: A Translation for the 21st Century* New York: New City Press, 1992.

Hirsch-Luipold, Rainer. "Klartext in Bildern. *Alêthinos* Ktl., *Paroimia - Parrêsia, Sêmeion* Als Signalwörter für eine Bildhafte Darstellungsform im Johannes-Evangelium." In *Imagery in the Gospel of John. Terms, Forms, Themes, and Theology of Johannine Figurative Language*, edited by J. Frey, van der Watt, J.G., Zimmermann, R., 61-102. Tübingen: Mohr Siebeck, 2006.

Hoskyns, E. *The Fourth Gospel*. 2 ed. 2 vols. London: Faber & Faber, 1947.

Howard-Brook, Wes & Gwyther, Anthony. *Unveiling Empire. Reading Revelation Then and Now*. Maryknoll: Orbid Books, 2000.

Huber, Lynn R. *Like a Bride Adorned. Reading Metaphor in John's Apocalypse*. Emory Studies in Early Christianity; New York & London: T & T Clark, 2008.

Irmie, C. & Focsa, M. *Romanian Icons Painted on Glass*. London: Thames & Hudson, 1970.

Johns, Loren L. *The Lamb Christology of the Apocalypse of John*. WUNT 167; Tübingen: Mohr Siebeck, 2003.

Keener, Craig S. *The Gospel of John. A Commentary*. 2 vols. Peabody: Hendrickson, 2003.

Keller, Helen. *The Story of My Life*. New York: Modern Library, 2003.

Kerr, A. *The Temple of Jesus' Body. The Temple Theme in the Gospel of John*. JSNT Sup 220; London & New York: Sheffield Academic Press, 2002.

Klink, Edward W. III *The Sheep of the Fold. The Audience and Origin of the Gospel of John*. SNTSMS 141; Cambridge: Cambridge University Press, 2007.

Köstenberger, Andreas J. *John*. Baker Exegetical Commentary on the NT. Grand Rapids: Baker Academic, 2004.

Köstenberger, Andreas J. & Swain, Scott R. *Father, Son and Spirit. The Trinity and John's Gospel*. NSBT 24. Downers Grove: InterVarsity Press, 2008.

Koester, Craig R. *The Dwelling of God. The Tabernacle in the Old Testament, Intertestamental Jewish Literature, and the New Testament*. CBQMS 22. Washington: Catholic Biblical Association of America, 1989.

———. *Revelation and the End of All Things*. Grand Rapids: Eerdmans, 2001.

———. 'Revelation's Visionary Challenge to Ordinary Empire', *Int* 63 (2009): 5-18.

———. 'Roman Slave Trade and the critique of Babylon in Revelation 18', *CBQ* 70 (2008): 766-86.

———. *Symbolism in the Fourth Gospel: Meaning, Mystery, Community*. 2nd ed. Minneapolis: Fortress, 2003.

———. 'What Does It Mean to Be Human? Imagery and the Human Condition in John's Gospel.' In *Imagery in the Gospel of John. Terms, Forms, Themes, and Theology of Johannine Figurative Language*, edited by J. Frey, Van der Watt, J.G., Zimmermann, R., 403-20. Tübingen: Mohr Siebeck, 2006.

———. *The Word of Life. A Theology of John's Gospel*. Grand Rapids: Eerdmans, 2008.

van Kooten, George H. 'The Year of the Four Emperors and the Revelation of John: The 'pro-Neronian' Emperors Otho and Vitellius, and the Images and Colossus of Nero in Rome', *JSNT* 30 (2007): 205-48.

Kovacs, Judith & Rowland, Christopher. *Revelation. The Apocalypse of Jesus Christ*. Blackwell Bible Commentaries; Oxford: Blackwell, 2004.

Kraybill, J. Nelson. *Imperial Cult and Commerce in John's Apocalypse*. JSNTSS 132; Sheffield: Sheffield Academic Press, 1996.

Kruse, Colin. 'Sin and Perfection in 1 John', *AusBR* 51 (2003): 60-70.

Kysar, Robert. *Voyages with John. Charting the Fourth Gospel*. Waco, Texas: Baylor University Press, 2005.

Lee, Dorothy. *Flesh and Glory: Symbol, Gender and Theology in the Gospel of John*. New York: Crossroad, 2002.

——. 'The Gospel of John and the Five Senses', *JBL* 129 (2010): 115-27.

——. 'The Gospel of John: Symbol and Prologue', *Conversations* 2 (2, 2008). http://ctm.uca.edu.au/

——. 'The Heavenly Woman and the Dragon: Re-readings of Revelation 12' in F.D. Glass & L. McCredden (eds.), *Feminist Poetics of the Sacred. Creative Suspicions*. Oxford: Oxford University Press, 2001: 198-220.

——. '"In the Spirit of Truth": Worship and Prayer in the Gospel of John and the Early Fathers'. *Vigilianae Christianae* 58 (2004): 227-97.

——.'John'. In *The New Interpreter's Bible: One Volume Commentary*, edited by B.R. Gaventa & D. Petersen, 709-34. Nashville: Abingdon, 2010.

——. 'Partnership in Easter Faith: The Role of Mary Magdalene and Thomas in John 20', *JSNT* 58, (1995): 37-49.

——. 'Paschal Imagery in the Gospel of John: A Narrative and Symbolic Reading', *Pacifica* 24 (2011): 13-28.

——. *The Symbolic Narratives of the Fourth Gospel. The Interplay of Form and Meaning*. Sheffield: Sheffield Academic Press, 1994.

——. *Transfiguration*. London/New York: Continuum, 2004.

——. 'Turning from Death to Life, A Biblical Reflection on Mary Magdalene (John 20:1-18)', *Ecumenical Review* 50 (1998): 112-20.

Léon-Dufour, Xavier. *Lecture De L'evangile Selon Jean*. 3 vols, Parole De Dieu. Paris: Editions du Seuil, 1988, 1990, 1993.

Lescher, Bruce H. & Elizabeth Liebert (eds.) *Exploring Christian Spirituality. Essays in Honor of Sandra M. Schneiders*. New York: Paulist, 2006).

Lieu, Judith. 'Scripture and the Feminine in John.' In *A Feminist Companion to the Hebrew Bible in the New Testament*, edited by A. Brenner, 225-40. Sheffield: Sheffield Academic Press, 1996.

————. *The Second and Third Epistles of John.* Edinburgh: T & T Clark, 1986.

————. *The Theology of the Johannine Epistles.* Cambridge: Cambridge University Press, 1991.

————. 'Us or You? Persuasion and Identity in 1 John', *JBL* 127 (2008): 805-19.

Lightfoot, R.H. *The Gospel Message of St Mark.* Oxford: Clarendon, 1950.

Lincoln, Andrew T. 'The Beloved Disciple as Eyewitness and the Fourth Gospel as Witness', *JSNT* 85 (2002): 2-36.

————. *The Gospel According to Saint John.* Black's MT Commentary. Peabody" Hendrickson, 2005.

————. *Truth on Trial: The Lawsuit Motif in the Fourth Gospel.* Peabody, MA: Hendrickson, 2000.

Lindars, Barnabas. *The Gospel of John.* London: Oliphants, 1972.

Lindberg, David. *Theories of Vision from Al-Kindi to Kepler.* Chicago: Chicago University Press, 1976.

Lioy, Dan. *The Book of Revelation in Christological Focus.* Studies in Biblical Literature 58; New York: Peter Lang, 2003.

Loader, William. *The Johannine Epistles.* London: Epworth, 1992.

Lossky, Vladimir. *The Mystical Theology of the Eastern Church.* ET: Crestwood, New York: St Vladimir's Seminary Press, 1998.

Maccini, R.G. *Her Testimony. Women as Witnesses According to John.* Sheffield: Sheffield Academic Press, 1996.

McCahill, Catherine M. *'Making God Known': Jesus, the Teacher of the Fourth Gospel and the Contemporary Christian Religious Educator.* PhD Thesis, Melbourne College of Divinity, Dalton McCaughey Library, 2006.

McDonald, Grantley. *Raising the Ghost of Arius. Erasmus, the Johannine Comma and Religious Difference in Early Modern Europe* (unpub. ms).

McHugh, John E. *A Critical and Exegetical Commentary on John 1-4.* ICC; London/New York: T & T Clark, 2009.

McNeill, J.T. (ed.). *Calvin: Institutes of the Christian Religion.* Philadelphia: Westminster, 1960.

Malina, Bruce J. *On the Genre and Message of Revelation. Star Visions and Sky Journeys.* Peabody: Hendrickson, 1995.

Marshall, I. Howard *The Epistles of John.* Grand Rapids: Michigan, 1978.

Martyn, J. Louis. *The Gospel of John in Christian History*. New York: Paulist, 1978.

————. *History and Theology in the Gospel of John*. 2nd ed.; Nashville: Abingdon, 1979.

Mathewson, David. *A New Heaven and a New Earth: The Meaning and Function of the Old Testament in Revelation 21.1-22.5*. JSNTS 238; Sheffield: Sheffield Academic Press, 2009.

Medina, John J. *Brain Rules. Twelve Principles*. Seattle, WA: Pear Press, 2008.

Metzger, Bruce M. *A Textual Commentary on the Greek New Testament*. 3rd ed.; London & New York: United Bible Societies, 1975.

Michaelis, W. "*horaô* et al.", *TDNT* V: 315-82.

Minear, Paul S. 'Far as the Curse is Found: The Point of Revelation 12:15-16' *NovT* 33 (1991): 71-7.

Moloney, Francis J. 'In the Bosom of' or 'Turned towards' the Father? *AusBR* 31 (1983): 63-71.

————. *The Gospel of John*, Sacra Pagina 4. Collegeville, MN: The Liturgical Press, 1998.

————. 'The Gospel of John: as Scripture'. *CBQ* 67 (2005): 454-68.

————. *The Gospel of Mark: A Commentary*. Peabody: Hendrickson, 2002.

————. 'The Gospel of John: The "End" of Scripture'. *Interpretation* 63 (2009): 356-66.

————. *Signs and Shadows. Reading John 5-12*. Minneapolis: Fortress, 1996.

Mounce, Robert H. *The Book of Revelation*. NICNT; 2nd ed.; Grand Rapids: Eerdmans, 1998.

Moyise, S. (ed.), *Studies in the Book of Revelation*. Edinburgh & New York: T & T Clark, 2001.

Need, Stephen W. 'Re-reading the Prologue: Incarnation and Creation in John 1.1-18', *Theology* 106 (2003): 397-404.

Nes, Solrunn. *The Mystical Language of Icons*. 2nd ed.; Grand Rapids: Eerdmans, 2005.

————. *The Uncreated Light: An Iconographical Study of the Transfiguration in the Eastern Church*. Grand Rapids: Eerdmans, 2007.

Newport, Kenneth G.C. *Apocalypse and Millemium. Studies in Biblical Eisegesis*. Cambridge: Cambridge University Press, 2000.

Neyrey, Jerome H. *The Gospel of John*. NCBC; Cambridge: Cambridge University Press, 2007.

————. 'Worship in the Fourth Gospel: A Cultural Interpretation of John 14-17', *BTB* 36 (2006): 107-17, 155-63.

Nielsen, Jesper Tang. 'The Narrative Structures of Glory and Glorification in the Fourth Gospel'. *NTS* 56 (2010): 343-66.

Nineham, Dennis E. *The Gospel of St Mark*, Penguin Gospel Commentaries. Hammondsworth, Middlesex: Penguin, 1963.

O'Day, Gail R. "John." In *The Women's Bible Commentary*, edited by C.A. Newsom & S.H. Ringe, 293-304. London: SCM, 1998.

————. '1, 2,3 & 3 John' in Newsom, C.A. & S.H. Ringe (eds.), *The Women's Bible Commentary*. London: SPCK, 1992: 374-5.

Okure, T. *The Johannine Approach to Mission. A Contextual Study of John 4:1-42*. Tübingen: J.C.B. Mohr, 1988.

Painter, John. *1, 2, and 3 John*. Sacra Pagina 18; Collegeville: Liturgical Press, 2002.

Painter, J., Culpepper R.A. & Segovia, F.F., ed. *Word, Theology, and Community in John*. St Louis, MO: Chalice, 2002.

Parsenios, George L. *Departure and Consolation. The Johannine Farewell Discourses in Light of Greco-Roman Literature*. SNT 117; Leiden: Brill, 2005.

Parsons, Mikeal. *Body and Character in Luke and Acts: The Subversion of Physiognomy in Early Christianity*. Grand Rapids: Baker Academic Press, 2006.

Perkins, Pheme. 'The Johannine Epistles'. In R.E. Brown, J. A. Fitzmyer, & R.E. Murphy (eds.), *The New Jerome Biblical Commentary*. London: Geoffrey Chapman, 1990.

Phillips, P.M. *The Prologue of the Fourth Gospel. A Sequential Reading*, Library of NT Studies 294; London: T & T Clark, 2006.

Pines, Maya. 'More Than the Sum of Its Parts', Part 4. In 'Seeing, Hearing and Smelling the World', Howard Hughes Medical Institute. http://www.hhmi.org/senses/a110.html.

Pippin, Tina. *Death and Desire. The Rhetoric of Gender in the Apocalypse of John*. Westminster: John Knox, 1992.

Plummer, Alfred. *The Gospel According to St John*. Cambridge: Cambridge University Press, 1905.

de la Potterie, Ignace. 'L'emploie de *eis* dans Saint Jean et ses incidences théologiques'. *Biblica* 43 (1962): 366-87.

Powell, Samuel M. *A Theology of Christian Spirituality*. Nashville: Abingdon, 2005.

Prévost, Jean-Pierre. *How to Read the Apocalypse* (ET; New York: Crossroad, 1993.

Ramelli, Ilaria. '"Simon Son of John, Do You Love *Me*?" Some Reflections on John 21:15', *NovT* 50 [2008]: 332-50.

Rensberger, David. *The Epistles of John*. Louisville: John Knox, 2001.

Resseguie, J.L. *Revelation Unleashed. A Narrative Critical Approach to John's Apocalypse*. BIS; Leiden: Brill, 1998.

Roloff, Jürgen. *The Revelation of John. A Continental Commentary*. ET: Minneapolis: Fortress, 1993.

Rowland, Christopher. 'Imagining the Apocalypse', *NTS* 51 (2005): 303-27.

Sheridan, Ruth. 'The Paraclete and Jesus in the Johannine Farewell Discourse', *Pacifica* 20 (2007): 125-41.

Schnackenburg, Rudolf. *The Gospel According to St John*. 3 vols. New York: Seabury (vols 1-2); Crossroad (vol 3), 1980 & 1982.

———. *The Johannine Epistles. Translation and Commentary*. ET: New York: Crossroad, 1992.

Schneiders, Sandra M. 'The Raising of the New Temple: John 20,19-23 and Johannine Ecclesiology', *NTS* 52 (2006): 337-55.

———. *'Written That You May Believe'. Encountering Jesus in the Fourth Gospel*. 2nd ed. New York: Crossroad, 2003.

Schnelle, Udo. *Das Evangeliums nach Johannes*. Leipzig: Evangelische Verlagsanstalt, 1998.

———. 'Johannine Theology: Introduction to the Christian Faith'. In *Theology of the New Testament*. ET: Grand Rapids: Baker Academic, 2009: 669-750.

———. 'Revelation: Seeing and Understanding'. In *Theology of the New Testament*. ET: Grand Rapids: Baker Academic, 2009: 751-72.

Schreiter, Robert J. *In Water and In Blood. A Spirituality of Solidarity and Hope*. New York: Crossroad, 1988.

Schüssler Fiorenza, Elisabeth. *The Book of Revelation: Justice and Judgment*. 2nd ed.; Minneapolis: Fortress Press, 1998.

———. *Revelation: Vision of a Just World*. Edinburgh: T & T Clark, 1993.

Scott, Martin. *Sophia and the Johannine Jesus* (Sheffield: Sheffied Academic Press, 1992.

Segovia, Fernando F. *The Farewell of the Word. The Johannine Call to Abide*. Minneapolis: Fortress, 1991.

Seim, Turid Karlsen. 'Descent and Divine Paternity in the Gospel of John: Does the Mother Matter?' *NTS* 51 (2005): 361-75.

Senior, Donald. *The Passion of Jesus in the Gospel of John*, The Passion Series 4. Collegeville, MN: Liturgical Press, 1991.

Sheldrake, Philip F. *Explorations in Spirituality: History, Theology, and Social Practice*. New York: Paulist, 2010.

Sheldrake, Philip F. *Spirituality and Theology: Christian Living and the Doctrine of God.* London: Darton, Longman, & Todd, 1998.

Sheridan, Ruth. 'The Paraclete and Jesus in the Johannine Farewell Discourse. *Pacifica* 20 (2007): 125-41.

deSilva, David A. *Seeing Things John's Way. The Rhetoric of the Book of Revelation*. Louisville: Westminster John Knox, 2009.

Skaggs, Rebecca & Doyle, Thomas. 'Violence in the Apocalypse of John', *CBR* 5 (2007): 220-34.

Smalley, Stephen S. *1, 2, 3 John*. Waco, Texas: Word Books, 1984.

———. 'John's Revelation and John's Community', *Bulletin of the John Rylands University Library of Manchester* 69 (1987): 549-71.

Smith, D. Moody. *First, Second, and Third John*. Interpretation; Louisville: John Knox, 1991.

———.*John*. ANTC; Nashville: Abingdon, 1999.

———. *John among the Gospels*. 2 ed. Columbia: University of South Carolina Press, 2001.

———. 'John: Historian or Theologian?', *BR* 20 (2004): 22-31, 45.

Strecker, Georg. *The Johannine Letters. A Commentary on 1, 2, and 3 John*. Minneapolis: Fortress, 1996.

Sweet, John. *Revelation.* 2nd ed. London: SCM, 1990.

Talbert, C.H. *The Apocalypse. A Reading of the Revelation of John*. Louisville: Westminster John Knox, 1994.

Talbert, C.H. *Reading John. A Literary and Theological Commentary on the Fourth Gospel and the Johannine Epistles. London:* SPCK, 1992.

———. *Reading John. A Literary and Theological Commentary on the Fourth Gospel and the Johannine Epistles*. London: SPCK, 1992.

Thatcher, Tom (ed.). *What We Have Heard from the Beginning: The Past, Present, and Future of Johannine Studies*. Waco: Baylor University Press, 2007.

Thatcher, Tom & Moore, S.D. (eds.). *Anatomies of Narrative Criticism. The Past, Present, and Futures of the Fourth Gospel as Literature*. Atlanta: SBL, 2008.

Thettayil, Benny. *In Spirit and Truth. An Exegetical Study of 4:19-26 and a Theological Investigation of the Replacement Theme in the Fourth Gospel*. Leuven: Peeters, 2007.

Thomas, John Christopher. *Footwashing in John 13 and the Johannine Community*. JSNTSup 61; Sheffield: JSOT Press, 1991.

————. 'The Literary Structure of 1 John', *NovT* 40 (1998): 369-81.

Thompson, Marianne Meye. '"Every Picture Tells a Story". Imagery for God in the Gospel of John.' In *Imagery in the Gospel of John. Terms, Forms, Themes, and Theology of Johannine Figurative Language*, edited by J. Frey, Van der Watt, J.G., Zimmermann, R., 259-77. Tübingen, 2006.

————. *The God of the Gospel of John*. Grand Rapids: Eerdmans, 2001.

————. *1-3 John*. IVPNTCS; Downers Grove: InterVarsity Press, 1992.

————. 'Reflections on Worship in the Gospel of John', *Princeton Seminary Bulletin* 19 (1998): 259-78.

————. "Worship in the Book of Revelation". *Ex Auditu* 8 (1992): 45-54.

Tovey; Derek. 'Narrative Strategies in the Prologue and the Metaphor of *Logos* in John's Gospel'. *Pacifica* 15 (2002): 138-153.

van Kooten, George H. 'Thje Year of the Four Emperors and the Revelation of John: The 'pro-Neronian" Emperors Otho and Vitellius, and the Images and Colossus of Nero in Rome'. JSNT 30 (2007): 205-48.

van Tilborg, Sjef. *Imaginative Love in John*. Leiden: Brill, 1993.

Tolmie, D.F. *Jesus' Farewell to the Disciples. John 13:1-17:26 in Narratological Perspective*. Edited by R.A. Culpepper & R. Rendtorff, Biblical Interpretation Series 12. Leiden/New York/Köln: Brill, 1995.

Tovey, Derek. *Jesus: Story of God. John's Story of Jesus*. Adelaide: ATF Press, 2007.

Tovey, Derek. 'Narrative Strategies in the Prologue and the Metaphor of *ho Logos* in John's Gospel'. *Pacifica* 15 (2002): 138-153.

Tyson, John R. *Invitation to Christian Spirituality. An Ecumenical Anthology*. New York/Oxford: Oxford University Press, 1999.

Van Kooten, George H. 'The Year of the Four Emperors and the Revelation of John: The "pro-Neronian" Emperors Otho and Vitellius, and the Images and Colossus of Nero in Rome'. *JSNT* 30 (2007): 205-48.

Wainwright, Arthur W. *Mysterious Apocalypse. Interpreting the Book of Revelation*. Abingdon: Nashville, 1993.

Weder, H. 'Deus Incarnatus: On the Hermeneutics of Christology in the Johannine Writings'. In *Exploring the Gospel of John: In Honor of D. Moody Smith*, edited by R.A. Culpepper & C.C. Black, 327-45. Westminster: John Knox, 1996.

Westcott, B.F. *The Gospel According to St John. The Authorised Version with Introduction and Notes*. London: John Murray, 1882.

Wiles, Maurice F. *The Spiritual Gospel. The Interpretation of the Fourth Gospel in the Early Church*. Cambridge: Cambridge University Press, 1960.

Williams, Rowan. *On Christian Theology*. Edited by G. Jones & L. Ayres, Challenges in Contemporary Theology. Oxford: Blackwell, 2000.

———. *Silence and Honey Cakes: The Wisdom of the Desert*. Oxford: Lion Publishing, 2003.

Witherington, Ben. *John's Wisdom. A Commentary on the Fourth Gospel*. Cambridge: Lutterworth Press, 1995.

———. *Revelation*. NCBC; Cambridge: Cambridge University Press, 2003.

Woods, Richard. 'Seven Bowls of Wrath: The Ecological Relevance of Revelation', *BTB* 38 (2008): 64-75.

Wright, Judith. *A Human Pattern. Selected Poems*. Sydney: Angus & Robertson, 1990.

Wyatt, Nicolas. "Supposing Him to Be the Gardener" (John 20,15). A Study of the Paradise Motif in John', *ZNTW* 81 (1990): 21-38.

Yarbrough, Robert W. *1-3 John*. Baker Exegetical Commentary on the NT; Grand Rapids: Baker Academic, 2008.

Zimmermann, Ruben. 'Imagery in John. Opening up Paths into the Tangled Thicket of John's Figurative World'. In *Imagery in the Gospel of John. Terms, Forms, Themes, and Theology of Johannine Figurative Language*, edited by J. Frey, Van der Watt, J.G., Zimmermann, R., 1-43. Tübingen: Mohr Siebeck, 2006.